A GUIDE TO T

IRELAND WAY™

3rd Edition

BEARA-BREIFNE WAY & ULSTER WAY

Published by:
IRELAND WAY GUIDES
Galway City, Co. Galway, Ireland.
Email: caroline@theirelandway.ie
Website: www.theirelandway.ie

ISBN: 978-1-7390957-0-3
3rd Edition July 2022

Design and Typesetting by Caroline Allen

Printed and bound in the European Union.

Disclaimer

Hill-walking and mountaineering are risk sports. The author and Ireland Way Guides accept no responsibility for any injury, loss or inconvenience sustained by anyone using this guidebook.

Advice to Readers

The author has made every effort to ensure the accuracy of this guidebook. However, changes can occur after the book has been published, including trail route, signage and changes to rights of way. All prices quoted are correct at time of going to print. If you notice discrepancies between this guidebook and the facts on the trail, please let us know by emailing caroline@theirelandway.ie.

Image: Galtee Mountains, Glen of Aherlow

Contents

NOTE FROM THE AUTHOR

A Personal Journey

The inspiration for this book came from my long-distance hike of the 800km Camino de Santiago in 2013. If you have done the Camino or any other long-distance trail you will understand the mind-altering experience that such a long walk can be. Although this kind of journey can be very personal, I especially loved the simplicity of life. Each day involved eating, walking, social interaction and sleeping. It covers all of our basic needs and very little more. It showed me how little we need in order to feel happy.

Walking is a kind of meditation, especially when it is long distance. Daily stresses and responsibilities slowly fade from your mind to leave wide open space, presence. Walking helps the mind to calm down, to rest, so that one can start to see more clearly their life's challenges. One can find answers or reach a state of peace.

The Emerald Isle of Ireland gets enough rain that the landscape is always green. The people in the quaint little villages with strong Irish and Northern Irish accents will guide you along your journey with a welcoming smile. Hiking through Ireland, south and north, has enabled me to see the island through tourist's eyes and gain a deeper appreciation for the landscape, friendly people and its rich history.

I present you with this guidebook and hope that it will accompany you on one of the most memorable journeys of your life.

Buen camino agus go n-eirí an bother leat!

Caroline

Image: Caha Mountains overlooking Glengarriff Forest

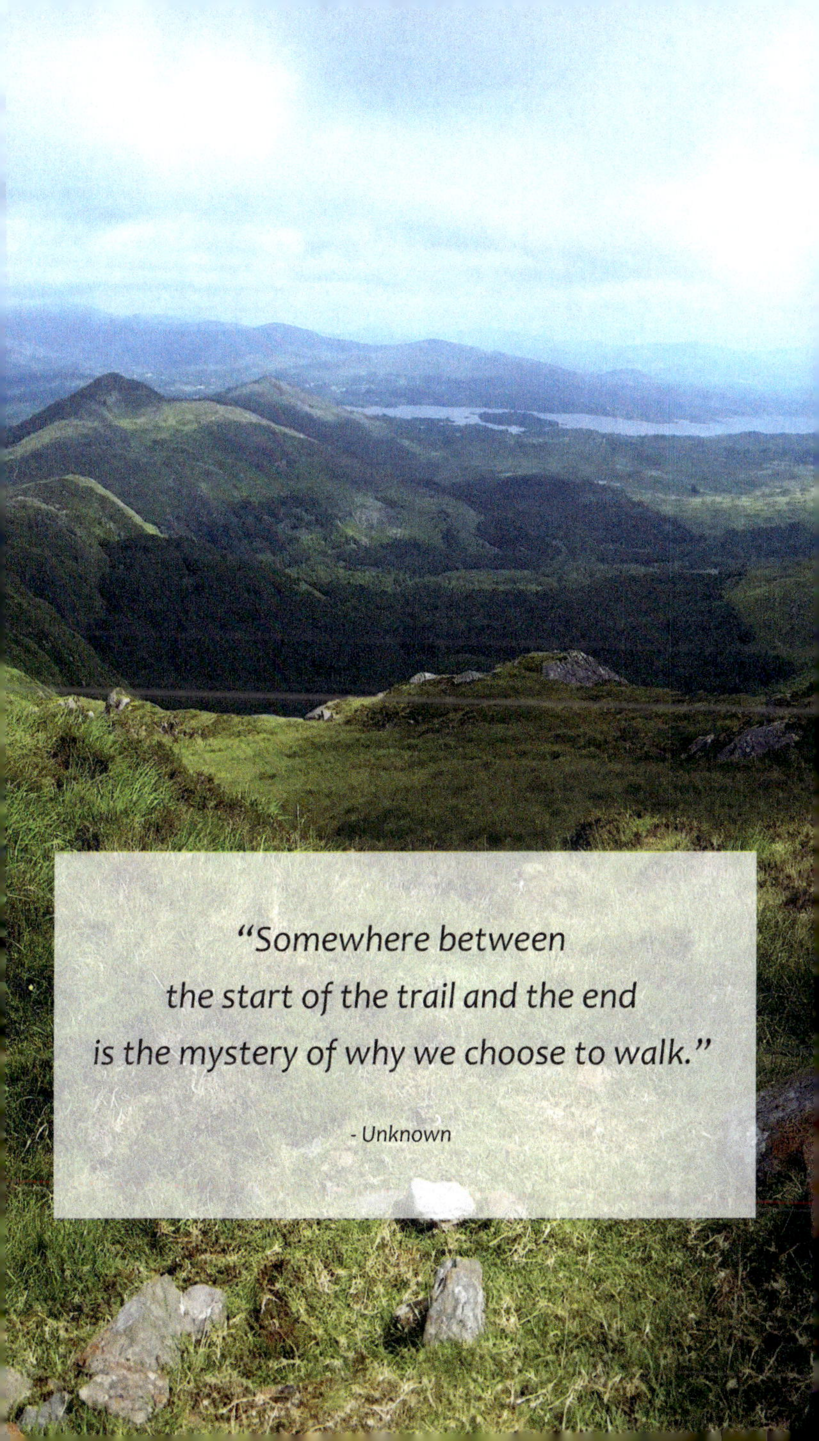
"Somewhere between
the start of the trail and the end
is the mystery of why we choose to walk."
- Unknown

Acknowledgements

I would like to give a sincere thank you to the following people who inspired, helped and encouraged me to write this book:

My parents, Rita and David Allen; my hiking buddies David Heneghan, Ursula and Margaret Cullagh, Gearóid O'Connor, Terence Killeen, Francesco Richichi, Anna Kolasa, Jagoda Bursa, John O'Mahony, Audrey Moore and Joe Connolly; for their continuous support and encouragement: Nick Tosh and Agnieszka Wychowaniec; for their assistance with historical references: Gearóid O'Connor and Stan Reynolds.

Thank you to Jim O'Sullivan, the man behind the Beara-Breifne Way, Matt Ryan of the Ormond Way, Mike Moroney for help with mapping, the farmers, land-owners and many other people involved in the development of the new Beara-Breifne Way trail. It is truly a wonderful way to explore Ireland and will give walkers for many generations a journey to remember.

Thanks also to the Causeway Coast and Glens Borough Council for the improvements they are making to the Ulster Way, and the Ballycastle Tourist Information Office who provide certificates to hikers at the end of their journey.

Lastly, I thank the Camino de Santiago for inspiring me to write this guidebook. The Camino was such an amazing experience that I wanted others to be able to have a 'camino experience' in Ireland.

Go raibh míle maith agaibh!

Image: Lough Meelagh

THE IRELAND WAY

Stage Summary

Stage	Way Name	Kilometres	Miles
1	Beara Way	57.5	35.7
2	Slí Gaeltacht Mhuscraí	71.6	44.5
3	North West Cork Way	40.2	25
4	Ballyhoura Way	87.2	54.2
5	Multeen Way	35.5	22.1
6	Ormond Way	85.8	53.3
7	Hymany Way	94	58.4
8	Suck Valley Way	66.5	41.3
9	Lung/Lough Gara Way	44.6	27.7
10	Miner's Way	53	32.9
11	Leitrim Way	22.1	13.7
12	Cavan Way	22.3	13.9
13	Bellcoo to Belleek	45.9	28.5
14	Belleek to Lough Bradan Forest	50.6	31.4
15	Lough Bradan Forest to Gortin	56.2	34.9
16	Gortin to Moneyneany	36.6	22.7
17	Moneyneany to Dungiven	21.3	13.2
18	Dungiven to Castlerock	56.1	34.9
19	Castlerock to Portstewart	16.2	10.1
20	Causeway Coast Way	49.3	30.6
	Total Distance:	**1,012.5**	**629**

BEARA-BREIFNE WAY

List of Maps, Towns & Facilities

Accommodation | Shop | Restaurant/Café /Pub Serving Food

Post Office | ATM | Doctor | Pharmacy | Washer/Dryer

Ruin of Kealkill Castle

Map	Town/Place	Facilities							Page
	STAGE 10 - MINER'S WAY								**143**
42	Ballinafad	A	S		PO				145
43	Castlebaldwin	A	S	R					149
43	Highwood								152
44	Ballyfarnon	A	S	R	PO				153
44	Keadue	A	S	R	PO				156
45	Knockvicar		S		PO				156
	STAGE 11 - LEITRIM WAY								**159**
45	Leitrim Village	A	S	R	PO	€			161
46	Drumshanbo	A	S	R	PO	€	D	P	161
47	Lough Allen	A							163
47	Ballinagleragh	A	S						163
	STAGE 12 - CAVAN WAY								**165**
48	Dowra		S	R	PO				166
49	Blacklion	A	S	R	PO		D		169

Accommodation | Shop | Restaurant/Café /Pub Serving Food

Post Office | ATM | Doctor | Pharmacy | Washer/Dryer

THE ULSTER WAY

List of Maps, Towns & Facilities

Accommodation	Shop	Restaurant/Café /Pub Serving Food		
Post Office	ATM	Doctor	Pharmacy	Washer/Dryer

Before You Go

How Long Does it Take to Walk?

To walk the entire Ireland Way takes roughly forty days. It will depend on each individual, their level of fitness and the weather. It is also good to take rest days as you need them.

The Ireland Way Passport

While on their journey, walkers and cyclists can carry the Ireland Way Passport: a document with which the walker/cyclist authenticates his/her progress by obtaining stamps along the way. Many towns have Beara-Breifne Way stamps in the accommodation, post office or local shop. This passport will get you a hiker's discount in some accommodations, and enable you to collect an Ireland Way Certificate from the tourist office in Ballycastle.

Slí Gaeltacht Mhuscraí

Walkers in the Caha Mountains

When to Go

The best time to do the Ireland Way is during the Summer months from **May to August,** as there is less rain and the ground in the boggy hills will be drier and easier to walk on. It will be warm most days and is ideal for camping. Come prepared with sun-cream and rain gear!

September and October will reveal the most beautiful Autumn colours as the leaves fall from the trees. Blackberries are everywhere and ripe for picking in September. Some Septembers are warm, and other years can be cold and wet. October is usually cold, wet and windy. These would be the final months in the year for camping but pack warm clothes and a good sleeping bag.

November to February is the least popular time to do the Ireland Way as the days are short with sunrise at 8am and sunset by 5pm. Heavy rainfall, strong winds and fog particularly on the hills and mountains can make it difficult to navigate and unsafe in remote areas. Some accommodation closes for Winter.

March to April, although wet, the weather is beginning to warm up and the countryside can be very pleasant with new-born lambs, calves and foals, as well as daffodils and cherry blossom trees in bloom.

How to Get There

Dublin Airport or Dublin City to Cork City

Buses available from Dublin Airport or Dublin City to Cork City include Air Coach, GoBé and Bus Eireann. The journey takes 3.5 hours from the airport. You can also travel by train from Heuston Station (www.irishrail.ie). The train takes 2.5 hours and costs €20-€65 for a one-way adult ticket (cheaper if booked well in advance).

Cork City to Castletownbere

At weekends some buses may only go as far as Glengarriff and a taxi is required from Glengarriff to Castletownbere. Check bus times in advance of travel in case of any changes.

1) Bus Eireann, number 236 bus, 3 hours. Buy your ticket at Cork Bus Station (not online). **Mon to Sat 08:30**, arrives 11:30 and **14:30**, arrives 17:40. **Sun 10:30**, arrives 13:20.

2) Harrington's private bus company: white mini-bus leaves from beside Cork Bus Station (near the Spar shop on Parnell Place), 2.5 hours. *Booking by phone is essential*: +353 (0)27 74003. **Mon to Sat (excluding Thurs) 18:00**, arrives 20:15. **Sun 19:35**, arrives 21:45.

3) O'Donoghue's Bus, Thurs only 18:00, +353 (0)27 70007.

Travel Times

The Google Maps app is the easiest ways to check travel times for bus and rail services in Ireland. Alternatively, use www.buseireann.ie for bus times and www.irishrail.ie for train times. For Northern Ireland use www.translink.co.uk.

Fitness Requirements

A reasonable level of fitness is required to undertake the challenge of hiking the Ireland Way. For the most part, the terrain consists of gently sloping hills, though there are also a few steep slopes along the way in the mountainous areas. As approximately 50% of the trail is on country roads, hikers tend to quickly get sore feet so extra cushioning or insoles are recommended as well as products for blister prevention and care.

Accommodation

There are not many hostels or budget accommodations. Hostels start from around €20, B&Bs (Bed & Breakfast), guesthouses and hotels will start at around €45 per person for a double or twin room, and from €55 for one person in a single room. This price usually includes breakfast. Prices in this guidebook are for two people sharing. AirBnB (www.airbnb.ie) has been included in some towns to give more accommodation options. It is always best to book your accommodation in advance, especially in the smaller towns which only have one B&B. Accommodation can fill up fast on bank holiday and public holiday weekends, especially during the summer months. Note that most of the B&Bs only accept cash and small villages may not have a bank or cash machine.

Washing Clothes

Some towns have a launderette or public washer/dryer at the petrol station. You could also ask at the accommodation as some may allow you to use their washing machine.

Emergency Numbers for Republic of Ireland
Emergency Services: 112 or 999 (free)

Emergency Numbers for Northern Ireland
Emergency Services: 999 (free). Non-Emergency Police number: +44 (0)845 600 8000 or +44 (0)28 9065 022.

The trail through Clonbrock

Carrowkeel Megalithic Tomb

Clothing and What to Bring

- 2 T-shirts
- 1 warm top
- 2 x Trousers
- Underwear
- Socks
- Waterproof jacket with hood
- Waterproof hiking boots
- Waterproof trousers
- Small quick-drying towel
- Small soap/shampoo
- Toothbrush/toothpaste
- Backpack with rain cover
- High-visibility vest
- Medical supplies, plasters
- Waterproof poncho
- Torch/head-light
- **GPS, Internet & Phone:** GPS will be essential until all the way-markers and signposts are in place. It is recommended to purchase an Irish SIM card with unlimited internet. Three Mobile have a SIM card for €20 with unlimited internet for 28 days and includes some EU data allowance which may be sufficient for use in Northern Ireland as well. There is a Three Mobile shop in Dublin City and Cork City centre. Alternatively purchase a second SIM card when you reach Northern Ireland

Optional

- Hiking poles - very useful for mountains and boggy land
- Waterproof socks (if you don't bring them you will wish you had!)
- Flashing red light for your back in fog or in autumn/winter for extra visibility on roads
- High-visibility arm bands or backpack cover
- Sun hat & sun glasses - summer only
- Sun cream - summer only

"The weather isn't bad here. It only rained twice this week, first for three days and then for four days. Monday was so windy one of the chickens laid the same egg four times. "
- Letter from Irish Mother to her Son

Caha Mountains, Cork

Language

The primary language spoken in Ireland is English. Some of the western parts speak primarily in Gaelic and English is their second language. You may hear some locals speaking in Gaelic on your journey, particularly in the first half of the trail. Below are some phrases you may like to use. Ask the locals how to pronounce them!

Go raibh maith agat	Thank you
Dia dhuit	Hello
Dia is Mhuire dhuit	Hello (in response to the first Hello)
Sláinte!	Cheers!
Conas atá tú?	How are you?
Tá mé go maith!	I am good!
Slán	Goodbye
Cad is anim duit?	What is your name?
______is anim dom	My name is _______
Craic agus ceol	Fun and music
Bean an Tí	Woman of the House
Siopa	Shop
Gaeltacht	Irish-speaking region
Cnoc, Slieve	Hill, Mountain
Bóthar, Boreen	Road, Small road
Teach Tabhairne	Pub
Lough	Lake
Slí	Way

Other words to note:
Bank/Public Holiday: Similar to Federal Holiday or National Holiday in the United States.
Self-Catering: This type of accommodation usually requires you to stay for a minimum number of nights and therefore has been excluded from this book.
En-suite: Bedroom with private bathroom.

How to Use This Guidebook

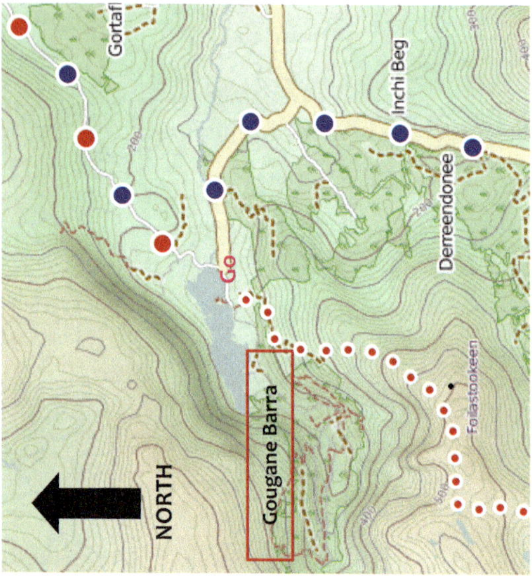

For **orientation,** the place names on the map always indicate the direction of **North.**

Bold pink text on the map indicates the location of accommodation using the first two letters. **The Gougane Barra Hotel** is shown here as **Go**.

All villages and towns on the trail are indicated with a red box.

Prices for accommodation will vary depending on the season and availability. The below will give you a rough guide to the prices.

€ / £	up to 50	Accommodation on the trail
€€ / ££	51 - 80	Accommodation off the trail
€€€ / £££	81+	

Walking trail on road

Walking trail off-road

Optional detour such as forest loop walk

Cycle Route

Carriganass Castle

Site of interest

Follow the **Beara-Breifne Way signposts** and the **yellow hiker icon on black background.**

In some places without arrows there maybe **yellow paint** on posts or rocks. Ignore trail arrows in any other colour.

On the Ulster Way follow the **blue and yellow leaf icon**. Sometimes there will be a **yellow arrow on blue background.**

On the maps, roads highlighted like this in blue, red or purple are cycle-ways and can be ignored.

PART 1:

Beara-Breifne Way

Slí Beara-Breifne

Castletownbere to Blacklion

Stages: 1 - 12

Distance: 680.3 km / 422.7 miles

Counties: Cork, Kerry, Limerick, Tipperary, Offaly, Galway, Roscommon, Sligo, Leitrim, Cavan

Hikers in the Caha Mountains

The March of Donal Cam O'Sullivan Beare

The Beara-Breifne Way follows the 14-day march of the last great Irish Chieftain Donal Cam O'Sullivan Beare. Following the Battle of Kinsale in 1601 where the Irish and Spanish were defeated by the forces of Queen Elizabeth I, Donal Cam fled back to Beara. He put three hundred of his followers, particularly women and children, onto Dursey Island for safety. The British besieged and levelled his castle at Dunboy and then proceeded to Dursey island to massacre the people there. Donal Cam and his remaining one thousand followers hid in the mountains near Glengarriff for a few months. The British army captured his cattle leaving them with no food to get through the winter. Donal Cam had no choice but to flee, heading north to his friends, the O'Rourkes in Breifne, Co. Leitrim. Their march began on 31st December 1602.

The Beara-Breifne Way Today

The creation of the Beara Breifne Way trail is the largest community-led project in Ireland to date and is led by Jim O'Sullivan. Many community groups and committees along the trail route have joined forces to create the trail based on the epic journey of Donal Cam O'Sullivan Beare, using local knowledge and expertise. The trail takes in many sites of historical interest as well as landscapes of natural beauty. This trail is thanks to the hard work of the groups involved, and the kind co-operation of approximately 400 farmers along the trail. To date the trail has cost over €3 million to develop.

Please note that dogs are not permitted on the Beara-Breifne Way trail and the trail is closed to the public on January 31st each year.

STAGE 1:

Beara Way

Slí Beara

Castletownbere - Adrigole - Glengarriff - Kealkill

Distance:	57.5 km / 35.7 miles
Difficulty:	Strenuous
County:	Cork
OSI Maps:	Discovery Series 84 & 85

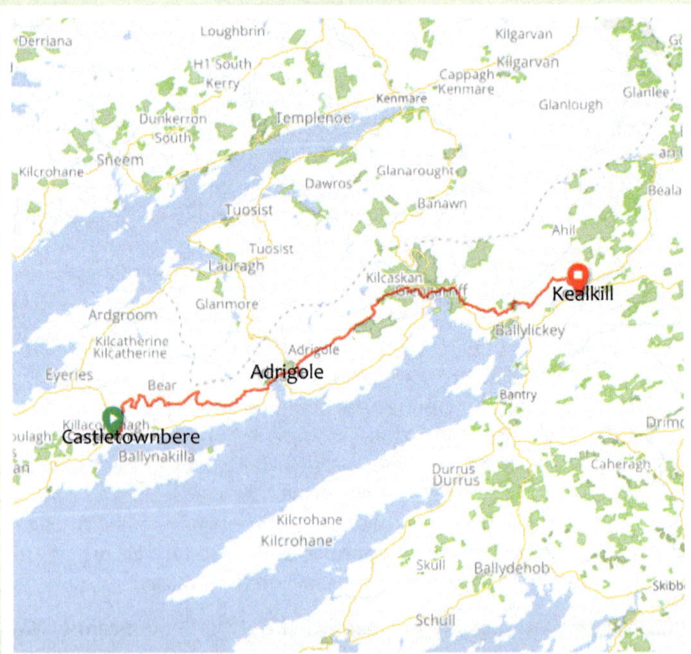

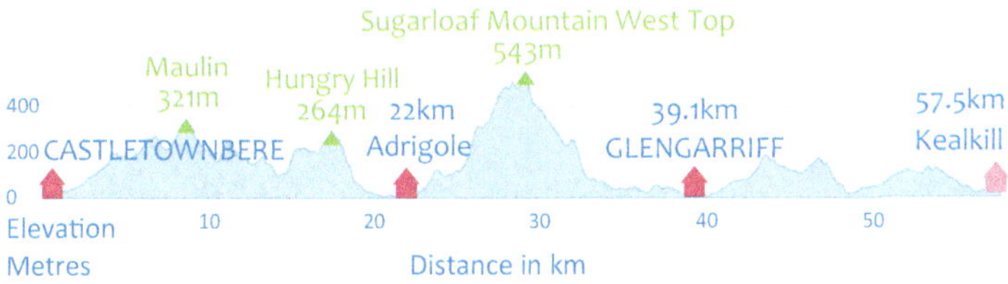

Wedge Tomb overlooking Castletownbere

[0km/0mi] Castletownbere

A S R PO € D P

(Baile Chaisleáin Bhéarra)

The starting point of the Ireland Way is Castletownbere, also known as Castletown-Berehaven. It is a colourful fishing village and one of the five main fishing ports in Ireland with the second-safest natural harbour in the world.

If you arrive in Castletownbere the day before you begin your hike, you can take a stroll to visit the ruin of Dunboy castle. It is 3.6 km/2.2 miles following the main road west of Castletownbere. Follow signs for Dunboy Castle or Puxley Mansion which is located beside the castle ruin. You will see the gatehouse ruin along the main road, marking the entrance to the Dunboy Estate. The estate was given to the Puxley family in the 1700's. They were a wealthy family who brought copper mining to the area. Several Puxley generations later the mines ran dry and when Henry Puxley's wife died in childbirth he decided to leave Ireland and left the mansion with it's caretakers. In 1921 the IRA set the mansion on fire, convinced that it would soon house English troops. The current Puxley Mansion is an impressive restoration project, intended to become Ireland's first six-star hotel until it ran out of money in 2008.

Ruin of Dunboy Castle

The March of Donal Cam O'Sullivan Bere

Donal Cam was not at Dunboy Castle when it fell under attack by the British. O'Sullivan's men defended the castle but were unsuccessful. Those who survived the initial attack spent the night in the darkness of the cellar, surrounded by the wounded and dying. In the morning twenty-six of the men surrendered from the cellar where "...there lay a great heap of bodies and arms, the whole hall ran streams of blood". One man in the cellar who was badly wounded stumbled toward barrels of gunpowder with a lit candle in order to kill himself and the enemy but he was quickly captured and stabbed to death. All of the men who surrendered were later executed. On the 22nd June 1602 the remaining walls of Dunboy Castle were blown up. You can see parts of the walls that remain today.

Camping is available at the back of **McCarthy's Bar**, Main Street, enquire at the bar; **Summer Hill B&B**, +353 (0)27 70417, +353 (0)86 2226271, www.ireland-guesthouse.com; **Sea Breeze B&B**, +353 (0)27 70508, www.seabreez.com; **Black's Seapoint Lodge**, +353 (0)27 70292; **Island View House**, +353 (0)27 70415, www.islandviewhouse.com; **Lugano Guest House**, +353 (0)27 70116; **Rodeen Country House**, +353 (0)27 70158, www.rodeencountryhouse.com. **Knockanroe**, +353 (0)27 70029.

At the east end of Castletownbere village over the bridge you will see a sign for the Beara Way. This section is well signposted though the posts can be tricky to spot at times. You will begin on a beautiful little road with a trickling stream alongside it. When you get to a gate, take the stile over it. There will be many of these stiles along the Way as

Lackawee
Derryclancy
Bawnard
Gortatornora
Maulin
Knocknagree
Knocknagree E-Top
Knocknagree SE-Top
Park Lough
Hungry Hill
Kilmackowen
Tooreen Beg
Pullincha
Bealalocpa
Cloontreem
Curryglass
Foildarrig
Derreentaggart
Derrymihan
CASTLETOWNBERE
1 mi.
1 km
DROUM

they take you in and out of private property and farmland. When you get to the end of this rough road you will be surrounded by long grass. The next way-marker is to the right. Go back a few metres before the mound with the way-marker and you will see a raised 'path' that will keep you out of boggy wet grass. I only noticed this on my second trek up these mountains as sheep were walking on it! Way-markers on these hills are quite far apart, but visible.

The trail passes by the ruin of a **wedge tomb**, with it's cap-stone long fallen off. A few kilometres into the trail it will seem like you are being directed over a fence to go back down the hill: this is correct, over you go! As you ascend further up into the mountains you will walk along a large stream and cross a small bridge. From here you will descend to a large pond called **Park Lough** which is roughly half way to Adrigole. At Park Lough there is the option to leave the trail and go down to the main road. If you think you will not arrive to Adrigole before sunset then it is recommended to leave the trail now, unless you are planning to camp in the mountains. Due to traffic, the main road to Adrigole is not safe for walking so a taxi is recommended. Also bear in mind that you could be waiting an hour for a taxi. **Shanahan's Atlantic Cabs**: +353 (0)27 70116, +353 (0)86 2461877; **Beara Cabs**: +353 (0) 87 6494796; **AD Hackney Service**: +353 (0)87 2845796.

Lough Toberavanaha

After the lough prepare for another ascent. It can get very wet in the long grass here. It is where I learned that my waterproof boots were not waterproof at all! You will soon see **Hungry Hill** (Cnoc Daod) in the distance, the highest peak of the **Caha Mountains** at 685m. The trail goes around Hungry Hill before the final boggy descent into Adrigole.

[22km/13.7mi] Adrigole

A S

Eadargóil - 'Between two inlets'

The only accommodation in Adrigole is **Hungry Hill Lodge**. You can get drinks and frozen pizza at the lodge if the nearby *Peg's Shop* is closed by the time you arrive. Alternatively there is a kitchen in the lodge where you can cook your own food.

2 Adrigole

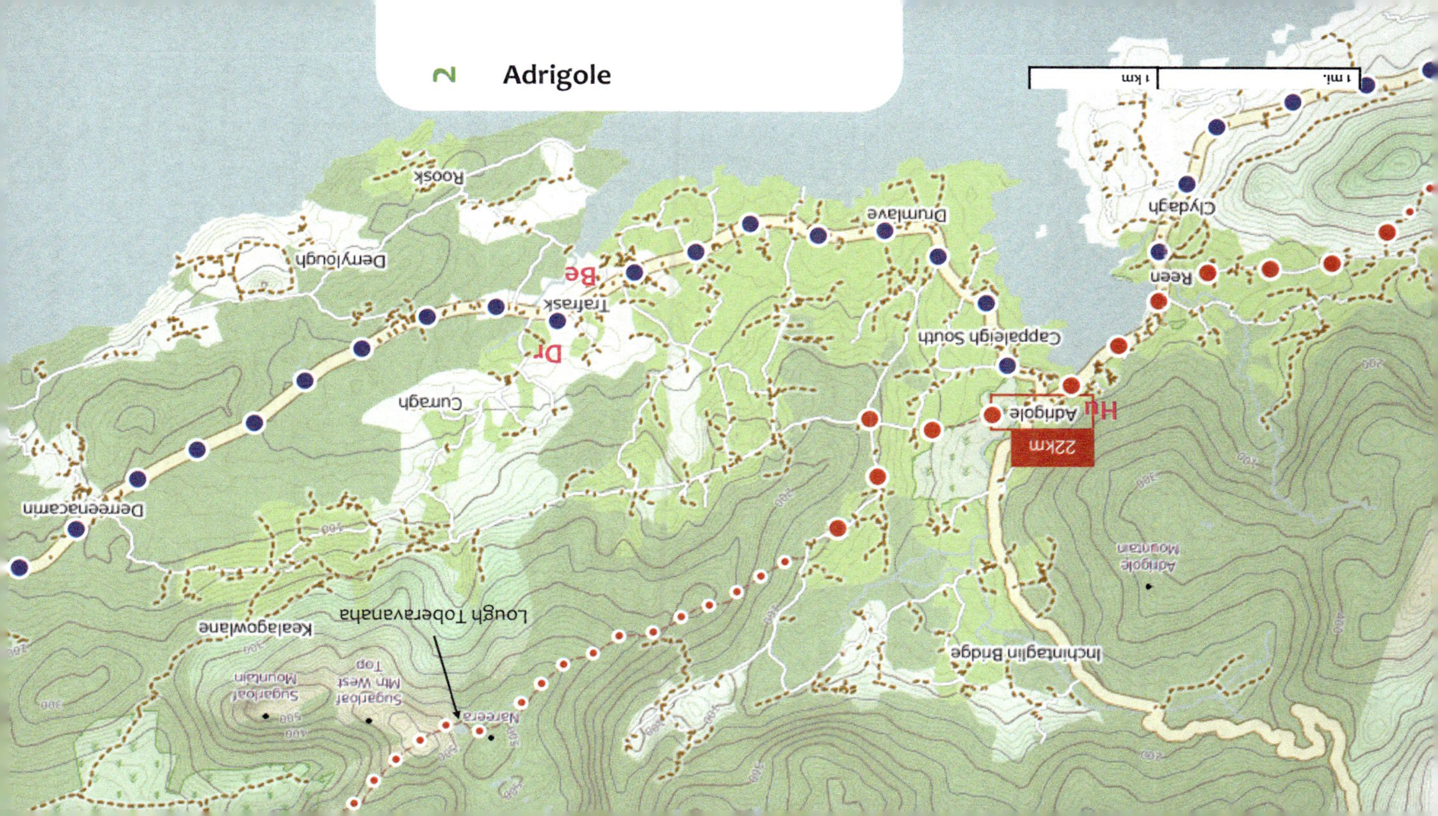

Derreenacarrin
Kealagowlane
Sugarloaf Mountain
Sugarloaf Mtn West Top
Lough Toberavanaha
Nareera
Curragh
Derrylough
Roosk
Trafrask
Dr
Be
Drumlave
Cappaleigh South
Adrigole
Hu
22km
Inchintaglin Bridge
Adrigole Mountain
Reen
Clydagh
1 km
1 mi.

Hungry Hill Lodge (hostel & campsite, closes in winter months) +353 (0)27 60228, www.hungryhilllodge.com. It is often fully booked out and is closed in winter months; Beechmount B&B, Trafask, East Adrigole: a few kilometres from Adrigole but the kind owner will collect you, +353 (0)27 60075; Dromagowlane B&B, +353 (0)27 60330, www.dromagowlanehouse.com.

Leaving Adrigole you will enter a forested area and pass over a metal grate bridge. The terrain will be rough fields, some road and then up into the mountains. Way-markers can be hard to spot in places but look carefully and you will see them. You will follow a fence for some time and also be provided with an "emergency exit" down to the main road should you require it. A few kilometres later you will arrive at a **Lough Toberavanaha** which is a good spot for lunch before the next ascent. Stunning views from the top await, looking towards Glengarriff and **Glengarriff Forest Park** and rolling mountains for miles into the distance. You will walk along the mountain ridge for a while before a final descent into Glengarriff. 6.5km/4miles before Glengarriff is Coomarkane Visitor Centre (+353 (0)27 68326) which includes camping and glamping facilities. Pop in for a cup of tea and check out Audrey's Bronze-work studio and shop. Soon you will enter **Glengarriff Forest Park**. In the park you can either follow the road all the way to the town (actual trail route) or you can take a left turn (marked by a painted arrow on the road) in through the forest. This is not the actual trail but is off-road and you get to explore the forest; though it is followed by 1km on a busy road into Glengarriff town. There is a hard-shoulder to walk along.

Glengarriff Forest Park

3 Glengarriff

[17.1km/10.6mi] Glengarriff

A S R PO € D P

An Gleann Garbh - 'Rough Glen'

Glengarriff is a popular stop for tourists and boasts many natural attractions. **Glengarriff Forest Park** has some of the oldest birch and oak groves left in Ireland. You can take a short steep path up to **Lady Bantry's Lookout** to see beautiful views of West Cork. The Italian Gardens can be visited on **Garnish Island** by boat if you have time. The **Martello round tower** on the island was built to keep watch due to the threat of a Napoleonic invasion.

Glengarriff is a lovely town in which to take a rest day should you need one as there are several sites to explore. Knee or foot injuries tend to happen in the first few days of the Ireland Way with the steep ascents and descents and uneven terrain. The next two days will also be mostly off-road uneven terrain which will continue to challenge those lesser-used muscles. You have over 900km left so take care in these strenuous early days of your journey. There is also a pharmacy here if you get blisters like I did!

Blue Pool Hostel, +353 (0)27 55829, +353 (0)869112050, www.bluepoolhostel.com: **Bay View Boutique Guest House**, +353 (0) 27 63030, www.bayviewboutiqueguesthouse.com; **Carraig Dubh House B&B**, +353 (0)27 63146; **Cottage Bar & Restaurant**, +353 (0)27 63226; **Island View House**, +353 (0)27 63081, www.islandviewhouse.net; **Magannagan Farm**, +353 (0)27 63361, www.bearawaybb.com; **Oakfield B&B**, +353 (0)27 63371; **Rockwood House**, +353 (0)27 63097, +353 (0)86 8292541; **The Heights Farmhouse B&B**, +353 (0)27 63088; **River Lodge B&B**, +353 (0)27 63049, +353 (0)87 6728615; **Arches B&B**, +353 (0)27 63836, www.archesglengarriff.com; **Casey's Hotel**, +353 (0)27 63010, www.caseyhotelglengarriff.ie; **Glengarriff Eccles Hotel**, +353 (0)27 63003, www.eccleshotel.com; **Glengarriff Park Hotel**, +353 (0)27 63000, www.glengarriffparkhotel.com. **The Perrin Inn B&B**, +353 (0) 27 63226. **Glengarriff Caravan & Camping Park**, +353 (0)27 63154, email: glengarriffccp@gmail.com.

View from hillside overlooking the bay

Leaving Glengarriff there is 3.3km to walk along a busy road, passing **Bamboo Park**. The trail is well waymarked and the yellow man will direct you when to cross the road and turn left off the main road. Climb into the hills alongside pylons. There was one

Farmhouse Ruin

incorrect way-marker up the hill but follow where the path is most worn and keep the sea in view, turning away from the pylons rather than following them to the very top. After you descend the hills out of the long knee-high grass you will follow a narrow tarmac road for a while until turning right through a metal gate. Walk through a small forest and the trail will take you through fields with stunning views over Bantry Bay.

It was along here that I remember stopping for a rest and enjoying the spectacular view of the coastline and the bay dotted with islands; the largest being **Whiddy Island** with **Sheep's Head** peninsula in the distance. There must have once been sheep but it is now home to a large herd of goats.

A forest track will lead you to Coomhola (no facilities) where you will follow the road and take the bridge over Coomhola river. Follow the main road until taking a left to follow a gently winding road track occasionally coloured with purple heather during the summer months. Off road again and trekking through long grass, passing by a farmhouse ruin and here you may also pass through a field of cattle. The trail is overgrown but easy enough to navigate as you wade through the long grass and follow the way-markers. Take care on the last stretch on the winding road into Kealkill village.

The March of Donal Cam O'Sullivan Bere

Donal Cam and his followers hid in the valley just before Glengarriff for a few months, keeping their animals in a field close by. In December 1602 the English closed in, capturing Donal Cam's two thousand cows and four thousand sheep. With very little food left and winter setting in, Donal Cam knew that their only hope for survival was to make the journey to their friends, the O'Rourkes, in County Leitrim. On New Year's Eve in 1602, with approximately 1,000 followers, Donal Cam fled from the Beara Peninsula. The first day they walked twenty-six miles, stopping briefly at Gougane Barra.

Donal Cam's nephew Philip wrote an account of the journey about fifteen years later. From this we know that Donal Cam's followers included thirteen horsemen and around four hundred soldiers; the rest were foot followers, horseboys, women, old men and servants. All the roads were beset with enemies and a large sum of money was promised to whomever would slay Donal Cam.

STAGE 2:

Slí Gaeltacht Mhuscraí

The Muskerry Way

Kealkill - Gougane Barra - Ballingeary - Ballyvourney - Millstreet

Distance: 71.6 km / 44.5 miles
Difficulty: Strenuous
County: Cork
OSI Maps: Discovery Series 85 & 79

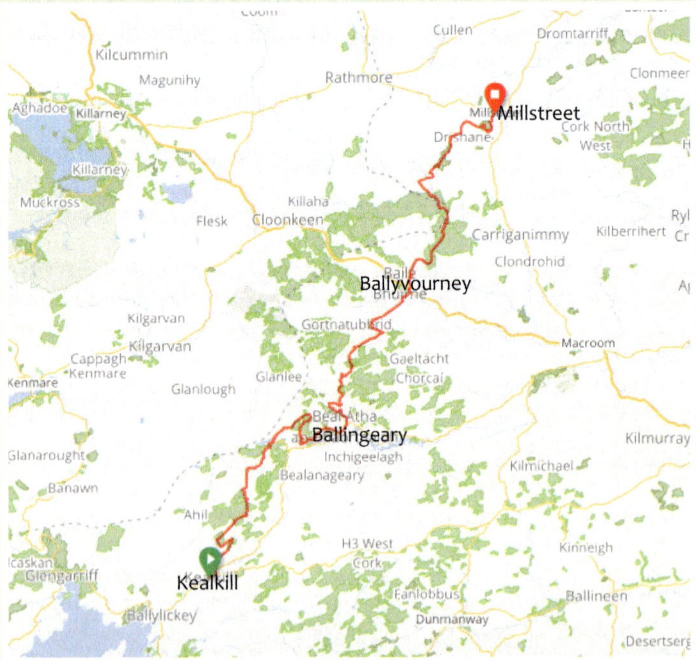

"Everywhere is within walking distance if you have the time."

- Steven Wright

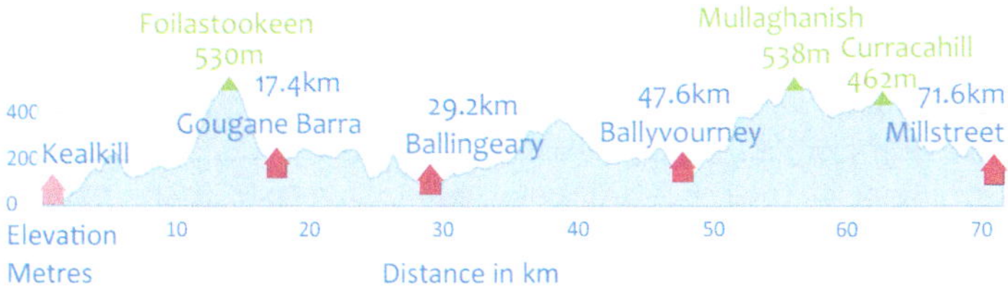

Slí Gaeltacht Mhuscraí (Muskerry Gaeltacht Way) is in the west of County Cork and joins Kealkill to Millstreet. There is a mix of forested areas, moorland and bogland with some beautiful views of mountains and lakes.

From Kealkill you will climb and descend the **Shehy Mountains** before arriving at Gougane Barra. This section should not be done in bad weather as visibility can be poor in thick fog. There are plans for a 'lower' route around the Shehy Mountains though it is not currently way-marked.

Slí Gaeltacht Mhuscraí

[18.4km/11.4mi] Kealkill

A S

An Choillchaoill

Kealkill has one shop (Burke's Gala) and two pubs. There are three accommodation options not far from the village by car; see details below. The ruin of **Carriganass Castle** once owned by Donal Cam's father, then his uncle and cousin sits beside the Owvane River.

The Bridge House, Pearson's Bridge, www.booking.com. The Bridge House offer a pick-up service from Kealkill. It is only a 4-minute drive and you can get meals in the bar. Alternatively you can take a 6-minute cab ride to **Ouvane Falls Inn**, +353 (0)27 50056, www.ouvanefalls.com; or **Aran Lodge**, www.aran-lodge.com, +353 (0)27 2750378; both in nearby town Ballylickey. The Ouvane Falls Inn has a bar and restaurant and is a short stroll from Aran Lodge. The Ouvane Falls Inn has traditional entertainment on Tuesday and Thursday evenings. **Ard na Greine**, Ballylickey, +353 (0)879786879. **A2B Cabs**, +353 (0)86 233 7574, also offers a bag drop service should you wish to walk without your backpack.

Leaving Kealkill follow the road for approximately 4km before reaching a grass track with a steep ascent. Over the hill you will descend along a grass track between pine trees. A wooden stile takes you onto a quiet road where you will walk towards **Kealkill Windfarm** for 2 km. A grass track and small forest will lead you to a road which

Carriganass Castle, Kealkill

4 Kealkill

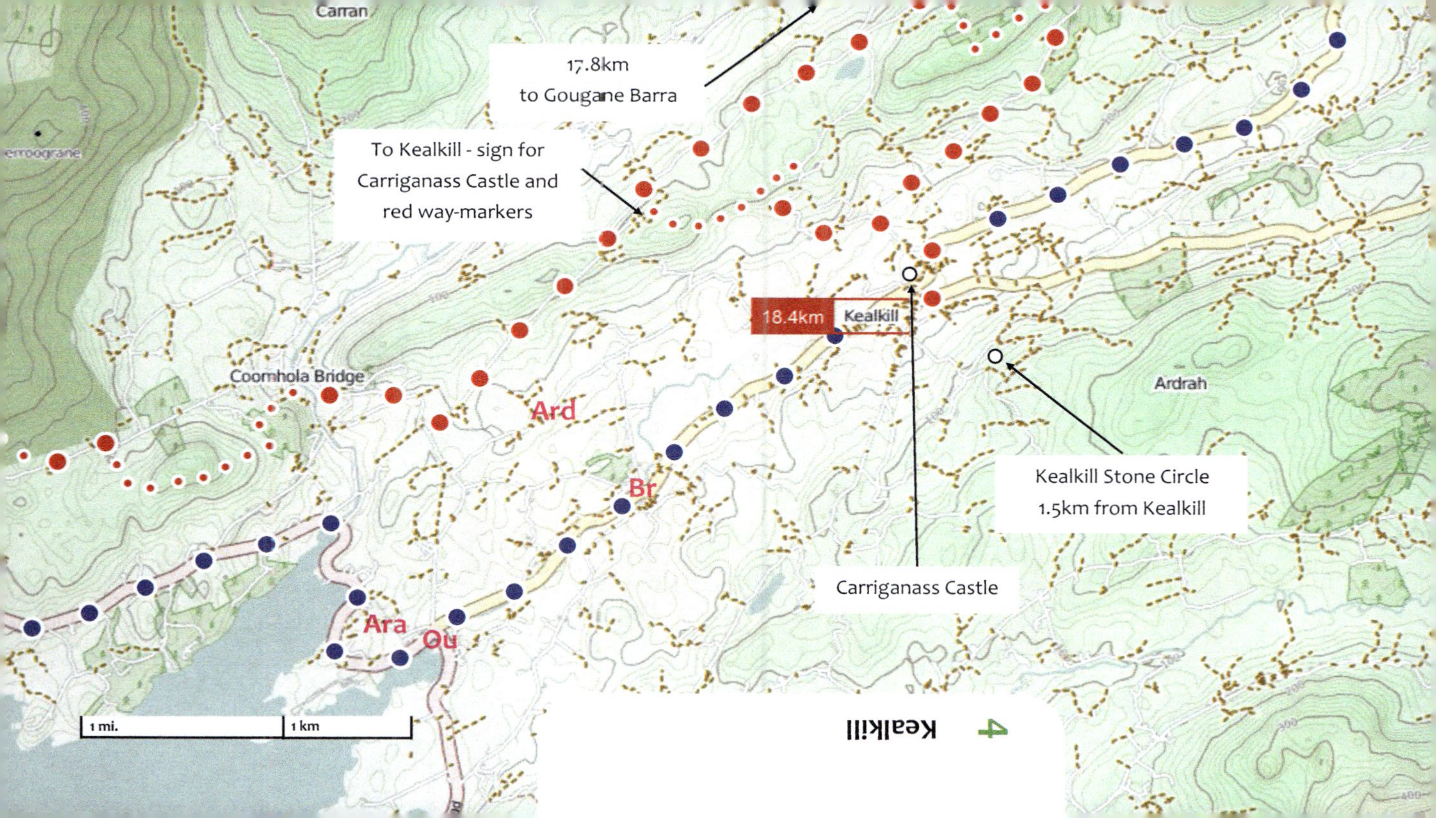
17.8km
to Gougane Barra
To Kealkill - sign for
Carriganass Castle and
red way-markers
18.4km
Kealkill
Carriganass Castle
Kealkill Stone Circle
1.5km from Kealkill
Ardrah
Coomhola Bridge
Carran
Ard
Br
Ara
Ou
1 mi.
1 km

passes by the windfarm and a field of Scottish Highland cattle. The farmer here hangs up the cattle skulls so it's a little eerie! A fairly steep climb up the Shehy Mountain will give you your last glimpses of Bantry Bay and the southern coastline. If it is foggy and you are unable to see the next signpost or painted yellow arrow along the top of the mountain, note that the trail follows straight alongside the fence until you reach a stile and two loughs and then continues alongside the fence to the right after the stile. The loughs are **Lough Fadda** on your left and the heart-shaped **Lough Namral** to your right. Turning right at Lough Namral the fence will take you to the top of **Foilastookeen**. Here there is a nice view of the River Lee Valley. From Foilastookeen walk down along the steep ridge, guided by the fence to your right. Take care on the steep descent into Gougane Barra as it can be very slippery when wet. Enjoy the breath-taking views of the lake on your way into the valley if you are lucky enough to have a clear day. A wide path will take you by some farm buildings and goats. After the last of the green stiles you will pass a circular thatched building which is a public toilet, and further along on your right is the Gougane Barra Hotel.

[17.4km/10.8mi] Gougane Barra A R

Guagán Barra - "The Rock of Barra"

The name 'Barra' refers to Saint Finbarr, patron saint of Co. Cork, who is said to have built a monastery here in the 6th century. The hotel was fully booked when I arrived due to a wedding (which happens regularly as it is a popular wedding venue). They didn't mind that I

Gougane Barra Lake and Chapel

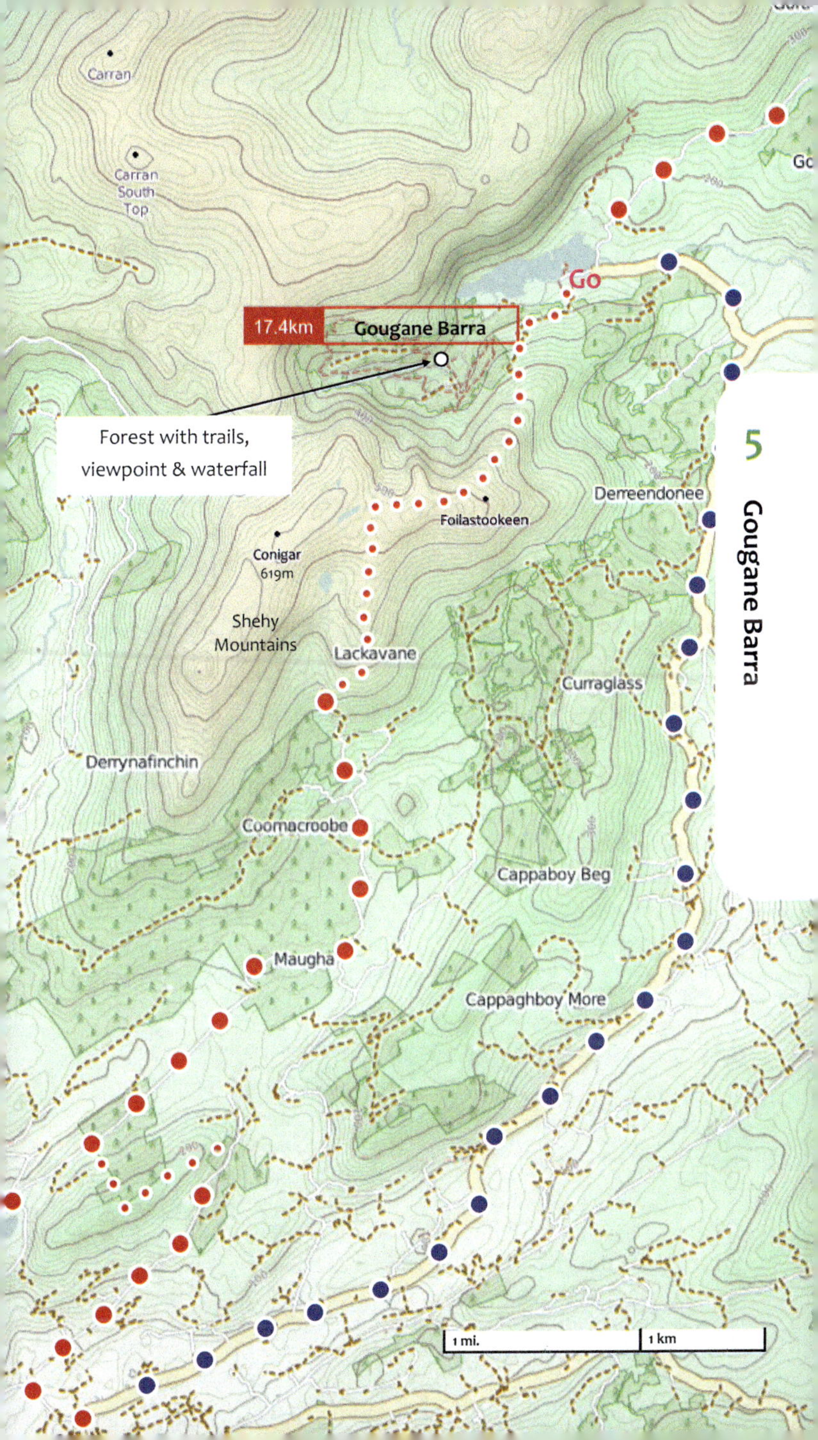
Carran
Carran South Top
17.4km
Gougane Barra
Forest with trails, viewpoint & waterfall
Foilastookeen
Conigar 619m
Shehy Mountains
Derreendonee
Lackavane
Curraglass
Derrynafinchin
Coomacroobe
Cappaboy Beg
Maugha
Cappaghboy More
1 mi.
1 km

was mucky and soaking through as they are well used to hikers here. The receptionist kindly booked me into Tír na Spideoga fishing lodge in Ballylickey, a short drive away. I had a lovely meal at the hotel while I waited for the taxi as there are no other shops or places to eat nearby.

Gougane Barra

Be sure to explore the small island on the lake and St. Finbarr's Oratory. This beautifully decorated 19th-century oratory is a destination for pilgrims who come to pray here. Opening hours 9am-6pm. Beside the oratory you will see a structure which dates from around 1700 and plaques showing the Stations of the Cross in Gaelic. This structure was built to represent the monastery which once stood here.

If you still have some energy left after your days hike, or if you take a rest day here, you can explore **Gougane Barra National Forest Park.** Allow one or two hours for this. It has several walking trails. Slí an Éasa will take you up to a waterfall, with a beautiful view of the valley when you climb to the top.

Gougane Barra Hotel, +353 (0)26 47069, www.gouganebarra hotel.com. The hotel may allow you to camp and use their facilities; enquire at reception. If the hotel is fully booked, take a taxi to accommodation listed for the next town, Ballingeary.

Famine Pot, Ballingeary

Leaving Gougane Barra you will walk along a gentle upward-sloping quiet road. After about 4 km, at a fork in the road take a right and another right shortly after. You will come to a small stone bridge; don't miss the left turn right before it with the black and yellow barrier. Follow this rough road and you will come to a grass track which may be overgrown with gorse. At the time of writing this I recall that it was necessary to crawl on hands and knees to get past the prickly gorse! Once back onto a small road you will walk along beside the river Lee on the way into Ballingeary.

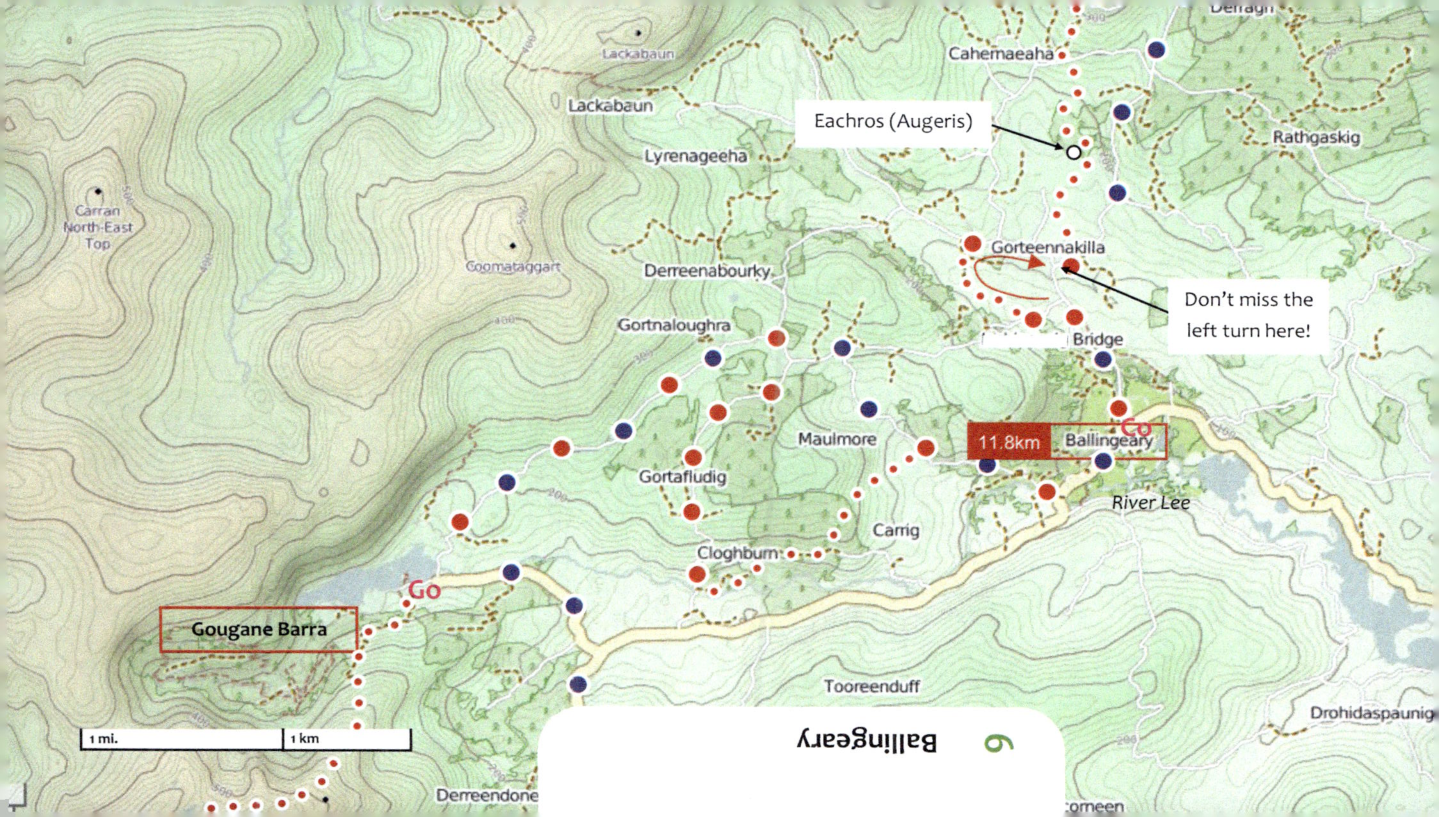
6
Ballingeary
Cahemaeaha
Eachros (Augeris)
Rathgaskig
Lackabaun
Lackabaun
Lyrenageeha
Carran North-East Top
Coomataggart
Gorteennakilla
Don't miss the left turn here!
Derreenabourky
Gortnaloughra
Bridge
Maulmore
11.8km
Ballingeary
Go
River Lee
Gortafludig
Carrig
Cloghburn
Go
Gougane Barra
Tooreenduff
Drohidaspaunig
1 mi.
1 km
Derreendone

[11.8km/7.3mi] Ballingeary

A S R PO D

Béal Átha an Ghaortaidh

Located in the Shehy Mountains in County Cork, Ballingeary is in the Gealtacht or Irish/Gaelic-speaking region. If you haven't heard Gaelic on your journey yet, you are likely to hear it spoken here. Over the stone bridge dated c.1800 you will see a large cast iron **'Famine Pot'**. It was provided by the owner of Coolmountain House a few miles away to give soup to those who were starving during the Great Famine of 1845 - 1852. Its last owners used it as a bathtub!

Curious Cattle

Take a taxi to **Tír Na Spideoga Fishing Lodge**, +353 (0)26 47151, www.pike-fishing-ireland.com. Ask to stay in one of the thatched cottages if they are available or stay in part of the main house which is over 100 years old; further away by taxi is **Mary Murphy's B&B**, Inshigeelagh, 086 3627209.

Important Safety Note about Cattle

A herd of cattle in a field are usually dairy cows or young bullocks and in my experience are generally safe to walk by. They are however very curious and will watch you, walk towards you and even surround you! Waving a hiking stick at them is often useful so you can pass by.

Bulls on the other hand are unpredictable and dangerous. They usually have a ring in their nose and are in a field on their own, though sometimes one might be mixed in with cows. Cows with calves are equally dangerous. Don't take any risks with cattle/bulls and take an alternative route if necessary. Do a quick scan for bulls before you enter every field. I recommend walking along the perimeter of fields with cattle so as to have a way of escape if necessary.

Author at the Church Ruin at Augeris. Photo by A. Moore.

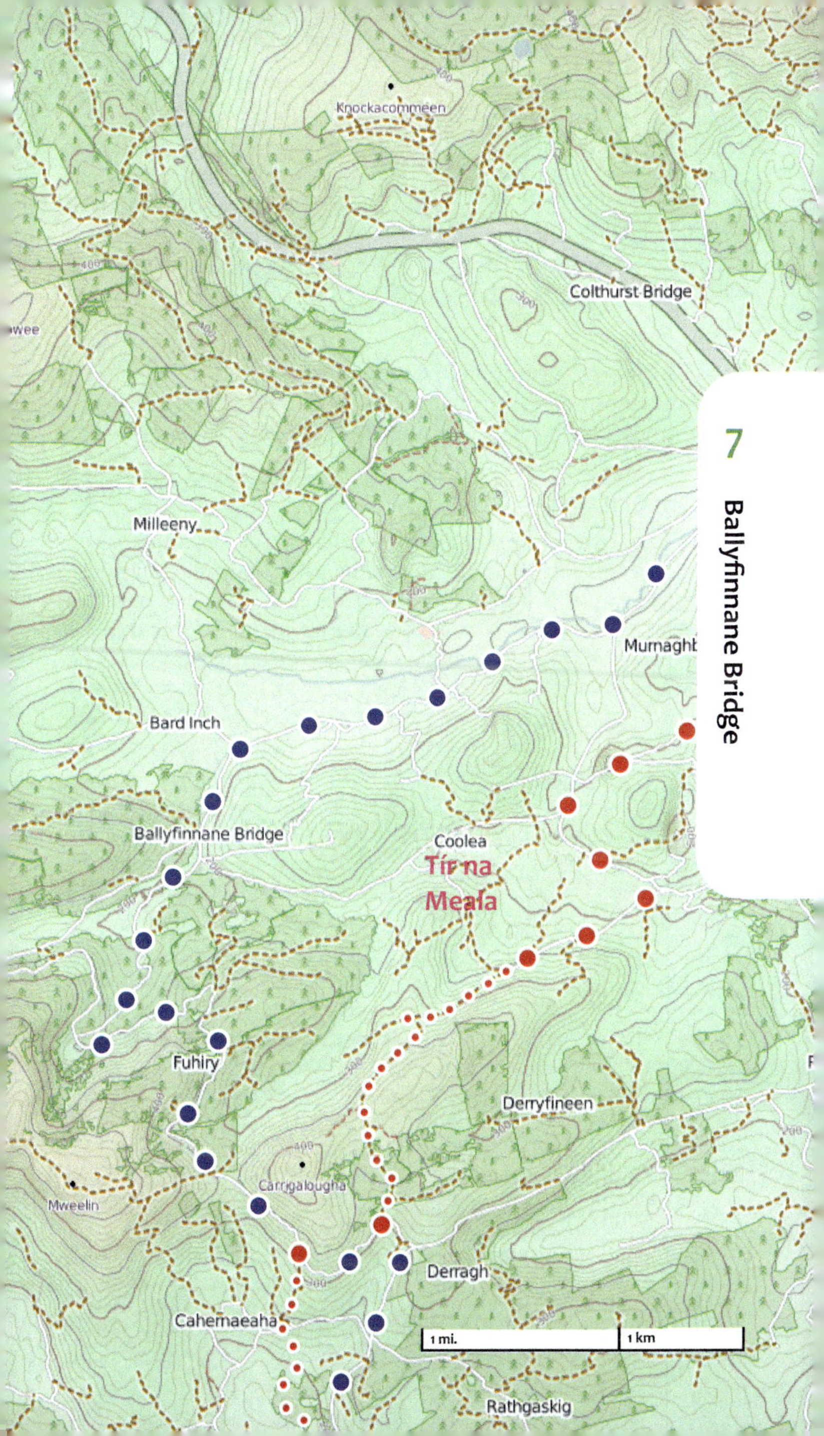
Knockacommeen
Colthurst Bridge
Milleeny
Bard Inch
Ballyfinnane Bridge
Coolea
Tír na Meala
Fuhiry
Derryfineen
Carrigalougha
Mweelin
Derragh
Cahernaeaha
Rathgaskig
1 mi.
1 km

First Rest since Setting Off from Glengarriff

Donal Cam and his people had their first night's rest at Augeris by a church ruin which would have been surrounded by forest at the time. They camped on religious ground for whatever protection it might provide them. During the night they let their horses roam about. Donal Cam's horse, named *An Cearc* (The Hen) broke his leg in a bog-hole during the night and drowned.

From Ballingeary most of the trail slopes gently uphill through fields until the forest on Carrigalougha hill and then it descends into Ballyvourney along a rough road and finally a quiet country road.

Tír na Meala B&B, Coolea, €€€, 1.5km off trail, +353 (0)26 45651, www.tirnameala-coolea.com.

Just before arriving in Ballyvourney you will see a wrought iron archway on your left for ***Tobar Ghobnatan***, or St. Gobnait's Holy Well. St. Gobnait was a 7th-century woman believed to have both curative and destructive powers. Donal Cam and his people stopped at St. Gobnait's shrine to pray, offer gifts and ask for protection. Just one year before, in 1601, Pope Clement VIII imparted a blessing for people who visited here. Pilgrims hang cloths, ribbons and trinkets from the 'wishing tree' and offer prayers. There are two taps nearby for pilgrims who wish to drink the water from the well. Further up the hill (go back out to the road and go right and right again) are the remains of a monastic settlement which include St. Gobnait's House, another well, and a statue of the Saint. Pilgrims walk around the stations, scratching crosses into the rocks and saying seven Our Father's, seven Hail Mary's and seven Glory Be's.

St. Gobnait's Shrine

[18.4km/11.4mi] Ballyvourney A S R D

Baile Mhúirne - "The Town of the Beloved"

The Abbey Hotel, +353 (0)26 45324, www.theabbeyhotel.ie; **The Mills Inn**, +353 (0)2645237, www.millsinn.ie. Live music on Friday nights.

Ballyvourney to Millstreet is well way-marked. There are a lot of electric fences on the first part of the off-road trail. The ascending

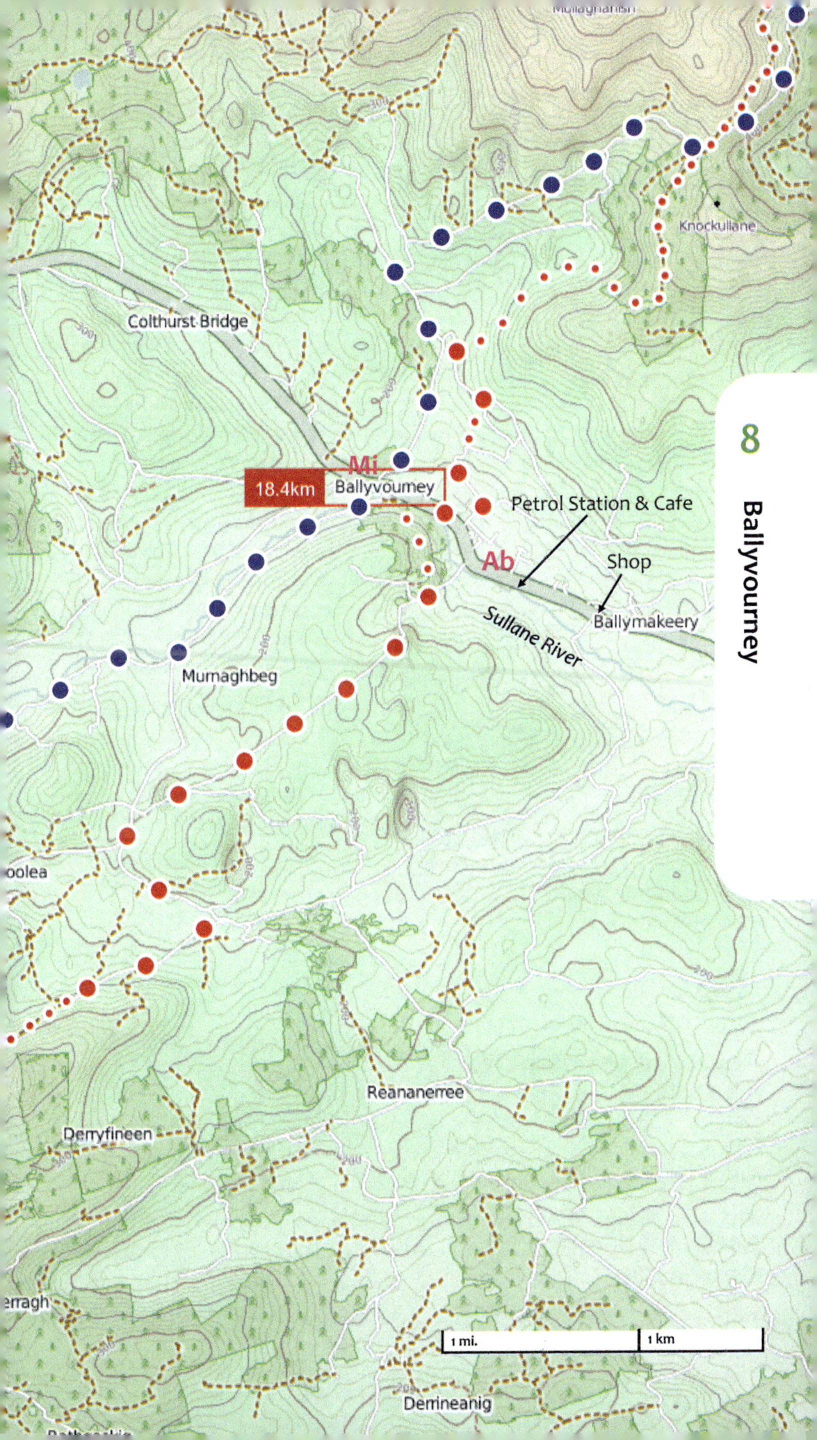
Knockullane
Colthurst Bridge
Mi
18.4km
Ballyvourney
Petrol Station & Cafe
Ab
Shop
Ballymakeery
Sullane River
Murnaghbeg
Reananerree
Derryfineen
Derrineanig
1 mi.
1 km

Slí Gaeltacht Mhuscraí

trail to **Mullaghanish mountain** can get waterlogged in winter months. If there is a signpost to say that it is waterlogged then follow the cycle route for a few kilometres until it joins up with the walking route again. The trail passes through some forested areas and there are lovely views on the approach to **Gneeves Windfarm**. You will walk right through the windfarm, and then along a boardwalk. After the boardwalk watch out for the way-markers. There is one off to your right that is easily missed. Follow a short distance of road before going up and around the fields of **Claragh Mountain**. Descend through a small forest. There is a stile at a small pond; be sure to take a left over the stile (it is marked incorrectly to turn right) and soon you will arrive at Millstreet.

Claragh Mountain

The end of the cycle trail joins up with the Duhallow Way trail so you should start to see signs with 'Beara-Breifne Way (Duhallow)'.

Attacked by the MacCarthys

Near Mullaghanish Donal Cam and his followers were attacked by the MacCarthys. It was the first time they had to fight since leaving Glengarriff two days before. The MacCarthys had previously been allies of the O'Sullivans but were now loyal to the queen. There was also a reward of £300 for the capture of Donal Cam.

The MacCarthys attacked them from the rear. Donal Cam had his soldiers turn suddenly to face their enemy. The MacCarthys suffered some casualties before fleeing back to their castle nearby.

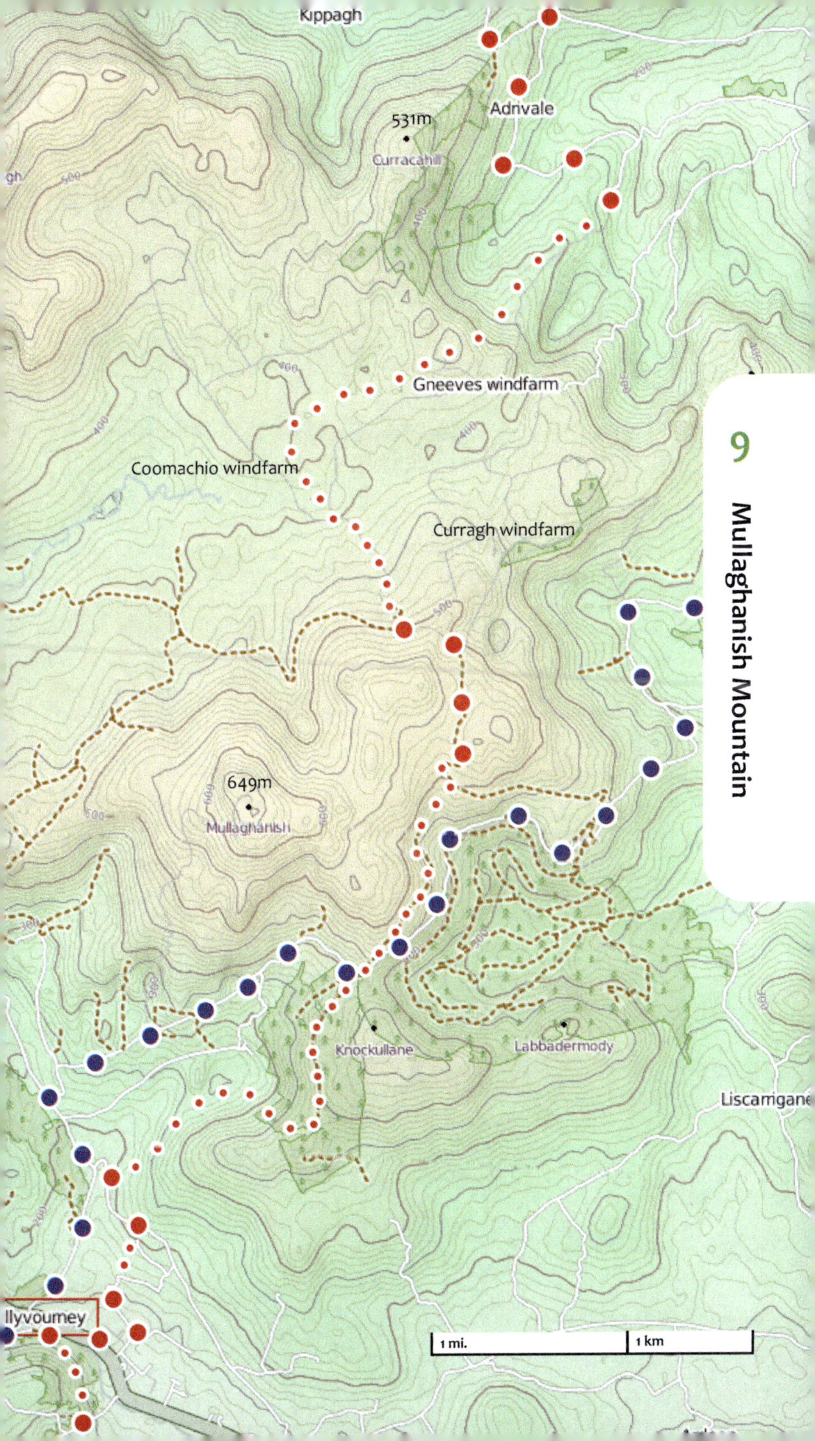
Kippagh
Adrivale
531m
Curracahill
Gneeves windfarm
Coomachio windfarm
Curragh windfarm
649m
Mullaghanish
Knockullane
Labbadermody
Liscarrigane
llyvourney
1 mi.
1 km

STAGE 3:

North West Cork Way

Slí Iarthuaisceart Chorcaí

Millstreet - Dernagree - **Newmarket** - Lismire - St. John's Bridge

Distance: 40.2 km / 25 miles
Difficulty: Moderate
County: Cork
OSI Maps: Discovery Series 79 & 72

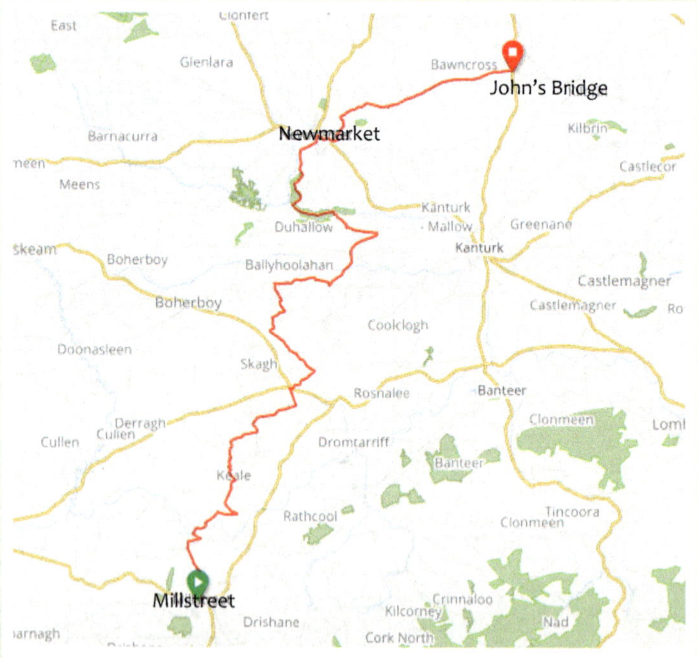

"Only one who wanders will find a new path."

- Norwegian Proverb

The North West Cork Way is signposted as Beara-Breifne Way (Duhallow), (not to be confused with the Duhallow Way, which runs perpendicular to it). The North West Cork Way is one of the last of the stages to be completed so you will notice it is less developed than the stages before it with most of the trail being on tarmac road.

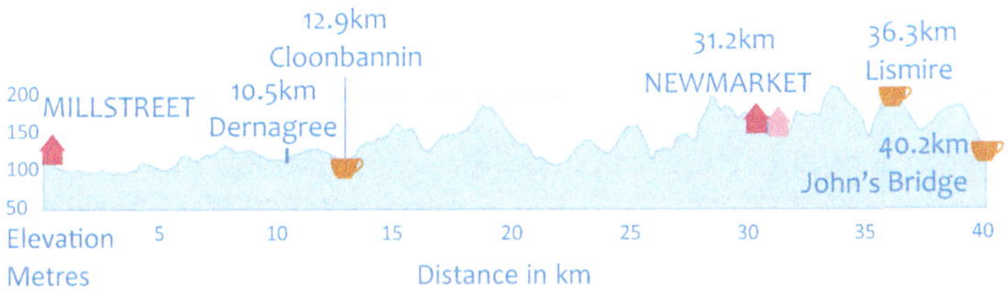

Pretty Cottage

[24km/14.9mi] Millstreet

A S R PO € D P W

Sráid an Mhuilinn

Millstreet has a population of around 1,500 and lies at the foot of Claragh Mountain. There is a B&B called Riverview House a few kilometres past the town that is recommended (see below).

The Wallis Arms Hotel, +353 (0)29 71445, www.wallisarmshotel.com; **The Laurels B&B**, +353 (0)87 2398335; **Knockdrish B&B**, 10-minute walk from town, +353 (0)29 70617.

Leaving Millstreet follow Station road towards the train station. Keep to the right after the train station and then take a left towards the bridge. There is an old way-marker from a time before the footbridge was built that indicates to keep going straight; so **don't miss the left turn**⍰ Cross the bridge over the **River Blackwater** which was built especially for the Beara-Breifne Way trail in 2016. There is a nice photo opportunity just before the bridge. If it is a hot day it is a lovely spot to wade in the river or go for a swim. Just past this bridge is **Riverview House B&B** €, (recommended & budget friendly), 0872479333. The lovely owner has walked the trail so is quite familiar with the trek you are undertaking. She is a 'trail angel' and offers pick-up and drop-off so you can walk without your backpack for a couple of days. You will be well looked after here!

River Blackwater

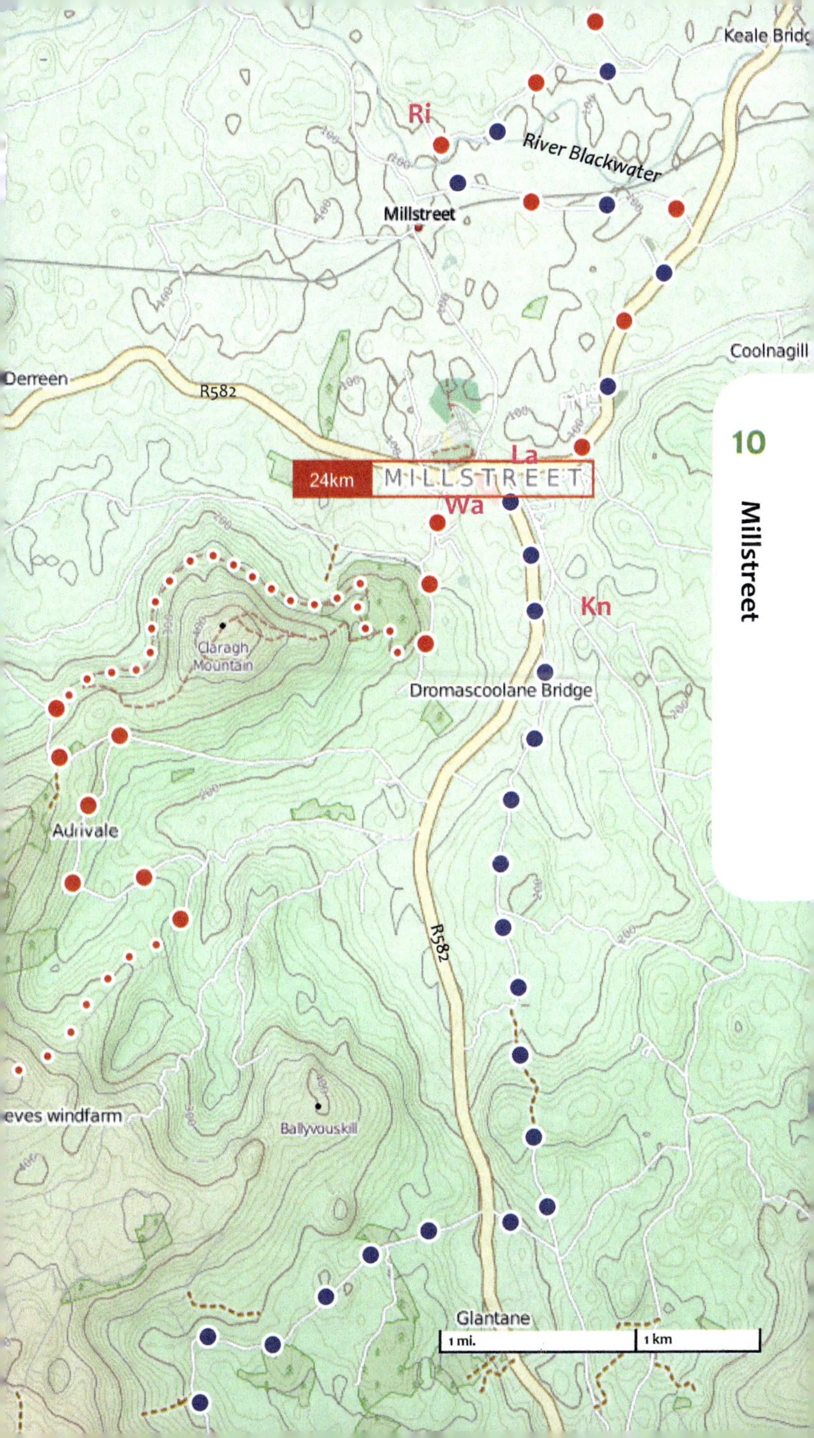
Keale Bridg
Ri
River Blackwater
Millstreet
Coolnagill
Derreen
R582
La
24km MILLSTREET
Wa
Kn
Claragh Mountain
Dromascoolane Bridge
Adrivale
R582
eves windfarm
Ballyvouskill
Glantane
1 mi.
1 km

Walkers on the road to Dernagree

Crossing the Blackwater

Donal Cam and his followers crossed the River Blackwater using steps that had been there for centuries. They were watched closely by the McCarthys on one side and the O'Keeffes on the other.

Beara-Breifne Way (Duhallow) Signpost

From the river Blackwater the trail follows along the river and in 1km at the T-junction turn right and then the next left and in 2.3km go right and then almost immediately left. Follow this narrow road for about 1km and at the T-junction turn right, and in another 1km turn left at the next T-junction and you will soon arrive in Dernagree.

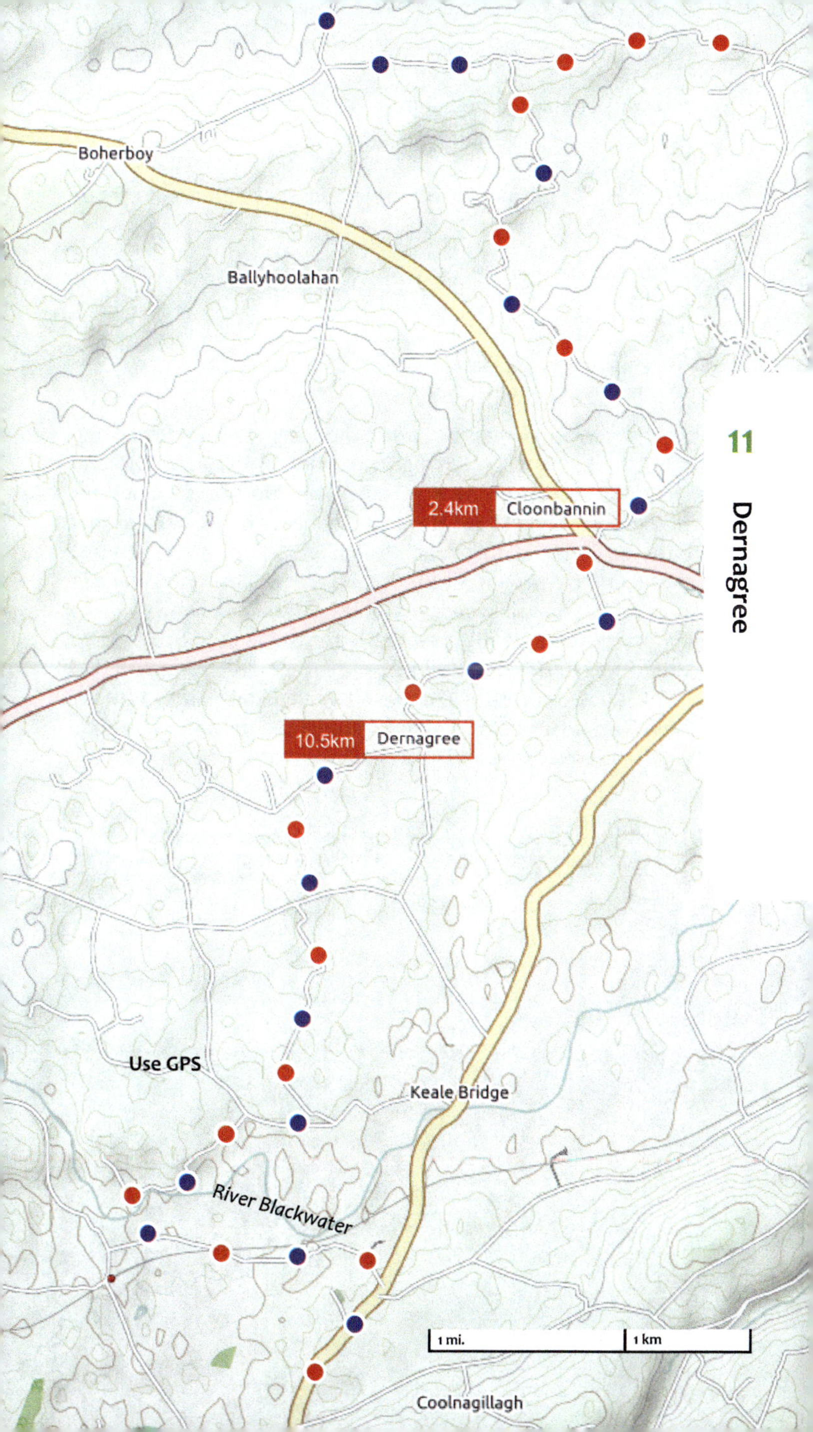
Boherboy
Ballyhoolahan
2.4km Cloonbannin
10.5km Dernagree
Use GPS
Keale Bridge
River Blackwater
1 mi.
1 km
Coolnagillagh

[10.5km/6.5mi] Dernagree/Derinagree

Doire na Graí

Dernagree has a large church and some houses. There are no shops or pubs.

2km past the church turn left and at the end of this road turn right into Cloonbannin.

[2.4km/1.5mi] Cloonbannin

S

Go past the car repair garage, small shop and pub and take the second left and in 1km go left again. Follow Drominagh road and gravel path for 3km, turn right at the T-junction and continue for another 2km. Turn right at the next T-junction. In 2.3km at the crossroads go left and follow this road for 2.3km, going straight through the first crossroads. At the second crossroads turn left and in 1.2km turn right. You will soon arrive at the **Dalua/Dallow River** which is a tributary of the River Blackwater. Enter the field to your left to get to the bridge. This is followed by a lovely trail through **Island Wood Park**. Look out for the tree with twelve trunks known locally as the **Twelve Apostles**. After 4km join onto the narrow Kerry road and then at the crossroads and church turn left into Newmarket.

Gate on the Beara-Breifne Way (Duhallow)

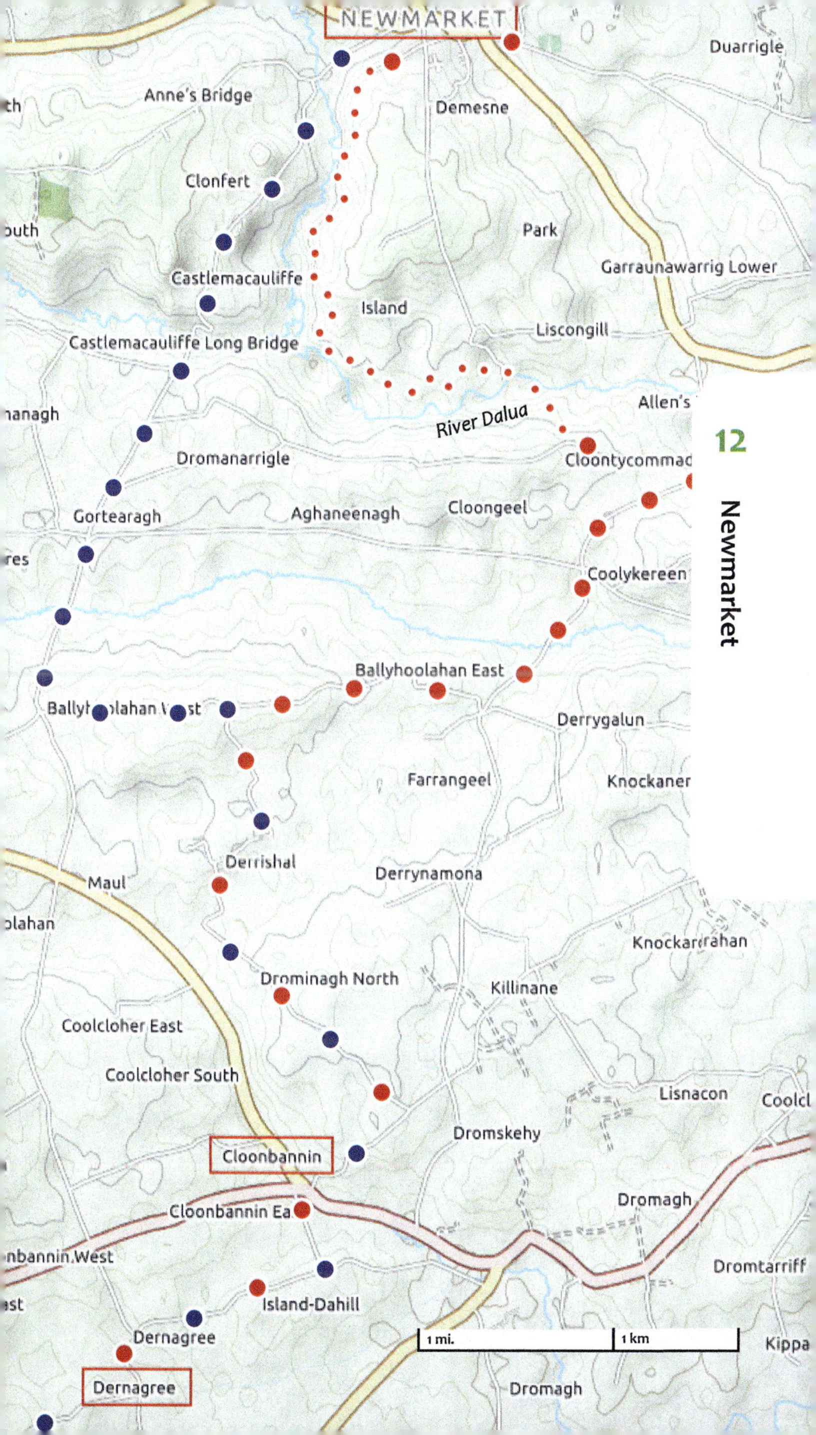
NEWMARKET
Duarrigle
Anne's Bridge
Demesne
Clonfert
Park
Garraunawarrig Lower
Castlemacauliffe
Island
Liscongill
Castlemacauliffe Long Bridge
Allen's
River Dalua
Dromanarrigle
Cloontycommac
Gortearagh
Aghaneenagh
Cloongeel
Coolykereen
Ballyhoolahan East
Derrygalun
Farrangeel
Knockaner
Derrishal
Maul
Derrynamona
Knockarrahan
Drominagh North
Killinane
Coolcloher East
Coolcloher South
Lisnacon
Dromskehy
Cloonbannin
Dromagh
Dromtarriff
Island-Dahill
Dernagree
1 mi.
1 km
Kippa
Dromagh

[18.3km/11.4mi] Newmarket

A S R PO € D P

Historical name: Aghatrasna, Áth Trasna in Gaelic

Newmarket has plenty of shops and places for food but no accommodation. Taxi: **Yellow Cabs**, Newmarket, +353 (0)21 487 444.

From High street turn right onto Church street and in 0.5km at the grotto turn left onto Pound Hill road. In 1.4km turn right at the fork in the road towards Lismire, onto Copsefield road. In 3km you will reach the crossroads at Lismire.

Scanlon's Bar with B&B, €€, Main Street, 02960003.

Crossing the River Allow

Donal Cam and his followers were attacked by the Barrys whilst crossing the River Allow. Three of his men were killed here, the last that they would be able to bury.

[5.1km/3.2mi] Lismire

S

Lios Maghaire - "Ringfort of the Plain"

There is a tiny park with seats and tables. The village has a plaque dedicated to the march of the O'Sullivan Beara clan. Further on past the crossroads there is a small shop just past the church.

2.5km past Lismire is **Kilmacow Cemetary** which is worth a look. Enter three gates to get to the graveyard. It is lush with greenery and has fine examples of **Irish High Crosses** and a holy well. You will reach the crossroads at St. John's Bridge further on down the road in 1.7km.

Lismire

13 Newmarket, Lismire, John's Bridge

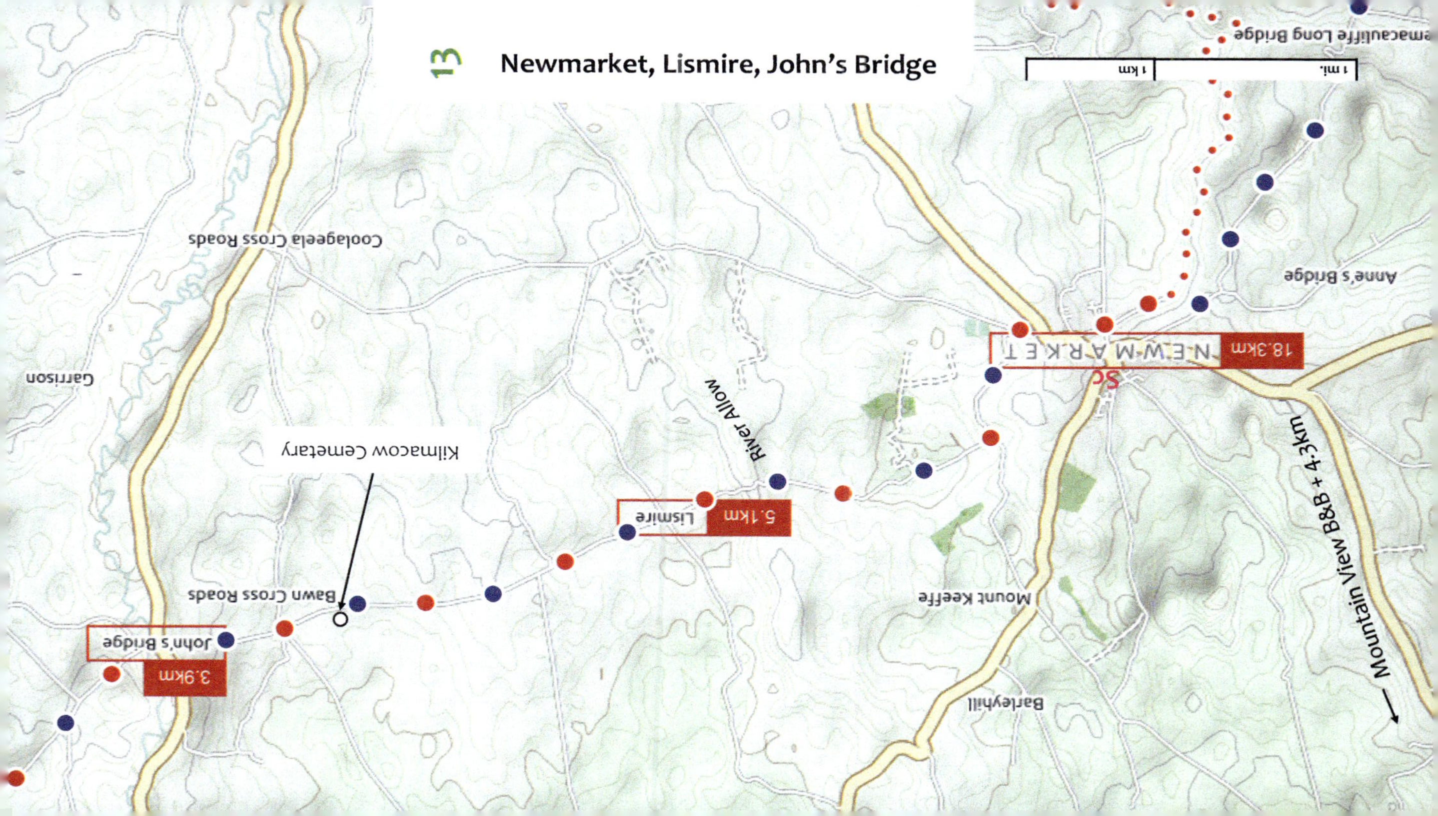

STAGE 4:

Ballyhoura Way

Bhealach Eabhra

St. John's Bridge - Liscarroll - **Churchtown** - **Ballyhea** - **Ballyorgan** - **Kilfinane** - Ballylanders - Galbally -**Glen of Aherlow** - **Tipperary**

Distance:	87.2 km / 54.2 miles
Difficulty:	Moderate
Counties:	Cork, Limerick, Tipperary
OSI Maps:	Discovery Series 72, 73, 74, 66

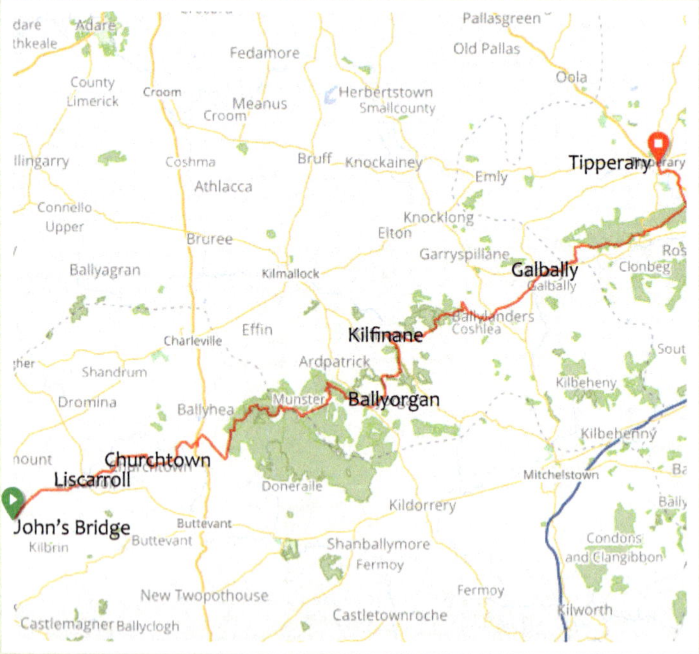

Statue of Christ, Slievenamuck

The **Ballyhoura Way** typically takes four days to walk. It was first opened in 1994 by President Mary Robinson. It is very well way-marked. You will walk on country roads for approximately 20km as far as Ballyhea, then off-road trails as you ascend into the **Ballyhoura Mountains**. Enjoy views over the **Golden Vale, Glen of Aherlow** and the **Galtee Mountains.**

It is recommended to stay in Ballyhea as it is a comfortable day's hike from Ballyhea to Ballyorgan over the Ballyhoura Mountains, or further on again to Kilfinane.

[3.9km/2.4m] St. John's Bridge S

Just a small shop here.

From John's Bridge to Liscarroll is all road.

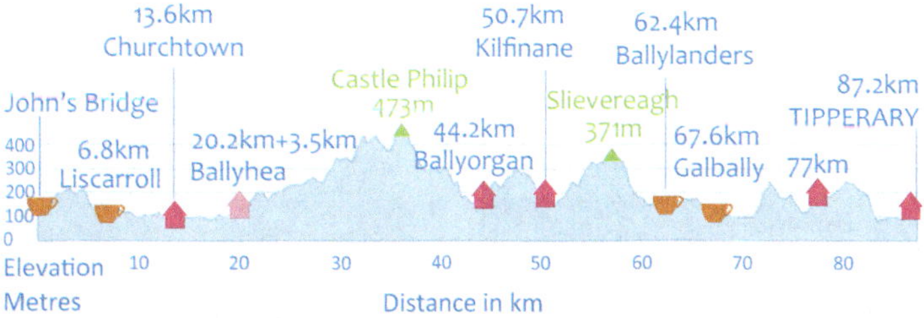

[6.8km/4.2mi] Liscarroll

R PO D

Lios Cearúill - "Carroll's Ringfort"

Liscarroll is a small quiet village. Take a left turn in the village and look out for a small unmarked pathway on the left to visit **Liscarroll Castle**. There is a pretty park right beside the castle which is a nice spot for a rest and you can get to the other side of the castle from here. 1.2 km past the castle is **The Donkey Sanctuary**. Admission is free and opening hours are Mon-Fri 9.00am to 4.30pm and Sat-Sun and Bank Holidays 10.00am to 5.00pm. If you arrive outside of opening hours you are still permitted to walk around the **Donkey Sanctuary Loop** trail. Phone: +353(0)2248395, www.thedonkeysanctuary.ie. Take care on the narrow roads to Churchtown.

Liscarroll Castle and the Barrys

On your way out of the town centre you will find the ruins of a large 13th-century Anglo-Norman fortress, Liscarroll Castle. It was the stronghold of the Barry's who had attacked Donal Cam as he crossed the River Allow. The O'Sullivans would have kept their distance from the castle and not gone through Liscarroll.

Donkeys! Image kindly provided by the Donkey Sanctuary

14 John's Bridge, Liscarroll

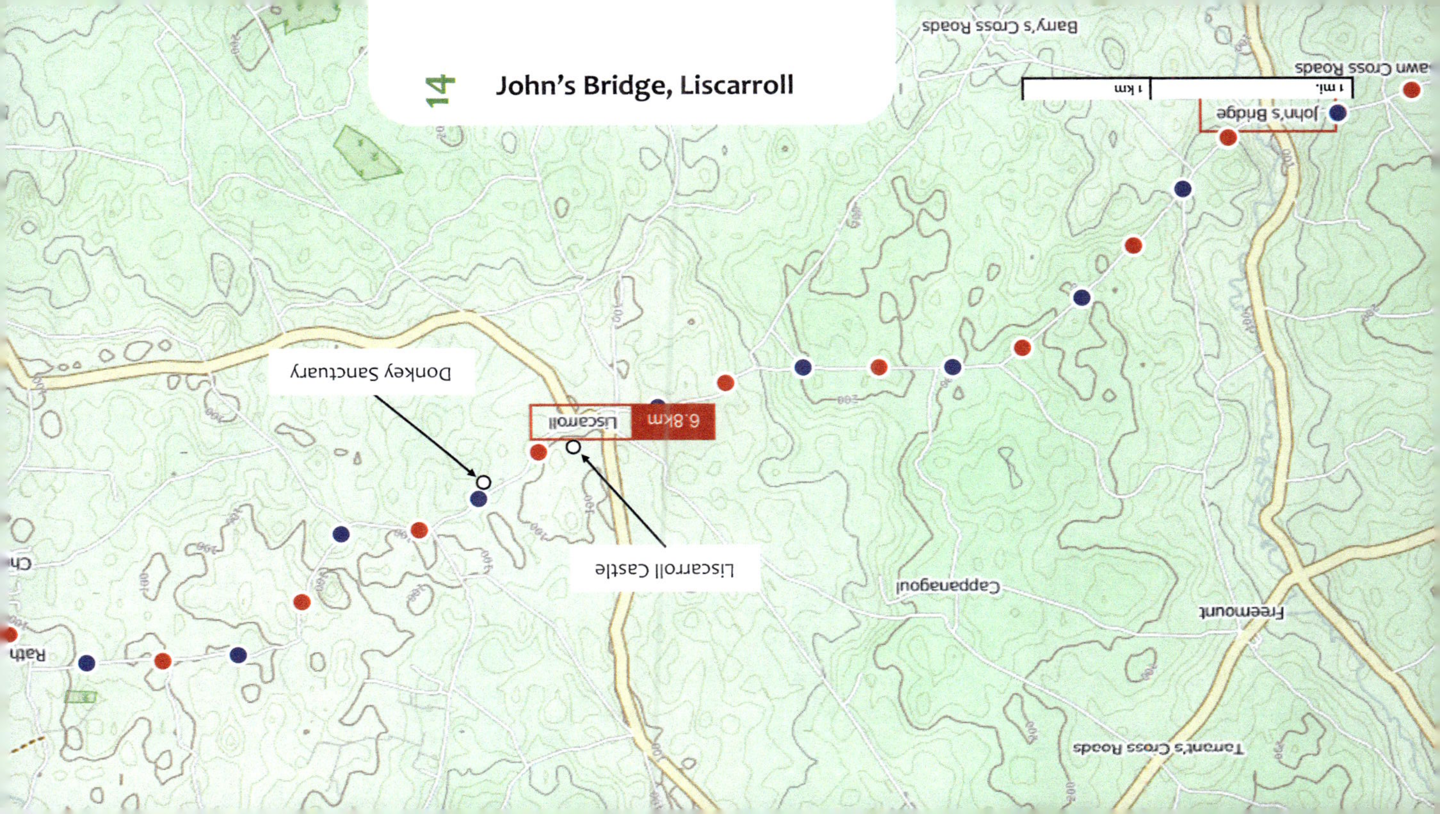

[6.8km/4.2mi] Churchtown

A R PO

Baile an Teampaill

Equine Sculpture, Churchtown

Near St. Nicholas church is **Pound Corner** where you can see a specimen of **Churchtown Marble**. This used to be the location of the town water pump. It is named **Pound Corner** as just behind the wall is where the landlord used to impound the animals of farmers who did not pay their rent. The **equine sculpture** in the town centre commemorates Vincent O'Brien who was a famous Irish racehorse trainer. The only accommodation in the town is Boss Murphy House which was built in the 1830s. Boss Murphy House, +353 (0)2259175 (accommodation), +353 22 23890 (bar), www.bossmurphys.ie.

Leaving Churchtown take care on the road for 2km. Turn left onto a smaller quiet road and go over a bridge. Walk alongside a small river then take a right over another bridge. Go over a stile and walk on rough track before crossing the N20 road. **Caution crossing this very busy road!!**

[6.6km/4.1mi] Ballyhea

A R

(+3.5km/2.2mi off trail to accommodation & restaurant)

Marengo Guest Accommodation B&B, Ballyhea, +353 (0)63 89658, www.booking.com. The friendly owners here may be able to collect you from the trail, ask when booking. There is a restaurant beside the B&B called Corbett Court. Innesfree B&B, Charleville (by taxi), +353 (0)63 81034.

COUNTY LIMERICK / CONTAE LUIMNIGH

After crossing the busy N20 road follow grass track then quiet country road. The first bit of off-road track has a tree-tunnel. On and off-road again a couple of times followed by a 2km grass track. Turn right into the forest where you will follow a rough road track for a few kilometres. The walking trail is criss-crossed with a mountain bike track so watch out for cyclists. The trails are kept separate for the

15 Churchtown, Ballyhea

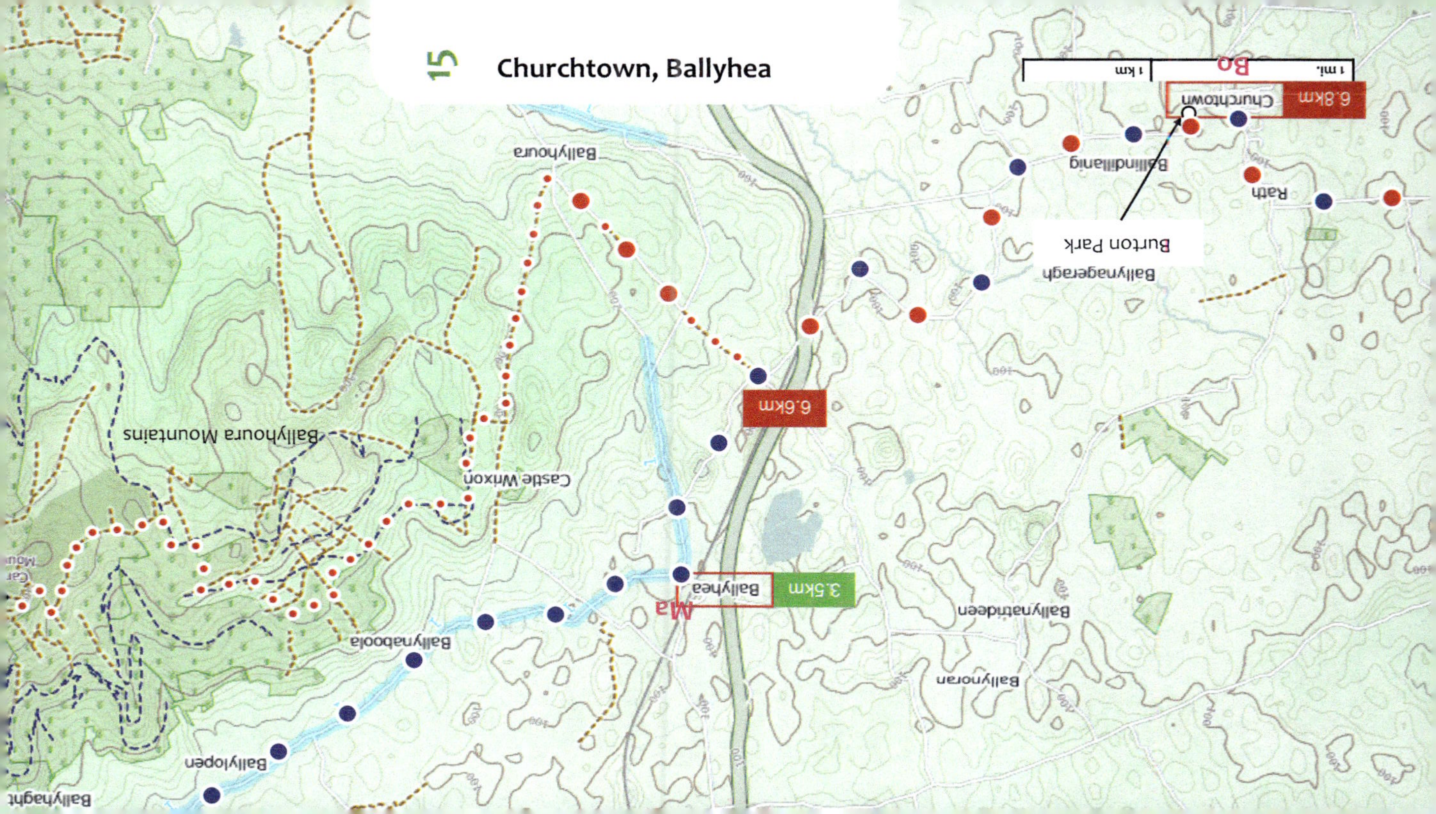

most part. There happened to be a mountain bike race on the second time I walked this section, about 30 or 40 cyclists whizzing past. Take a right up a steep rocky slope toward the summit of **Carron Mountain** with some stunning views behind you on the way up. From the top you can see for miles around and there is a cairn at the peak. Cross over to the next peak with its transmitter station. Soon you will be walking along the **Claidh Dubh**, or Black Ditch; an ancient linear earthworks dating from before 100AD. Gaelic folklore tells of a giant boar that created the ditch with his tusks, and also that it was a giant worm that created it. The purpose of this 20km ditch is unknown but theories are that it may have marked a territorial border, protected cattle from wild animals, defended ancient roads or prevented cattle raids. The next peak is called **Castle Philip** and is the highest point of the Ballyhoura Way and sits on the side of Seefin Mountain. Take a rest on the rocks here and enjoy the view before your final descent. The origin of the name Castle Philip is unknown but it is said to have been an outlaw's hideaway. It may refer to the natural rock formation nearby which from a distance looks like a castle ruin.

Castle Philip

On your descent the grass track leads onto a rough road which takes you down the side of the mountain. Leave this road and enter a pine forest trail with a bridge and waterfall.

At the bottom you will exit the forest at Trailriders Mountain Biking Centre and follow the road to the right. Look out for **Castle Oliver** in the valley below. At a fork in the road, follow the sign for Glenosheen. The next left turn takes you into Glenosheen. At the T-junction go right and walk carefully on the busy R152 road for 350 metres until you see a green stile on your left leading into **Glasure Wood**. A metal bridge leads you to *Ballyhoura Holiday Homes* and then to a main road where you can go right into Ballyorgan or left onto Kilfinane.

[24km/14.9mi] Ballyorgan

S R PO D P

Baile Uí Argáin

The Way passes by the outskirts of the village; however, the town has accommodation should you wish to stay here. **Lantern Lodge B&B**, +353 (0)63 91085, is in the centre of the tiny village opposite the cosy

16 Ballyorgan, Kilfinane

Village Inn. There is nowhere to get food in Ballyorgan but you can order takeout from Kilfinane. **Taxi:** Greg Conway, Kilmallock, 086 8140840, 06320150.

Look out for the **Castle Oliver Gate House** ruin on your left on your way out of Ballyorgan. Follow road and then grass track and road again into Kilfinane.

[6.5km/4mi] Kilfinane

A S R PO D P

Cill Fhíonáin - "Church of St. Finian"

Ballyhoura Hostel (recommended), +353 (0)63 91625, www.ballyhourahostel.ie; **Woodiew B&B**, AirBnB.ie; **Deebert House Hotel**, Kilmallock, 15-minute taxi, +353 (0)63 31200, www.deeberthousehotel.com; **Deebert B&B**, 15-minute taxi, +353 (0)6398106, www.deeberthouse.com.

Kilfinane Village

Follow the road out of Kilfinane and begin your ascent up **Slievereagh**. Just past the horse stud the trail takes a left turn up a dirt/grass track climbing further up. The trail levels out and then turns left into the forest. Cross a wooden bridge over a stream. Follow the grass track uphill until you reach a clearing. Continue straight and pass through a pine forest. Take a left onto rough road as you ascend further. At the next clearing take a right (the way-marker is a bit hidden here). Continue up until you pass by a black and yellow barrier. You will hear the whoosh of the windmill through the trees before you can see it. From here you will begin the descent of Slievereagh. Passing the windfarm the trail turns off to the left and down a steep grassy slope (slippery when wet! My hiking buddy John, wearing trainers instead of hiking boots, slipped on the wet grass numerous times!). Go left when you reach the narrow road below. Walking along the road, to your right you can see the two hills of **Knockalisheen**, and to the right are the **Galtee Mountains**.

Turn right when you reach the grotto. You will see Ballylanders village in the distance with a red building with the top of the church ruin rising above it. Behind the village are the Galtee Mountains. And to the left is **Castlecreagh**. The only place for food in Ballylanders is a shop. There is a seating area at the back of the shop should you need a rest stop.

17 Kilfinane, Ballylanders

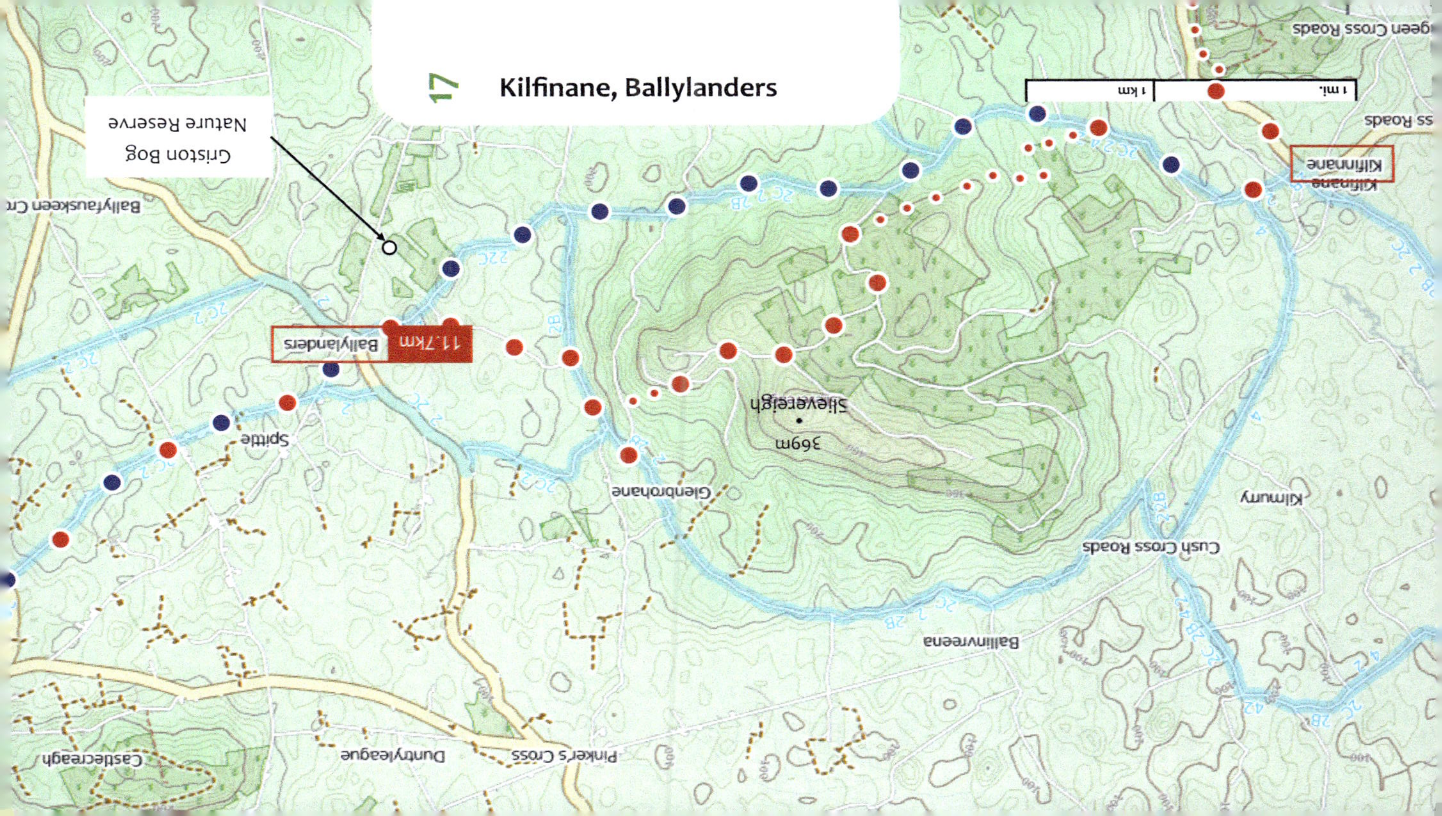

[11.7km/7.3mi] Ballylanders

S R PO D

Baile an Londraigh - "Town of De Landres"

Ballylanders Church Ruin

The ruin at the far end of the town was built in the 19th century as a Protestant church. You can go inside and explore the ivy-clad structure. **Griston Bog Nature Reserve** is 1 km from the village and is home to up to 75 bird species. If you visit the bog be sure to stick to the path as there are some hidden ditches. The trail around the bog is approximately 1 km.

Ballylanders to Galbally is all quiet country road and it is well way-marked. Shortly before Galbally you will cross two bridges over the River Aherlow.

[5.2km/3.2mi] Galbally

R

An Galbhaile - "Town of the strangers"

Galbally is located at the foot of the Galtee Mountains. Have a listen to a song with satirical lyrics called *The Galbally Farmer*. It was recorded by *The Dubliners* under the name *Darby O'Leary*. The Way passes by the edge of the town which has a couple of small shops should you need to stock up on food or water, and a small café.

Go back along the road on which you came into Galbally. 1.5 km out of the town is the ruin of **Moor Abbey,** founded between 1204 and 1212 and took three hundred years to complete.

Moor Abbey

At **Moor Abbey** turn right and very soon after a left into a field. Follow along the **River Aherlow**. Traverse a small metal bridge. Go over or under the electric fence, of which there are quite a few on this part of the trail. Continue along the river. Cross another electric fence, then a wooden bridge and continue

18 Galbally, Glen of Aherlow

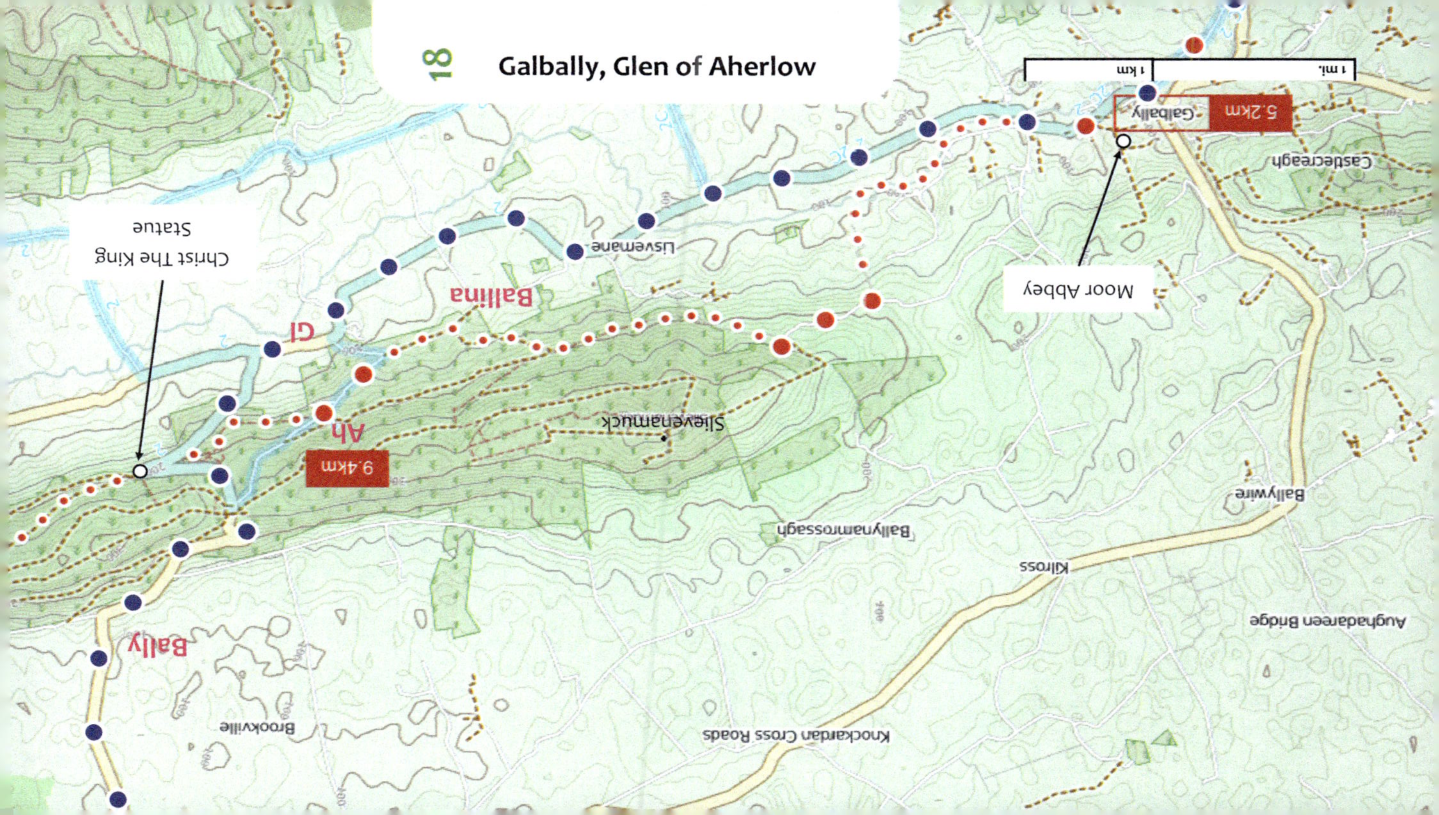

along the river. At around 2.4km there is a sign alerting you of the possible presence of a bull in the field and an alternative route map.

Not wanting to take any risks I took the alternative route along the road past a bungalow and green bridge. I ascended up a narrow country road until the end of the hedgerow and turned right. I hopped over an electric fence and after a narrow grassy path was about to hop over another electric fence when a bull popped his head around the bushes to see who the intruder was! Walking briskly away (for there was nothing but an electric wire between us) I made my way to the farmer's house and he said that I should have stayed along the river. He was very kind to walk me past the bull so I didn't have to go all the way back to the detour point. So do check the field to see if the detour is actually necessary. This spot has caused confusion for other hikers as well so hopefully it is resolved in time for your journey.

Follow along the river to one more bridge. There is a signpost here to go left along the side of the field. Go over a stile. Ascend through this field and exit it at the far end in the centre. Walk into the next field and continue again to the far side of the field. Cross a stream and go over a wooden stile. There is a fallen signpost here and another signpost just past it. Walk up through the field where there is a visible signpost and gate. Up again through the next field (and possibly another, I lost count!). Keep to the right and pass through a gap in the fence near the far end on the right. Through here go left and you will see two stiles. Walk on past them up again to the far end of the field. The next stile is to the left on the far side of the field. Over this is a road which you will follow to the right. Follow this to the end which will lead you through someone's backyard.

Ogham Stone

A track will lead you on the ascent up **Slievenamuck**. Through a gate and past an unused stile continue right along the track past a TV/radio mast (ignore red arrows which indicate the National Looped Walk). At around 5.6km past Galbally the track leads you into a forested area. In 0.4km don't miss the left turn off the road. There are two rocks to climb up on and a fallen signpost nearby. The red arrow points left but you will go right and follow the forest track. You will see a yellow arrow very soon confirming you are on the right track.

Keep following the yellow arrows through the forest track and ignore other colours. At around 8.3km pass by a black and yellow barrier and take a left as you join onto a narrow road. Follow way-markers to Aherlow House Hotel & Lodges. Taxis: Johnny Cotter: 0877111777; Drumms Taxi in Tipperary Town: 06252366, 087 8113040.

[9.4km/5.8mi] Glen of Aherlow (Aherlow House Hotel) A R

Gleann Eatharlaí

On Slievenamuck (Mountain of the Pig) enjoy the views from the **Christ the King statue** over the Glen of Aherlow valley and the **Galtee Mountains.** The landscape and picnic benches provide an ideal place to stop for a break. A little further on the trail is the **Aherlow House Hotel**, outside of which is an ancient **Ogham Stone**, an example of Ireland's earliest form of writing.

Aherlow House Hotel, +353 (0)62 56153, www.aherlowhouse.ie; **Ballinacourty House B&B**, +353 (0)62 56000, www.ballinacourtyhse.com; **Ballinacourty Caravan & Camping Park**, +353 (0)62 56559; **Glen of Aherlow Caravan & Camping Park**, Newtown, +353 (0)62 56555, www.tipperarycamping.com. **Ballyglass Country House**, +353 (0)6252104, www.ballyglasshouse.com.

From Aherlow House Hotel follow the trail through the carpark and veer right into the forest. Continue your ascent along the forest track. Take a right at a gap in the stone wall. The forest track will lead you up stone steps and further on to a large clearing with picnic benches and the **Christ the King Statue** overlooking the **Glen of Aherlow valley** and the **Galtee Mountains.**

Galtee Mountains

Continue on the trail past the statue. The rest of the trail over **Slievenamuck** is easy to follow along. When you come to a tarmac road turn left. Take the next turn right and you will soon arrive at a busy main road (N24, Bancha road). Keep to the small road on the left before coming out onto Bancha road. Take care crossing the road and walk along the narrow hard shoulder towards Tipperary Town. The road can be quite busy and does not leave much room for walkers. Take a left and cross the railway line and river Ara. Take a right into Tipperary Town.

STAGE 5:

Multeen Way

Slí Multeen

Tipperary - Donohill - Cappawhite - **Milestone**

Distance: 35.5 km / 22.1 miles
Difficulty: Moderate
County: Tipperary
OSI Maps: Discovery Series Sheet 66

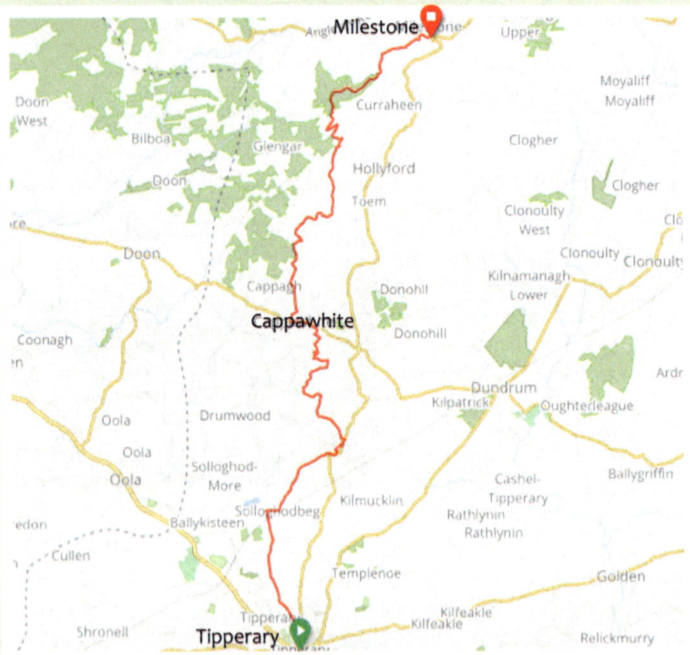

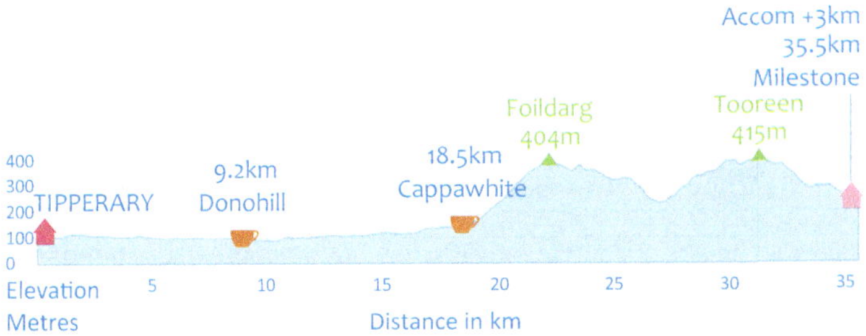

The trail takes you by Donohill Motte which is followed by an off-road track to Cappaghwhite, and then across Foildarg Hill which has an optional trail to the 440m summit. It is then mostly off-road to Milestone. There is not much accommodation on this trail so you may need to take a taxi back to Tipperary town for a place to stay.

[10.2km/6.2mi] Tipperary Town

A S R PO € D P

Tiobraid Árann - "The Well of the Arra"

Tipperary is a large town with plenty of facilities and a good place for a rest day. The town was once the site of a large British Army Barracks which was used as a military hospital during World War I. The song *It's a Long Way to Tipperary* was written in 1912 and first recorded by John McCormack.

Watch out for incorrect signposts in Tipperary as local kids like to turn them to face the wrong way both in the town centre and on your way out of the town! So check maps carefully and don't trust the way-markers; or any signposts for that matter!

Tipperary Town

Ach na Sheen Guesthouse, 062 51298, www.achnasheen.ie; **Aisling B&B**, 062 33307, www.aislingbedandbreakfast.com; **Emmet House B&B**, 33 Main Street, 062 51465, www.emmethouse bedandbreakfast.ie; **Central House B&B**, 44 Main Street, +353 (0)62 51117, www.centralhousebandb.com; **Royal Hotel**, Bridge Street, +353

(0)62 33244; **Times Hotel**, 13 St. Michael Street, +353 (0)62 31111; **Riverside House**, (1.5km from town), Galbally Road, +353 (0)62 51219, www.tipp-riversidehouse.com; **Ballykisteen Hotel & Golf Resort**, (5.8km from Tipperary Town), +353 (0)62 33333, www.ballykisteenhotel.com.

Leaving Tipperary and double-checking your map (because we don't trust the sign-posts here!) follow Davis street northwards out of the town. After 1km turn left onto Springfield road. In 1km veer right where there is a triangle of grass in the centre of the junction. In 2.5km pass through Bohertrime which has a pub . After 0.7km cross the bridge over a railway line and shortly after turn right towards Donohill. You will pass by **Soloheadbeg**, the location of the Battle of Sulcoit in 968 where King Mahon of Thomond along with his brother Brian Boru defeated Ivar, the Viking king of Limerick. Donal Cam also stopped here on his march north. Follow this road for just over 3km into Donohill.

[9.2km/5.7mi] Donohill

Dún Eochaille - 'Fort of the Yew Wood'

Donohill marks the heart of the 'Golden Vale'. It includes parts of counties Limerick, Tipperary and Cork and is said to be the best land in Ireland for dairy farming. Be sure to pop into Heffernan's Bar and Grocery shop for a rest and refreshments. Cross over the road and continue on for 0.5km and you will see **Donohill Motte** ahead of you. Go left and then go over a stile on your right into a field.

Donohill Motte

Pope's Bridge
Cauteen Bridge
9.2km
Donohill
Bananalleen
Moanmore
Soloheadbeg
Grange
Monard
Bohertrime
Cunningham's Cross Roads
Limerick Junction
Limerick Junction
Train Station for
Dublin, Cork, Galway
Ballyhoura Way
Davis Street
Cashel Road
Croque
10.2km
TIPPERARY
Bansha Road
Clonpet
Brookville
1 km
1 mi

The Siege of Donohill Motte

By the time Donal Cam and his followers reached Tipperary they had been walking for fours days and were starving, as they had only brought one days worth of provisions when they had set off from Glengarriff. His soldiers were barely able to stay awake with hunger weariness and fatigue. **Donohill Motte** was a defensive structure which housed the winter's food supplies of the local people. As well as it being the middle of winter the entire province was struggling against famine, inflicted deliberately by the English forces who had burned fields and slaughtered livestock throughout Munster. Having eaten only "plants and roots and leaves of trees" the previous night and facing the starvation of his people, Donal Cam besieged the motte from the local O'Dwyer clan. "Whatever prepared food was there, the first who entered devoured right off. The rest set themselves to feed on meal, beans and barley grains, like cattle." They drank water from the nearby well of St. James. The food-store was owned by the Lord of Ormond who sent his men after Donal Cam to get bloody revenge. They pursued and fought relentlessly.

Over the stile and into the field; there were cattle and one bull in this field when I was here so take care and stick to the road if you think it is safer to do so. Exiting the field onto laneway go right and then left on the road, then soon go left into another field. Go through fields and then track for 1.7km and at the road go right. Take the next left and in 1km at the crossroads turn right and soon after go right again through some fields, a small bit of road and then enter **Greenfield Park**. After 1.5km in Greenfield Park exit through a small carpark and turn right and then the next left down a laneway for 1.5km of track and fields. Exit onto the R505 and then go left for 0.5km into Cappaghwhite village.

Pond in Greenfield Forest

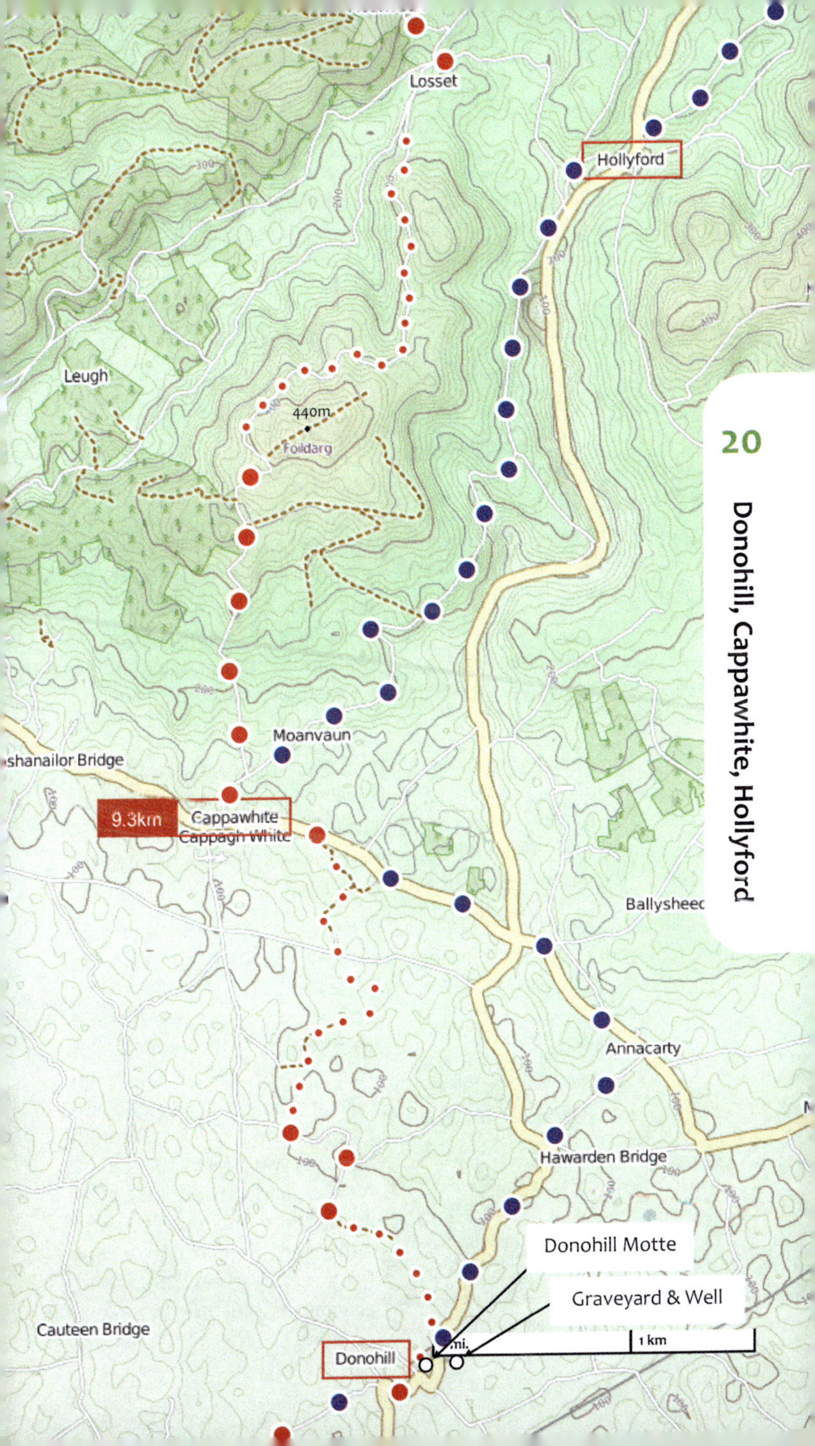
Losset
Hollyford
Leugh
440m
Foildarg
Moanvaun
shanailor Bridge
9.3km
Cappawhite
Cappagh White
Ballysheec
Annacarty
Hawarden Bridge
Donohill Motte
Graveyard & Well
mi.
1 km
Cauteen Bridge
Donohill

[9.3km/5.8mi] Cappawhite

R PO D P

An Cheapach n Bhfaoiteach - "White's Tillage Plot"

Cappawhite is a small village with a shop and some places to eat. It is 15 minutes by taxi back to Tipperary town should you wish to end your day's hike here.

Cappaghwhite

COUNTY TIPPERARY / CONTAE THIOBRAID ÁRANN

Hollyford (cycle trail only) PO

Áth an Chuilinn

The **old sweathouse** just outside of Hollyford is beehive-shaped with a small doorway and thick stone walls. It is an early type of sauna said to cure various types of ailments. After using the sauna, people would bathe in a nearby stream. It was said that this treatment would cure anyone of their ailment.

Leave Cappaghwhite by heading north on Church Street. After 0.5km turn left and begin your ascent up Foildearg Hill, reaching the peak in 3km with nice views behind you on the way up and more stunning views over the top. The trail descends for 5km, passing through a windfarm and then merging onto a narrow road.

Keep going straight after merging onto the road and soon come to a junction. Continue straight across the road, following the sign for Milestone and beginning your ascent up Tooreen Hill. After a short distance at a fork in the road go left. After 1.4km go over a stile on your right and follow the track through another wind farm for 3.8km. At the road go left and after 0.7km take the stile to your right and go through a few fields and then on road, arriving at Milestone in 2.2km.

Rainbow on the Multeen Way

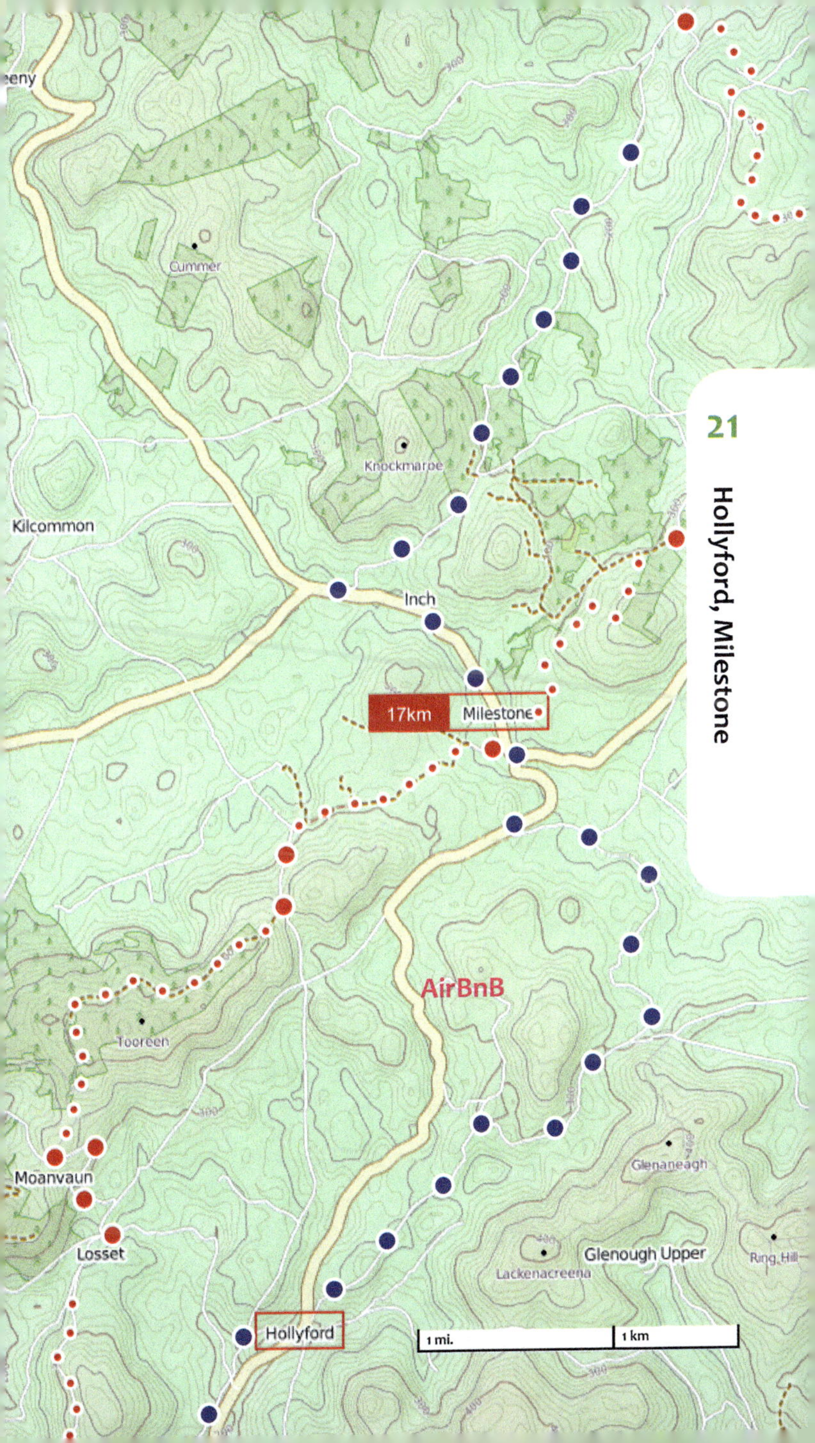
Cummer
Knockmaroe
Kilcommon
Inch
17km
Milestone
AirBnB
Tooreen
Moanvaun
Losset
Hollyford
Glenaneagh
Glenough Upper
Lackenacreena
Ring Hill
1 mi.
1 km

STAGE 6:

Ormond Way

Slí Ormond

Milestone - **Upperchurch** - Templederry - Toomevara - **Cloughjordan** - **Ballingarry** - Aglish - Lorrha - **Portumna**

Distance: 85.8 km / 53.3 miles
Difficulty: Moderate
Counties: Tipperary, Galway
OSI Maps: Discovery Series 66, 59, 53

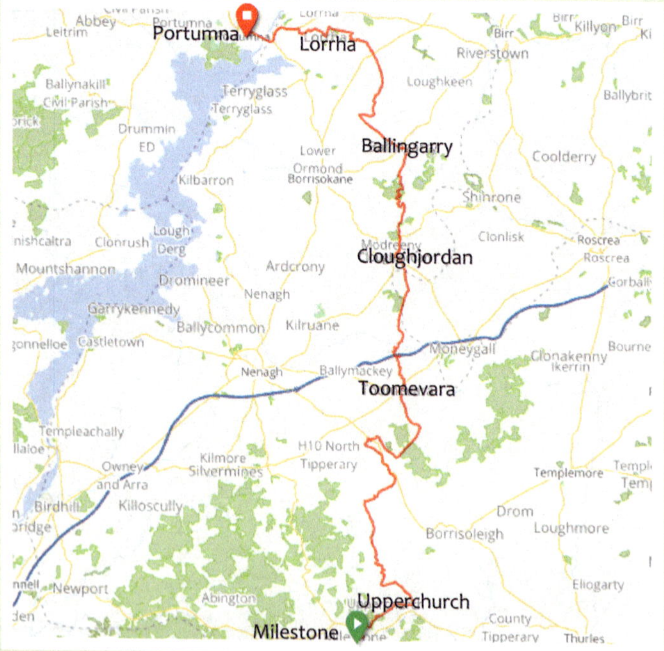

View on the Ormond Way

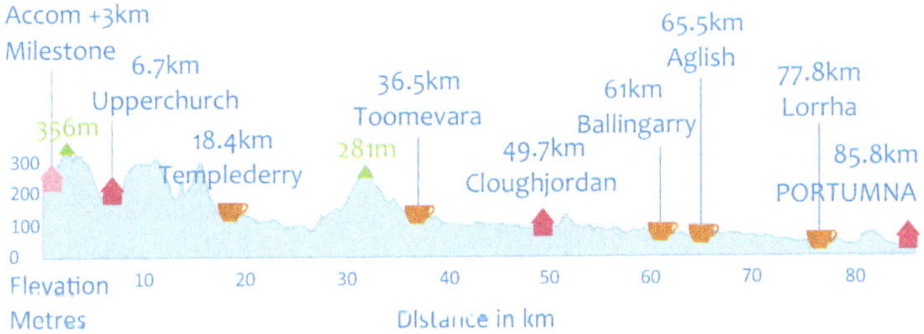

The Ormond Way is a brand new trail which was created thanks to the hard work and perseverance of local man Matt Ryan. It is fully way-marked and passes through many farms and fields.

[17km/10.5mi] Milestone (+3km/1.8mi off trail to accommodation) A

Cloch an Mhíle

There is nothing in Milestone since the local pub closed down. AirBnB about 3km off the trail, see map 21.

This section has lovely views as you rise and dip among the hills and valleys. From Milestone cross the R503 road, go over the stile and into a field. Cross several fields up-hill for 2km on grass track. Descend on a dirt track and then veer right into a field. Keep to the right to go under electric fences and over two stiles.

Exit onto a road and go right and at the next road go left for a short distance before going right over a stile and walk alongside a forest. Traverse several more fields. The field track follows alongside road and then exit onto the road as you descend into Upperchurch.

COUNTY TIPPERARY / CONTAE THIOBRAID ÁRANN

[6.7km/4.2mi] Upperchurch

A S R PO

Traditional music is played on Monday nights in Pa's Bar, Thursdays in Jim O'the Mills (by taxi, starts 9pm and is recommended for a late night trad session) and the first Friday of every month in Kinnane's. There is a small shop and post office further down the road past Pa's.

Pa's Bar and Hillview B&B

Hillview B&B, +353 (0)504 54363, 087 2645919 or book on AirBnB.

Leaving Upperchurch take the road headed north passing by the Sacred Heart Church and continuing on quiet road for 2.4km. Take a stile to your left and cross two fields followed by grass track between two forests. This turns into pebble track and then turn right over a stile. Cross several fields and exit over a stile onto a quiet boreen.

Veer right by an old stone farm building onto a dirt track. Descend a field and there is a stile at the bottom right hand side hidden in the corner. Exit next field through the gate at the far side.

Walk to the right on quiet road, cross **River Clodiagh** and climb over a stile to your right into a field. Walk through a track of low nettles and thorns and then through a field. Spot the Hazelnut tree just beside the next stile.

Exit onto the road and go left and over the next stile across the road into a field. This is a steep ascent followed by a steep descent. Exit onto road and go left continuing down hill. Follow the road and soon

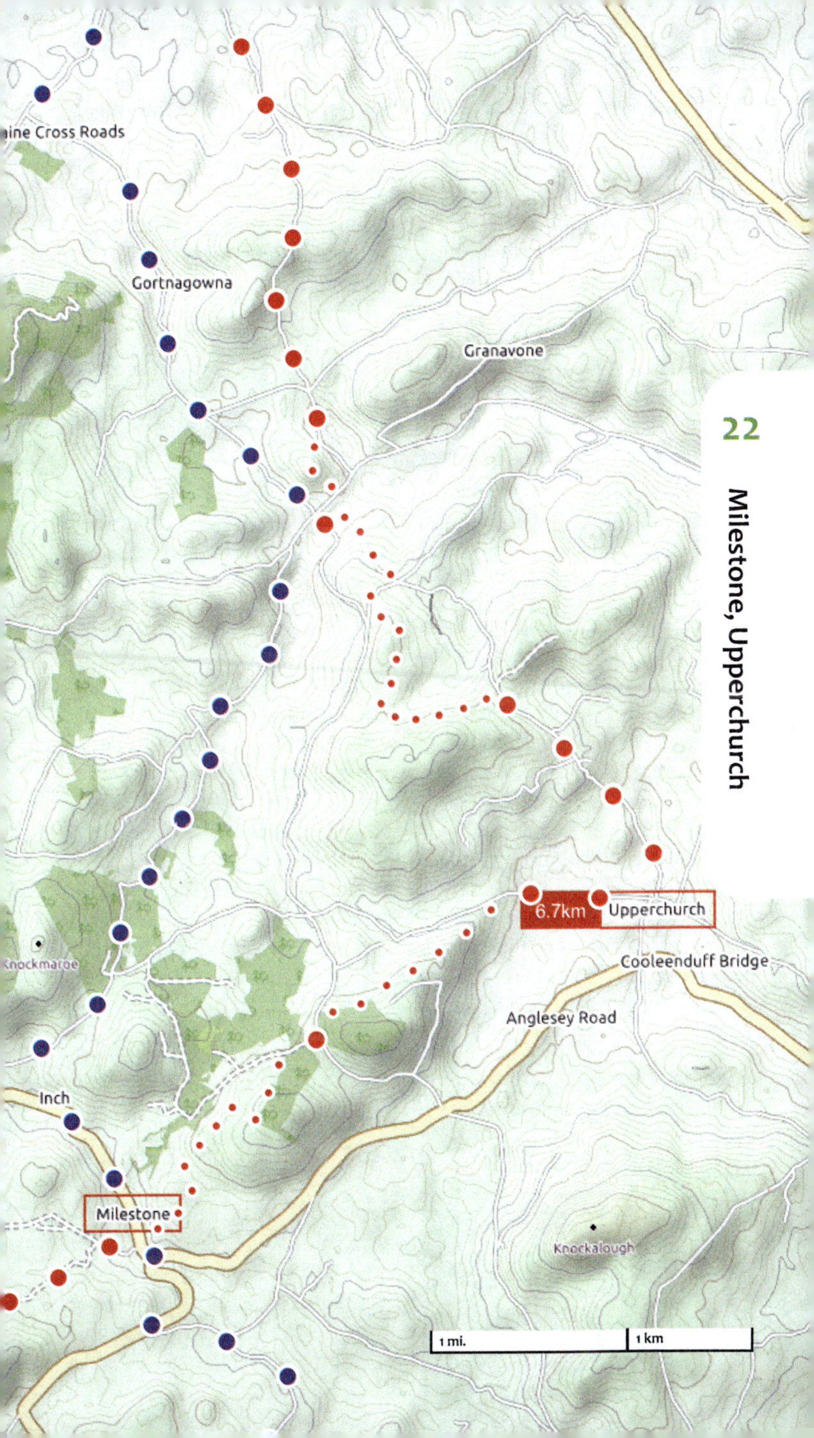

ine Cross Roads
Gortnagowna
Granavone
6.7km
Upperchurch
Cooleenduff Bridge
Anglesey Road
nockmaroe
Inch
Milestone
Knockalough
1 mi.
1 km

come to a dirt track. Descend the hill on a narrow tarmac road and go over a stile to your left. Keep to the right of this overgrown field and take the bridge over a stream. Go over the electric fence and continue along an overgrown track staying parallel to the road continuing through fields. Exit to the right back onto the road. Cross the **Nenagh River** shortly before arriving at Templederry. Turn right into Templederry village. There is a grocery shop just on your right.

[11.7km/7.3mi] Templederry

S D

Teampall Doire

Templederry Church

There is a small shop in this village. The Templederry Roman Catholic Church is built in the Gothic Revival style and has a large rose window and some impressive stained glass windows.

Pass through Templederry village and the next stile is just past the graveyard. Cross some fields and exit over a stile and bridge. Continue up the field and then cross the road to enter the next field. Keep to the left in this field and you will come to a track which continues along the ditch. Keep to the left and soon go left over the ditch and then right to the bridge. Keep along the right of the next few fields and follow alongside a stream. Exit the field by ascending a dirt track. Ignore the way-marker leading down towards the stream. Follow along the road then enter the field to the right at the electricity mast. The next stile its at the bottom far end of the field towards the road. Follow along the river for the next field and forest track. There is a **WASPS NEST** just as you exit the forest into a field. My friends and I got a few stings so move very quickly here!

Continue through the field and alongside the forest. Pass by a farm shed and descend into another forest track along the river. Exit onto a road and cross the bridge.

Latteragh Castle Ruin

Ascend the narrow road and past the next crossroads is the ivy-covered ruin of **Latteragh Castle** (only part of a wall remaining), first owned by the Kennedys and later by the Butlers. Further up the road is the site of **St. Odhran's Monastery** which has a 12th

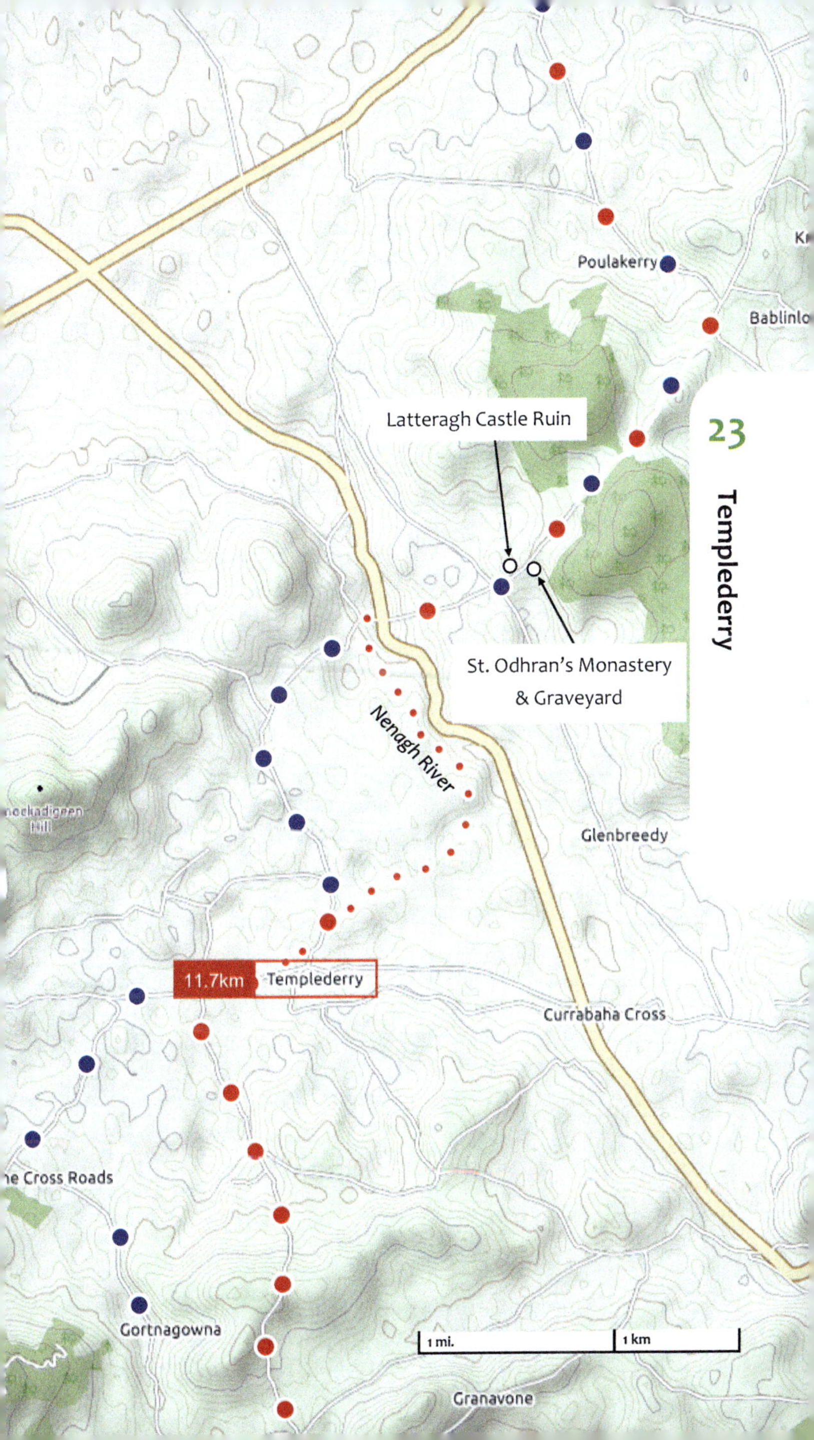
Poulakerry
Latteragh Castle Ruin
St. Odhran's Monastery
& Graveyard
Nenagh River
Glenbreedy
11.7km
Templederry
Currabaha Cross
Gortnagowna
Granavone
1 mi.
1 km

St. Odhran's Monastery

century church ruin and graveyard. This is another holy site where Donal Cam and his men stopped to rest for a night. Continue on this road for some lovely views from the tops of the hills. Take a left near the windfarm and descend into Toomevara for 3km, keeping right at the fork in the road.

[18.1km/36.5mi] Toomevara/Toomyvara

S PO P W

Tuaim Uí Mheára - "Tumulus of the O'Meadhras"

Beside St. Joseph's Church is the ruin of the **Toomevara Augustinian Priory** which was dedicated to St. Mary and founded in the 12th century. In the centre of the village is the **ruin of a church** which may have been built in the late medieval period. It has only one wall remaining as well as what may have been a priest's chamber at one end.

Augustinian Priory

Leave Toomevara on the busy R445 road for 0.7km, then go left onto Knockanpierce road for 0.5km and left again onto a narrow laneway and through some farmland for 1.2km. Back onto Knockanpierce road go left, then right at an old farmhouse. After 1 km you will cross the M7 motorway via an underpass. After the M7 go over a stile onto a farm track and walk through fields for 1km and exit onto a narrow country road. Go right and then take the next left and follow this road for 5km, crossing the Ollatrim river and continuing straight at the crossroads. At the T-junction go left and after 2.8km you will arrive in Cloughjordan shortly after crossing the Ballyfinboy river and a railway line.

[13.2km/8.2mi] Cloughjordan

A S PO D P

Cloch Shiurdáin - "Siurdán's Stone"

Entering Cloughjordan you will pass a shop on your left. The eco-village and Django's hostel are further up the street down a laneway on the right. Check out the new **Thomas MacDonagh Heritage Centre.**

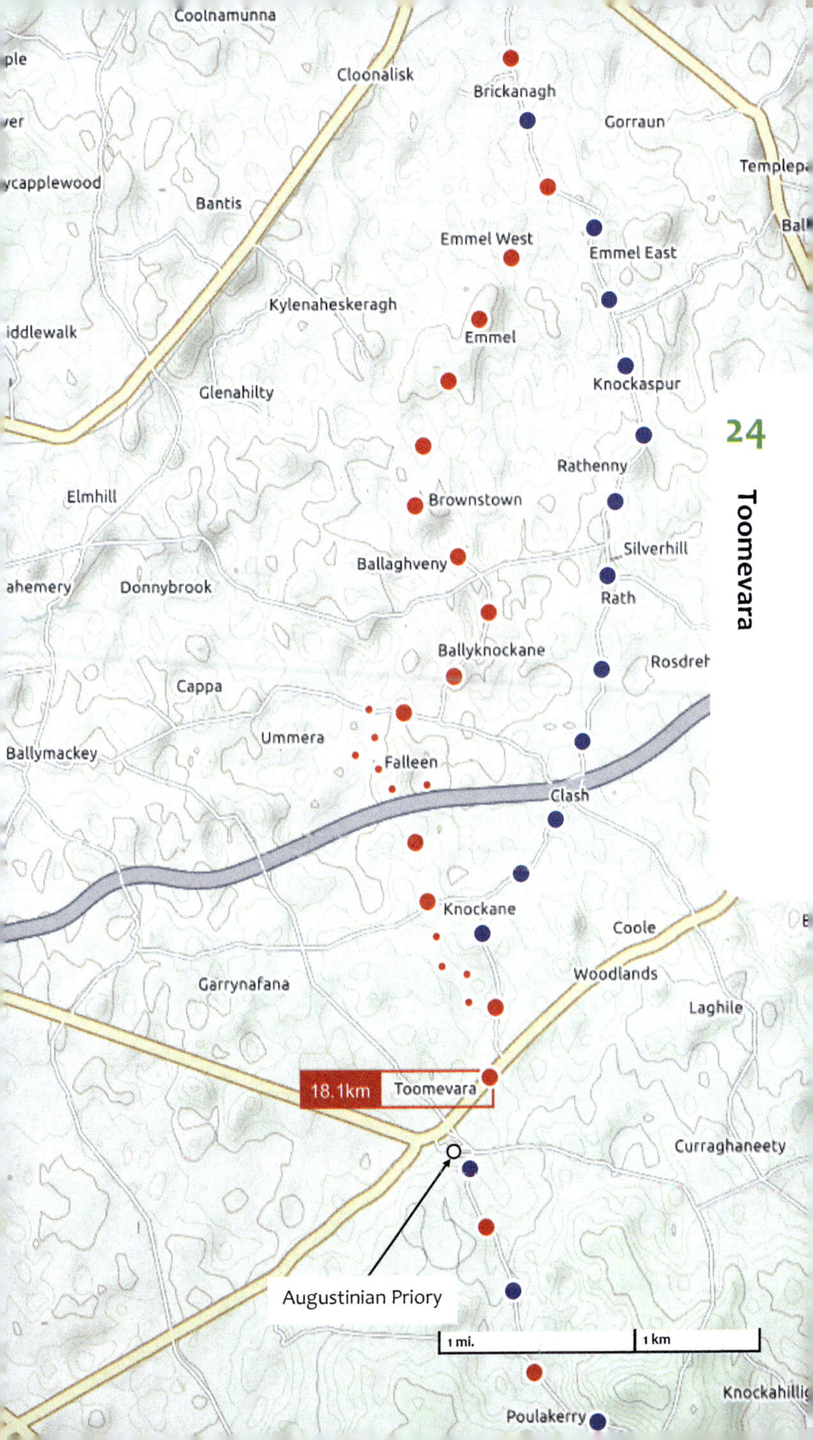
Coolnamunna
Cloonalisk
Brickanagh
Gorraun
Bantis
Emmel West
Emmel East
Kylenaheskeragh
Emmel
Glenahilty
Knockaspur
Rathenny
Elmhill
Brownstown
Silverhill
Ballaghveny
Donnybrook
Rath
Ballyknockane
Cappa
Ummera
Ballymackey
Falleen
Clash
Knockane
Coole
Woodlands
Garrynafana
Laghile
18.1km
Toomevara
Curraghaneety
Augustinian Priory
1 mi.
1 km
Poulakerry

Cloughjordan Eco-Village

MacDonagh was an activist, poet, teacher and one of the seven leaders in the 1916 Easter Rising. After learning about some of Ireland's most important history, relax in the cosy **Sheelagh na Gig** book and coffee shop with it's resident cat. The trail takes you through **Cloughjordan Eco-Village** where you can see the many types of eco-friendly buildings with solar panels. There are many vegetable gardens where residents grow much of their own food and some of the streets are lined with apple trees.

Django's Eco-Friendly Hostel €, (recommended), +353 (0)87 2569348, www.djangoshostel.com; **Cloughjordan House B&B**, +353 (0) 879690824; **Courtyard Antiques B&B**, +353 (0)86 2689499;

Follow the way-markers through the eco-village and exit onto the R491 main road and go left for 4.2km of road. There is a footpath until the crossroads where you continue straight along the R491. Veer left at the fork in the road where you will also see an entrance into **Knockanree Woods.** This is an optional 2.5km looped trail detour called Beech Trail which may in the future become part of the Ormond Way. Continuing on past the woods down a narrow road, take a left at the T-junction and then right into **Laghile Woods** for 3.7km of off-road track. Follow the path through the forest and after

Laghile Woods

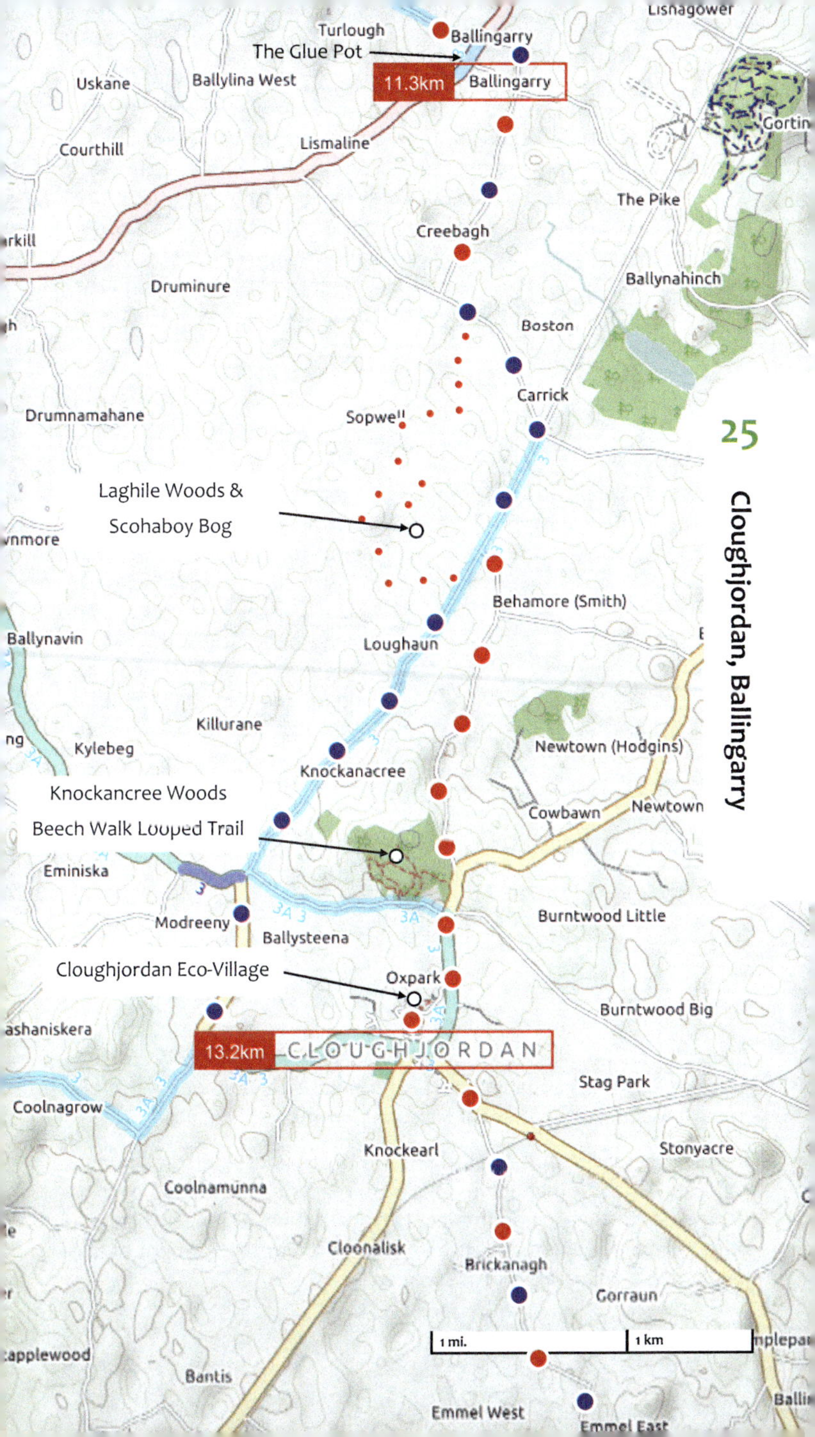
The Glue Pot
11.3km
Ballingarry
Turlough
Lisnagower
Uskane
Ballylina West
Courthill
Lismaline
Gortin
The Pike
Creebagh
Druminure
Ballynahinch
Boston
Carrick
Drumnamahane
Sopwell
Laghile Woods &
Scohaboy Bog
Behamore (Smith)
Ballynavin
Loughaun
Killurane
Kylebeg
Newtown (Hodgins)
Knockanacree
Knockancree Woods
Beech Walk Looped Trail
Cowbawn
Newtown
Eminiska
Modreeny
Ballysteena
Burntwood Little
Cloughjordan Eco-Village
Oxpark
Burntwood Big
13.2km
CLOUGHJORDAN
Stag Park
Coolnagrow
Knockearl
Stonyacre
Coolnamunna
Cloonalisk
Brickanagh
Gorraun
1 mi.
1 km
Bantis
Emmel West
Emmel East

about 2km the way-marker directs you to the right in through the trees for a pretty forest track, then a grass track alongside rows of deciduous trees and several fields (one with curious cattle who gathered around me, but as usual I stayed close to the electric fence just as a precaution!). Over the last stile and electric fence and go right on the quiet country laneway. At the end go left and then take the next right. Follow this road for 2.8km, going straight through the crossroads and passing by **Ballingarry Church** as you enter Ballingarry.

[11.3km/7mi] Ballingarry

Baile an Gharraí - "Town of the Gardens"

Ballingarry church was built in 1856 and features an octagonal spire. Stop at the **Glue Pot** pub for a rest. In Ballingarry go left and then right, following the sign for Aglish and you will reach it in about 4.5km. You don't need to go into the tiny village (unless you want to stop at the pub for another rest), so take a sharp right at the post box to continue on to the next town.

Ballingarry Church

[4.5km/2.8mi] Aglish

R

An Eaglais

There is a pub at the far end of the village.

Ballycormac House €€€, lovely accommodation and farm animals. Dinner is also available. (0)67 21129. **Conroy's Old Bar** €€€, self-catering and 2-nights minimum stay for unique accommodation in old pub, www.ConroysOldBar.com, also on AirBnB.

1.3km after leaving Aglish, at the fork in the road veer left. Follow this road for 5km and then come to a busy road. Cross the road over to the gate and continue on this laneway for a short distance. Then exit onto a small road and go left and then take the second right at the junction. 0.5km up this road is **Lackeen Castle**.

26 Ballingarry

Lackeen Castle

Lackeen Castle is a tower house built in the 12th century by the Kennedy clan. It is four-stories high and has a large fireplace. It has a straight staircase up to the first floor and spiral stairs to the higher floors, with a vaulted ceiling on the third floor. A 9th century manuscript was discovered in the walls of the castle. It had been used at St. Ruadhan's Monastery in Lorrha around 1050 and must have been moved to the castle for safe keeping. The manuscript is called the **Stowe Missal** and is currently stored in Dublin, however you can see images of the manuscript with a search on the internet. The manuscript is written in Latin with the last pages in Gaelic and contains some illustrations.

THE POOKA

IRISH MYTHS & LEGENDS

Local mythology tells a story of O'Kennedy from Lackeen Castle and how he managed to capture a Pooka. A Pooka/Phooka is a fairy shape shifter who can take on many different terrifying forms. One night, O'Kennedy chased some old hags who were stealing from a corpse that had been prepared for burial at the old Eglish (Aglish) Church. As the hags ran they called upon the Pooka to protect them. Surely enough a Pooka appeared and tried to attack O'Kennedy, with it red eyes and flames coming from it's nostrils. O'Kennedy was as fast as lightening and as strong as an ox and quickly hit the Pooka with his sword, sending it flying into the air. With a few flicks of his rope O'Kennedy had tied up the Pooka and slung it over his shoulder. It is rare for a Pooka to ever be captured and it swore and cursed as O'Kennedy took it back to Lackeen Castle. At the castle the Pooka shouted "If you dare to take me inside your castle, I shall burn you all with my breath!" One of O'Kennedy's loyal servants opened the castle doors but said "For goodness sake let it loose or none of us shall have any peace or a good night's sleep ever again!" O'Kennedy made the Pooka promise to not harm him or any generation of the O'Kennedy family and then set it free. Local people to this day have seen terrifying shadows about the castle late at night so keep an eye out for these devious creatures!

Passing by Lackeen Castle walk for 0.5km and then enter fields for 1.6km. On road again and take the next left into **Lorrha Bog**, walking along a raised laneway with occasional views into the bogland on both sides. After this is a grass track with rows of planted trees on either side, then a large field. When you come to old farm machinery and an large green shed, continue behind the shed and out onto the narrow road. Go left and arrive soon at Lorrha.

Help from the Monks of Lorrha

MacEgan, the high sheriff of Tipperary, ordered the monks of Lorrha to shun Donal Cam and offer him no aid; however, they ignored these orders and helped Donal Cam and his people.

[12.3km/7.6mi] Lorrha

S R

Lothra

Lorrha village is full of history and several ruins. St. Ruadhan founded a monastery here and on the site is the ruin of an 11th century church known as **St. Ruadhan's Abbey** (1). The south wall has a decorated doorway with floral motifs and also a pelican drawing blood from its chest - a symbol of Christ's sacrifice (2). The site also has the bases of two 8th century high crosses. The one pictured here (3) shows spirals and celtic knot patterns on its three panels. Above this you can see a faint row of horses.

(1) *St. Ruadhan's Abbey*

(2) *St. Ruadhan's Abbey Doorway*

(3) *Base of a High Cross*

Priors arrived in the 12th century who were devoted to St. Augustine and built the **Augustinian Priory** (4). On the top of the decorated doorway is a carving of a woman's head (5) with horned headdress. She was possibly the wife of a Norman lord who may have commissioned the building. The shelf above where the piscina (washing basin) used to be has a carving of a high cross on the top of it, only discovered in recent years.

The **Dominican Friary** (6) was built in the 13th century when Walter de Burgo, the Earl of Ulster, invited the Dominicans to Lorrha. The friars would have worked the nearby mill to make bread, an important food at the time.

In Lorrha turn right, following the sign for Portumna. After 1km go left for 2km of beautiful off-road track and then 4km of very busy road into Portumna which has little room for walkers.

(4) *Augustinian Priory*

(5) *Augustinian Priory Doorway*

(6) *Dominican Priory*

STAGE 7:

Hymany Way

Slí Hymany

Portumna - **Meelick** - Clonfert - (**Ballinasloe**) - **Aughrim** - (Ahascragh) - **Ballygar**

Distance:	94 km / 58.4 miles
Difficulty:	Moderate
County:	Galway
OSI Maps:	Discovery Series 53, 47, 40

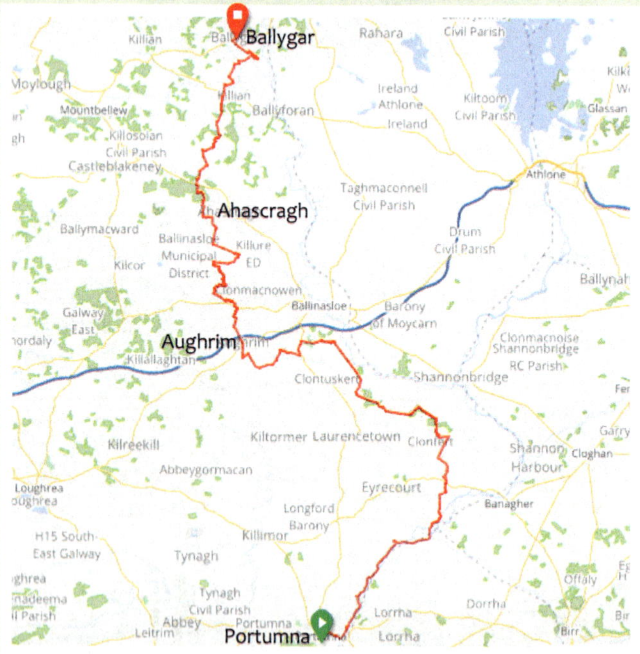

The **Hymany Way** brings you through County Galway and takes three days to walk. The Hymany Way was officially opened in 2010 by Jimmy McClearn, Mayor of County Galway. The first part of the trail is alongside the **River Shannon**, Ireland's longest river. I first walked this section on a very hot summers day and quickly realised there is almost no shelter from the sun all the way to Meelick, as most of the trail is on top of a levee. The River Shannon callows (area prone to flooding) are important for the variety of birdlife including Skylark, Reed Buntings, Meadow Pipit and Sedge Warblers, as well as the endangered Corncrake. I spotted many dragonflies, a variety of butterflies, frogs, a corncrake, swallows, grouse and buzzards. If the trail by the river is flooded, follow the signs for the alternative route.

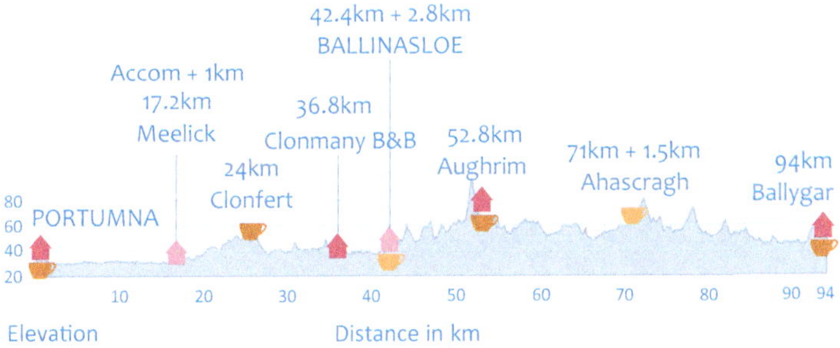

River Shannon, Portumna

[8km/5mi] Portumna

A S R PO € D P

Port Omna - "Landing Place of the Oak"

Portumna is a great town in which to spend a rest day. There is plenty to see here between the pretty village, the 17th-century **Portumna Castle** and **Portumna Forest Park** which has views over **Lough Derg** (map on page 102). Portumna Castle is open 24th March to 15th October daily and 16th October to 31st October weekends only. The entry fee is €4.

Accommodation is all in the town centre: **Pod Umna Glamping Village**, 090 975 4499, www.podumnavillage.ie; **Oaklodge B&B**, St. Brendan's Road, 090 974 1549, www.oaklodgeportumna.ie; **Portumna House**, 1 St. Brendan's Road, 090 9741078, www.portumnahouse.com.

Leave Portumna the way you entered and after 1km at the river and boats turn left and walk along the other side of the river. Take the stile rather than go through the gates so that you are walking off-road on top of the levee. You have 15.5km of mostly grass track to Meelick. The levee is a little overgrown with long grass in some parts but still very pleasant as it is here that you are surrounded with pretty butterflies, dragonflies and you may even spot a frog or two. Where the gravel road beside the levee ends, turn right through two gates and continue to walk along the levee. Approximately 2km before Meelick walk on the narrow road for a short stretch, and then hop

Portumna Castle

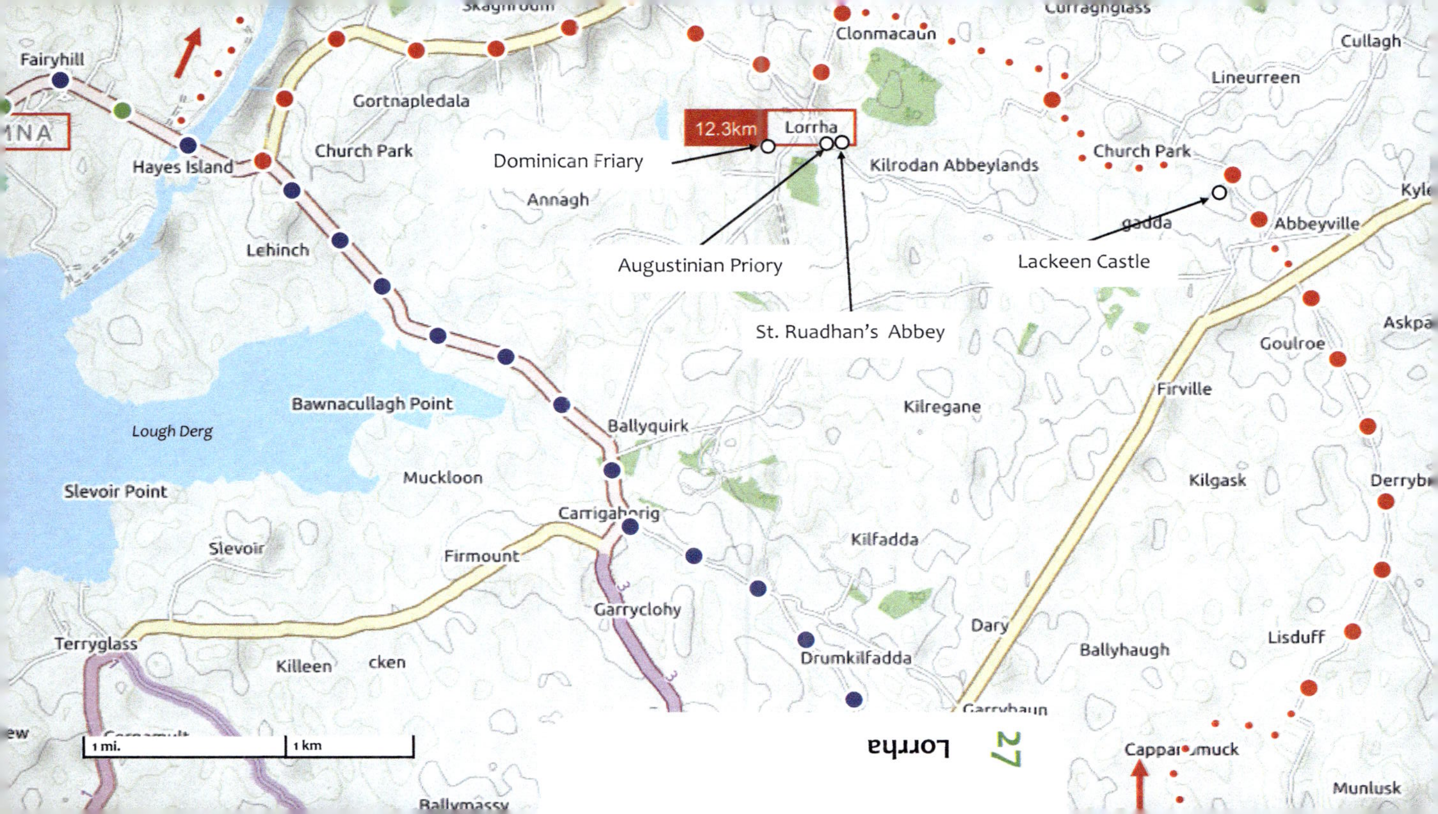
Fairyhill
Hayes Island
Gortnapledala
Church Park
Lehinch
Clonmacaun
Lorrha
12.3km
Dominican Friary
Augustinian Priory
St. Ruadhan's Abbey
Kilrodan Abbeylands
Annagh
Lineurreen
Cullagh
Church Park
Lackeen Castle
Abbeyville
Goulroe
Firville
Kilregane
Kilgask
Bawnacullagh Point
Lough Derg
Ballyquirk
Muckloon
Slevoir Point
Slevoir
Carrigahorig
Firmount
Garryclohy
Kilfadda
Dary
Drumkilfadda
Ballyhaugh
Lisduff
Terryglass
Killeen
1 mi.
1 km

over a stile to the right to walk on the levee yet again. Pass by a dam and continue along more levee with grass kept short by grazing sheep. Beautiful views of the Shannon on either side. In 1km you will pass **Meelick Weir** and shortly after arrive at Meelick Quay (known locally as Meelick Wall). There is no shop here, but some picnic benches for a rest by the river and **Meelick Church** is a short stroll away.

The Crossing of the Shannon

The MacEgans who owned Redwood Castle were loyal to the Queen. They were obliged to attack Donal Cam as he tried to cross the river Shannon with his followers. Stuck between the MacEgans and the River Shannon, Donal Cam ordered his men to build boats. One group of his followers built a currach and another built a coracle. They killed some of their horses to stitch the skins together and make the boats water-tight. They started to cross a quarter-mile of river under the cover of darkness. The smaller of the two boats sank. The larger boat was well made and carried thirty at a time. When two-thirds of them had crossed over, the MacEgans saw their chance to attack; however, Donal Cam had left his musketeers as the last to cross and they slayed MacEgan along with fifteen of his men.

Day hiker on the Hymany Way

River Shannon & Sheep on the Levee

[17.2km/10.7mi] Meelick

A

Míleac

Meelick Abbey

Meelick Abbey is the oldest Roman Catholic church in Ireland that is still in use for regular masses. It was built in 1414 by the O'Maddens as a Franciscan Friary. Traces of the transept chapel and friary can be seen in the ruin beside it.

Lynch's Farmhouse B&B (dairy farm 1km/0.6mi off trail, recommended for a farm experience), Mayour, Eyrecourt +353 (0) 909 675156, www.lynchsfarmhouse.com.

From Meelick turn inland for Eyrecourt (cycle trail) or Clonfert (walking trail).

Eyrecourt (cycle trail)

A

Dún an Uchta

Caslawn House, The Square, Eyrecourt, +353 (0)909 675469.

Walking from Meelick continue on past Meelick Quay along the narrow road for 2.8km, then turn left over two stiles just before an old stables building. Follow 0.6km of off-road track. Walk along the right side of two fields, cross a metal bridge and continue alongside the steam. The stile to exit the field is behind the house. The last time I hiked here, the next stile across the road was blocked off, however I was able to go left and then right to follow the road and re-join the trail. At the T-junction go right down a quiet road to where the road veers left and you will see **Kilnaborris Bog** to your right. At the next bend in the road go left over a metal bridge. There may be cattle in these fields so take care here. Go straight across three fields and you can see the top of Brackloon Castle in the distance, which is where you are going. Follow a laneway for 1.5km. At the road go right, but check out Brackloon Castle just on your left first.

Brackloon Castle

Our Lady of Clonfert Chapel

Brackloon Castle, now privately owned, was a 15th-century O'Madden stronghold. The name Brackloon comes from the Gaelic 'Breac Cluain', meaning 'Speckled Meadow'. This fortified tower house features strong walls, small windows, defensive turrets and a murder hole.

[6.8km/4.2mi] Clonfert

Cluaín Fearta

Continue right from the castle and you will soon arrive at **Our Lady of Clonfert Chapel**. It contains a **statue of the Madonna and Child** which dates from the late 13th or early 14th century. It is carved from a block of solid oak, hand painted and 4 feet in height. The statue had been found hidden inside a tree by men who were cutting it down. They cut the arm of the statue and according to local legend only noticed the statue when they saw blood coming from the severed arm. It is now the

Madonna & Child Statue

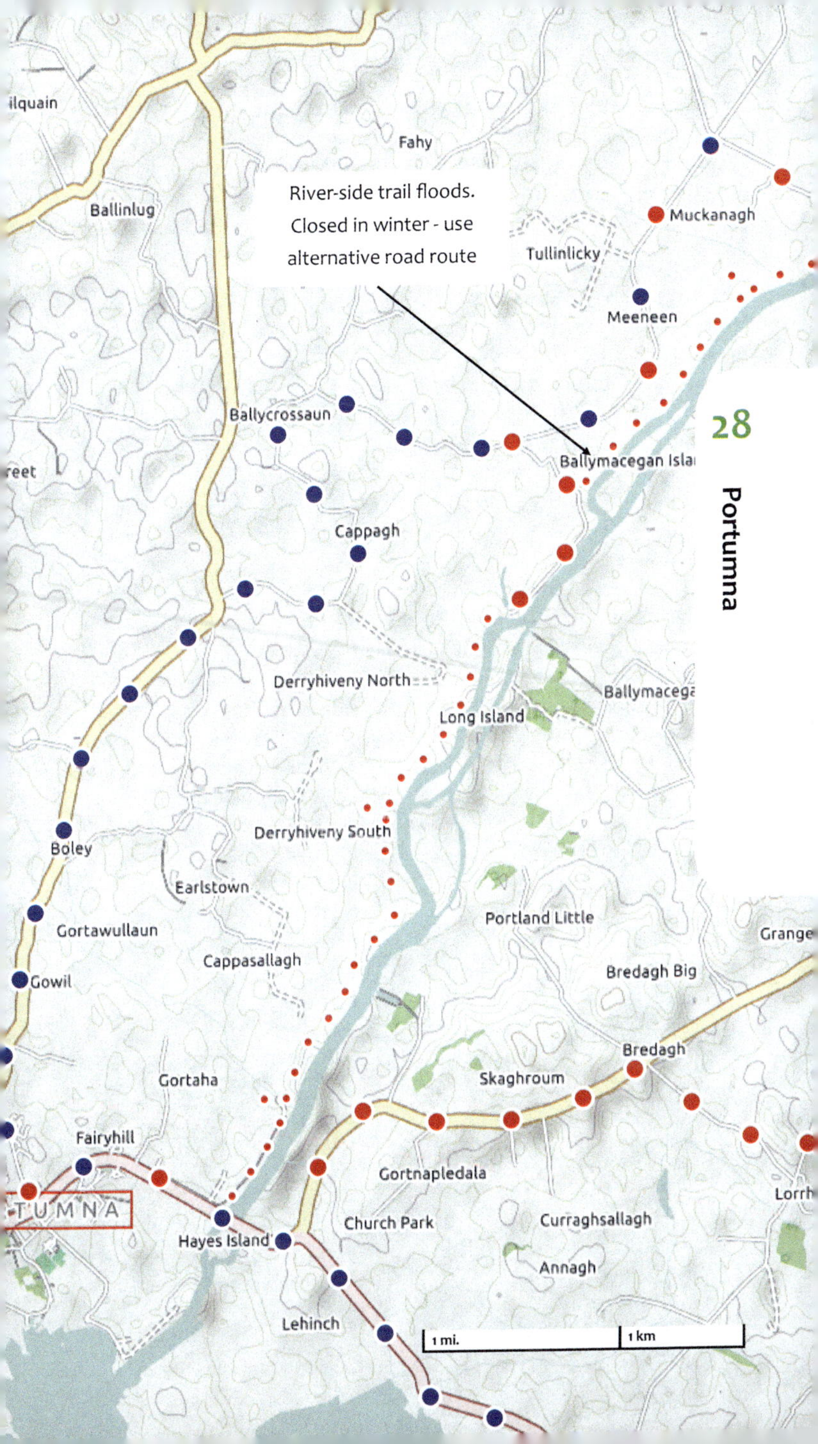
River-side trail floods. Closed in winter - use alternative road route
Fahy
Muckanagh
Tullinlicky
Meeneen
Ballinlug
Ballycrossaun
Ballymacegan Isla
Cappagh
Derryhiveny North
Ballymacega
Long Island
Derryhiveny South
Boley
Earlstown
Portland Little
Gortawullaun
Grange
Cappasallagh
Bredagh Big
Gowil
Bredagh
Skaghroum
Gortaha
Fairyhill
Gortnapledala
Lorrh
TUMNA
Church Park
Curraghsallagh
Hayes Island
Annagh
Lehinch
1 mi.
1 km

focus of a large pilgrimage which takes place here every May. Continue straight past the chapel for another 1.8km, going straight through the crossroads. The trail turns left at the Beara-Breifne Way information board, however, you can continue straight on for a short and worthwhile detour to visit St. Brendan's Tree and St. Brendan's Cathedral.

St. Brendan's Tree is covered in trinkets in memory of loved ones. Next to it is **St. Brendan's Cathedral**, which dates back to the medieval period. Founded by St. Brendan the Navigator, it was a centre for worship and learning. Its Romanesque doorway has beautifully carved sandstone. St. Brendan was buried here c. 580. In 1026 the King of Cenél Conaill began his pilgrimage from here to Rome, indicating the possible significance of the cathedral at that time. A church was recorded as being built here in 908. It is not known if this is the same structure, however it does have some features typical of this period. It is estimated that the Romanesque portal was constructed around the 12th century. Look out for the mermaid and wyfren (two-legged dragon from medieval mythology) stone carvings inside the cathedral which were added in the 15th century.

St. Brendan's Tree

Wyfren Stone Carving

St. Brendan's Cathedral

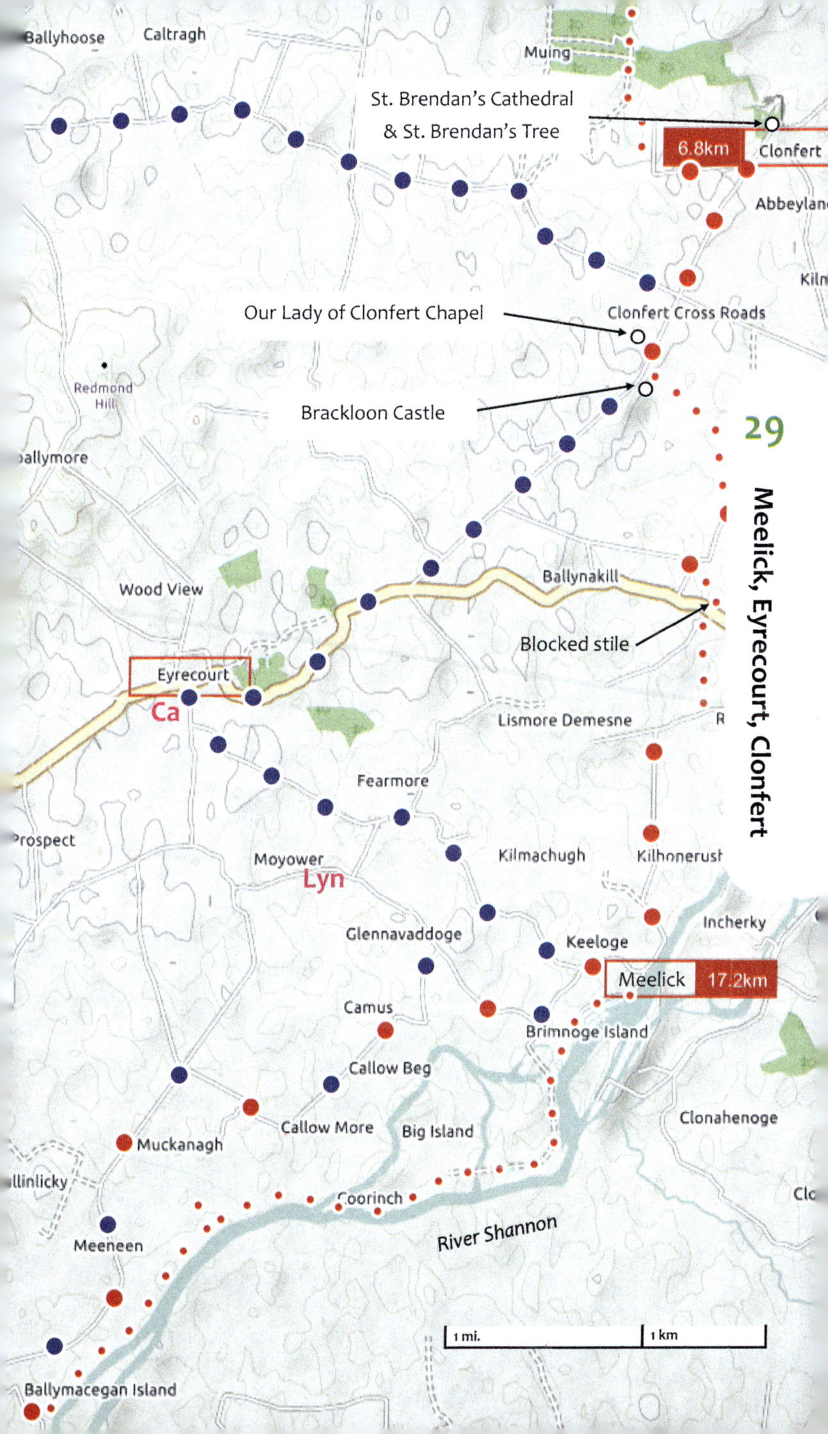
Ballyhoose
Caltragh
Muing
St. Brendan's Cathedral
& St. Brendan's Tree
6.8km
Clonfert
Abbeylan
Kil
Our Lady of Clonfert Chapel
Clonfert Cross Roads
Redmond
Hill
Brackloon Castle
allymore
Wood View
Ballynakill
Blocked stile
Eyrecourt
Ca
Lismore Demesne
Fearmore
Prospect
Moyower
Lyn
Kilmachugh
Kilhonerust
Incherky
Glennavaddoge
Keeloge
Meelick
17.2km
Camus
Brimnoge Island
Callow Beg
Clonahenoge
Callow More
Big Island
Muckanagh
llinlicky
Coorinch
Clo
River Shannon
Meeneen
1 mi.
1 km
Ballymacegan Island

From Clonfert make your way to Laurencetown (cycle trail) or towards Ballinasloe (walking trail).

Laurencetown (cycle trail)

S R D

An Baile Mór

Small shop and pub serving breakfast and lunch.

Back to the Beara-Breifne Way information board and after 0.6km on this quiet road, just past a bungalow on the left you will see a stile at the back of the property. Way-markers and stiles are all viewable through these fields. Exit the field onto a grassy laneway and go right. Over the next stile and continue straight onto a forest track along a stream. When the pine forest is on your left hand side there is an unmarked right turn between Alder trees. (If you miss this turn you will come to an impassable stream). At the bog go left into the trees, cross a wooden plank and walk beside a field of sheep. Follow a lovely trail through Clooncarta Woods for 3.5km, walking parallel to the vast Clooncarta bogland.

Clooncarta Woods & Bog

Exiting the forest you will follow a grassy track, then rough road. At the crossroads continue straight onto tarmac road. Soon you will come to **Laurencetown Heritage Trail** which is a very short boardwalk which overlooks restored bogland. Continuing on the way the road becomes surrounded by forest for a short distance and leads to Lismany.

[12.8km/8mi] **Clonmany B&B**, 0879815287.

Shortly after, you will see the ruin of the **Pollock Estate**, former home of local landlord Allan Pollock. Take the next right turn and after 1km turn left down a rough track for 3.7km and crossing the Ballinure river. This pleasant stretch goes through bogland along a drainage canal. Go over concrete steps into the Ballinasloe (Clay) Shooting Grounds and exit shortly after over another set of concrete

Laurencetown Heritage Trail

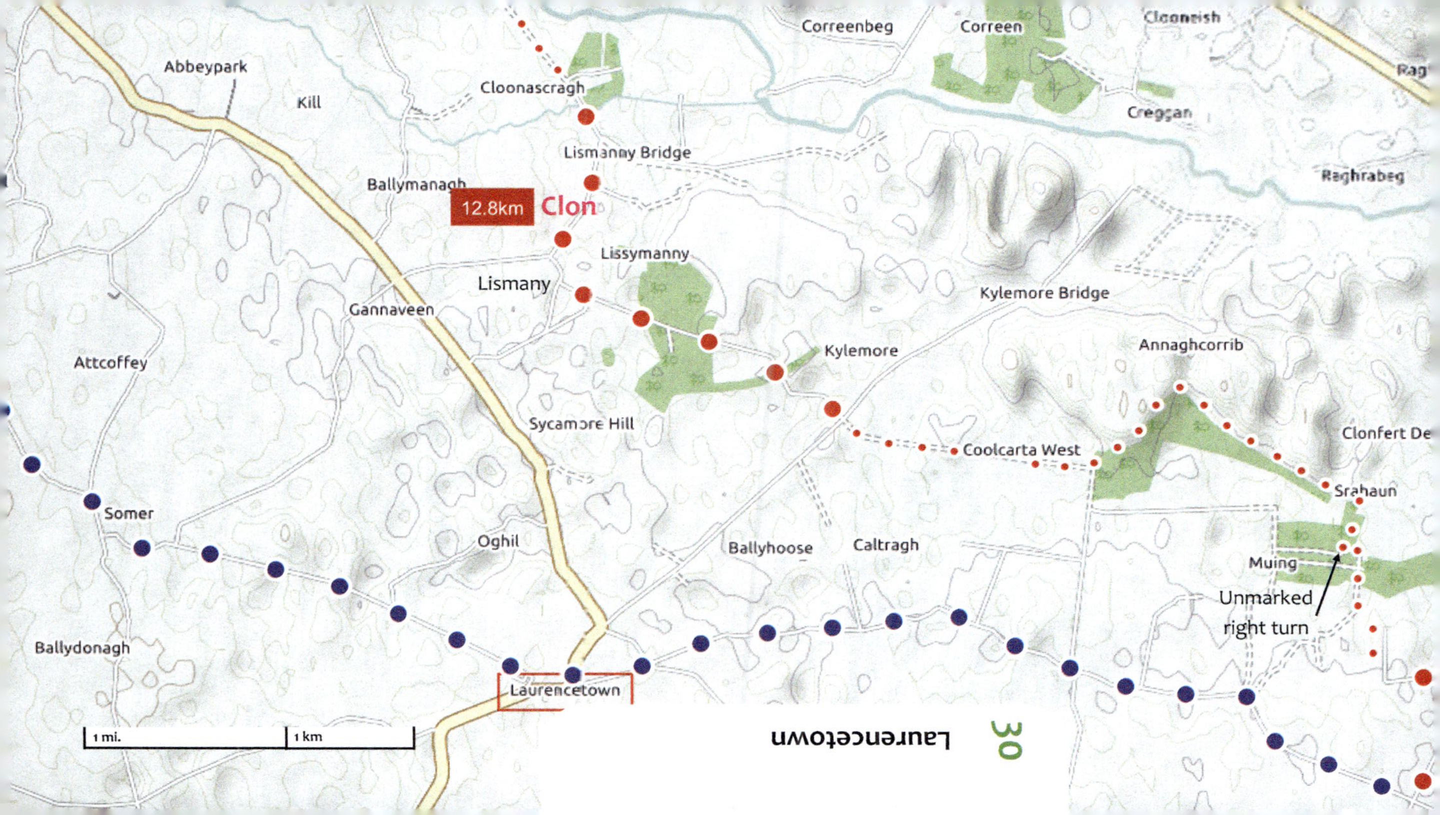

Correenbeg
Correen
Cloonеish
Abbeypark
Kill
Cloonascragh
Creggan
Rag
Lismanny Bridge
Raghrabeg
Ballymanagh
12.8km
Clon
Lissymanny
Lismany
Kylemore Bridge
Gannaveen
Annaghcorrib
Kylemore
Attcoffey
Sycamore Hill
Clonfert De
Coolcarta West
Srahaun
Somer
Oghil
Ballyhoose
Caltragh
Muing
Unmarked
right turn
Ballydonagh
Laurencetown
1 mi.
1 km

steps and go left onto a rough track. Take the next right and after 0.8km arrive at Poolboy Cottages road. Go right at the road and take the next left to continue on the trail or continue straight into Ballinasloe which is a medium sized town with plenty of shops and accommodation 3km off the trail.

[5.5km(+2.8km)/3.4mi(+1.7mi)] Ballinasloe

A S R PO € D P

Horse & Handler Sculpture, Ballinasloe

Béal Átha na Sluaighe - "Ford Mouth of the Hosts/Crowds"

Every October the **Ballinasloe Horse Fair** is held here - one of the oldest in Europe which dates back to the 18th century. It is now a part of a week-long festival. For more information check www.Ballinasloeoctober fair.com.

Gullane's Hotel, Main St., +353 (0)909 642220, www.gullanes hotel.com; **Hayden's Hotel**, Dunlo St., +353 (0)909 642347, www.haydens.ie; **Carlton Shearwater Hotel**, Marina Point, +353 (0) 909 630400, www.shearwater hotel.com; **Cloon Cummer B&B**, Creagh, +353 (0)905 (or 9096) 43983, www.clooncummer.com; **Moycarn Lodge & Marina Hotel,** +353 (0)909 645050, www.moycarnlodge.ie; **Nephin B&B** (1.8 km off the trail), +353 (0) 909 642685.

Bloodiest Battle for the O'Sullivans

This area was also a battle site for Donal Cam in January 1603 when he found his path blocked by eight hundred English. He was outnumbered but had no choice but to fight. Against all odds he lead his men to victory; it was his bloodiest battle. Many of his mercenaries now returned home. Weary and vulnerable, Donal Cam and his remaining people had to march 20 miles during the night to escape their enemy.

Leave Ballinasloe the same way you came into the town. Walk 3km south along Poolboy Cottages road and cross over motorway before joining back onto the trail. Turn right onto quiet rough road for 1.8km. The track will take you through the centre of Ballinasloe Golf Club. Then turn left onto busy road for 0.6km. Use space along verge on left of road for walking. At bend in the road there is no verge for a few metres so use caution. Turn right onto a smaller less-busy road for almost 2km and pass by a church. Then turn left onto a narrow

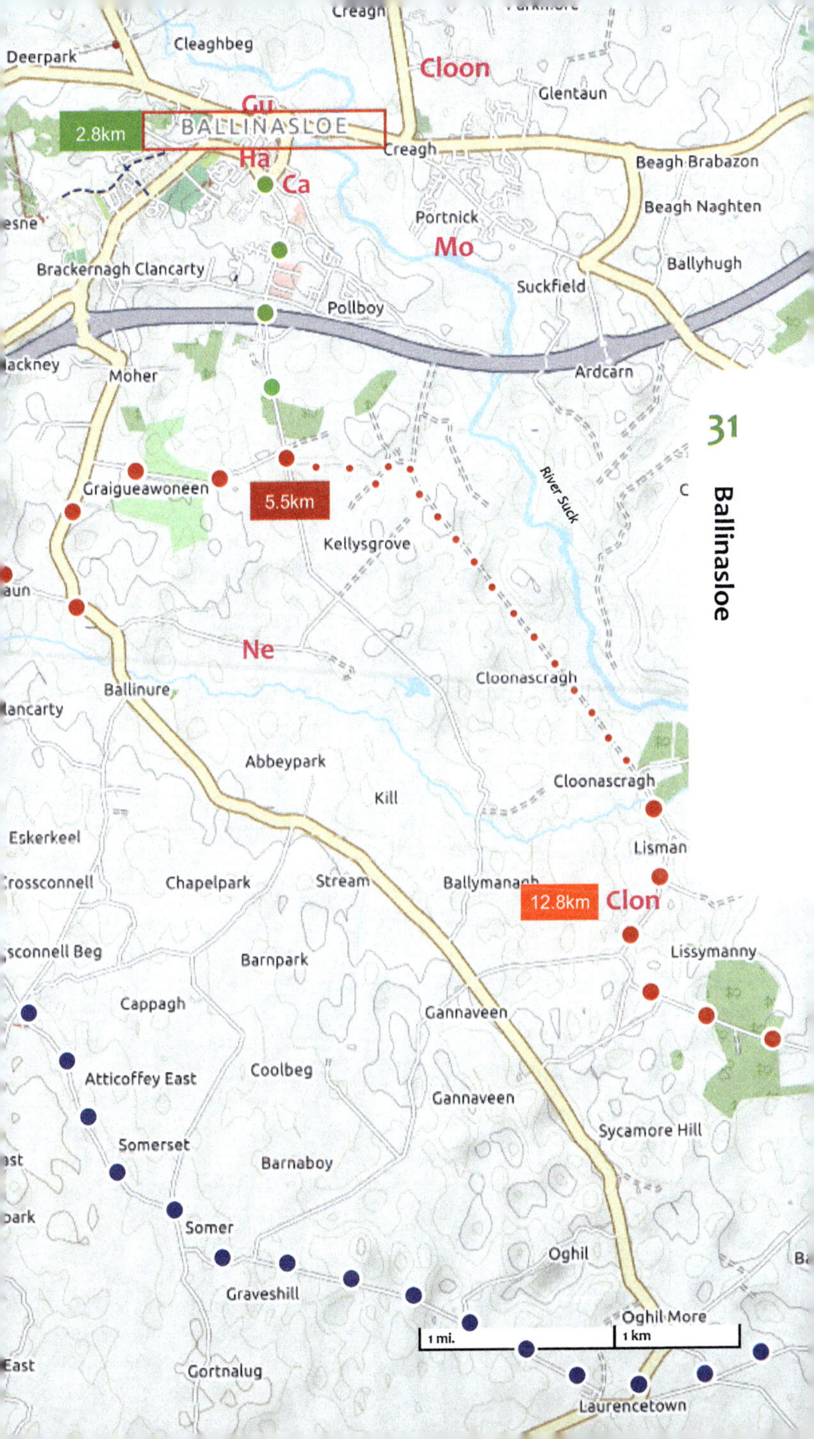
Cleaghbeg
Deerpark
Cloon
Glentaun
2.8km
BALLINASLOE
Gu
Ha
Ca
Creagh
Beagh Brabazon
Beagh Naghten
Portnick
Mo
Brackernagh Clancarty
Ballyhugh
Suckfield
Pollboy
Moher
Ardcarn
Graigueawoneen
5.5km
Kellysgrove
River Suck
Ne
Cloonascragh
Ballinure
Abbeypark
Cloonascragh
Kill
Eskerkeel
Lisman
Chapelpark
Stream
Ballymanagh
12.8km
Clon
Barnpark
Lissymanny
Cappagh
Gannaveen
Atticoffey East
Coolbeg
Gannaveen
Somerset
Sycamore Hill
Barnaboy
Somer
Oghil
Graveshill
Oghil More
1 mi.
1 km
Gortnalug
Laurencetown

road for 2.6km and right at Hurney's Forge and a white thatched cottage with some old farming machinery of the horse-drawn variety on display in the front garden. Walk for 1.6km along this road and you are in **Battle of Aughrim** territory. Several information boards around this area will tell you all about this famous battle of July 1691. Turn left over a stile and cross a few fields. Back on road go right and then left at the T-Junction and cross the busy R446 road to Aughrim village. Take the first left for the **Battle of Aughrim Visitor Centre** or continue straight for Valerie's Hostel & Bar.

[10.5km/6.5mi] Aughrim

A S R

Eachroim - "Horse Ridge"

Battle of Aughrim Visitor Centre

The **Battle of Aughrim** took place near here between the Jacobites and the forces of William III in July 1691. Drop into the **Battle of Aughrim Visitor Centre,** open Tues-Sat 10.30am-4.30pm, Sun 2pm-5pm during summer only.

Valerie's Hostel € (also a pub and serves food) +353 (0)90 9673734, +353 (0)86 2830673, www.valeries.ie; **Finn's B&B**, +353 (0) 90 9673726, email: ppfinn@eircom.net.

Leaving Aughrim, take the road between Valerie's and the church. After 1.6km and crossing over the M6 motorway turn right at the Golden Mile sign, then after 0.8km turn left down a laneway and soon come to a stile which takes you through two fields with the exit stiles being diagonally to the left. Exit onto a rough track by a stream and then onto road and go left for a short distance before turning right down a laneway. This takes you over a railway line to then enter a field with the stile diagonally to the left again. Into the second field the stile is over a little hill (don't mistakenly follow the track towards the farmhouse). In the third field go straight keeping along the left. At the fourth field watch out for the electric fence and take a left turn immediately after the

Donkeys on the Hymany Way

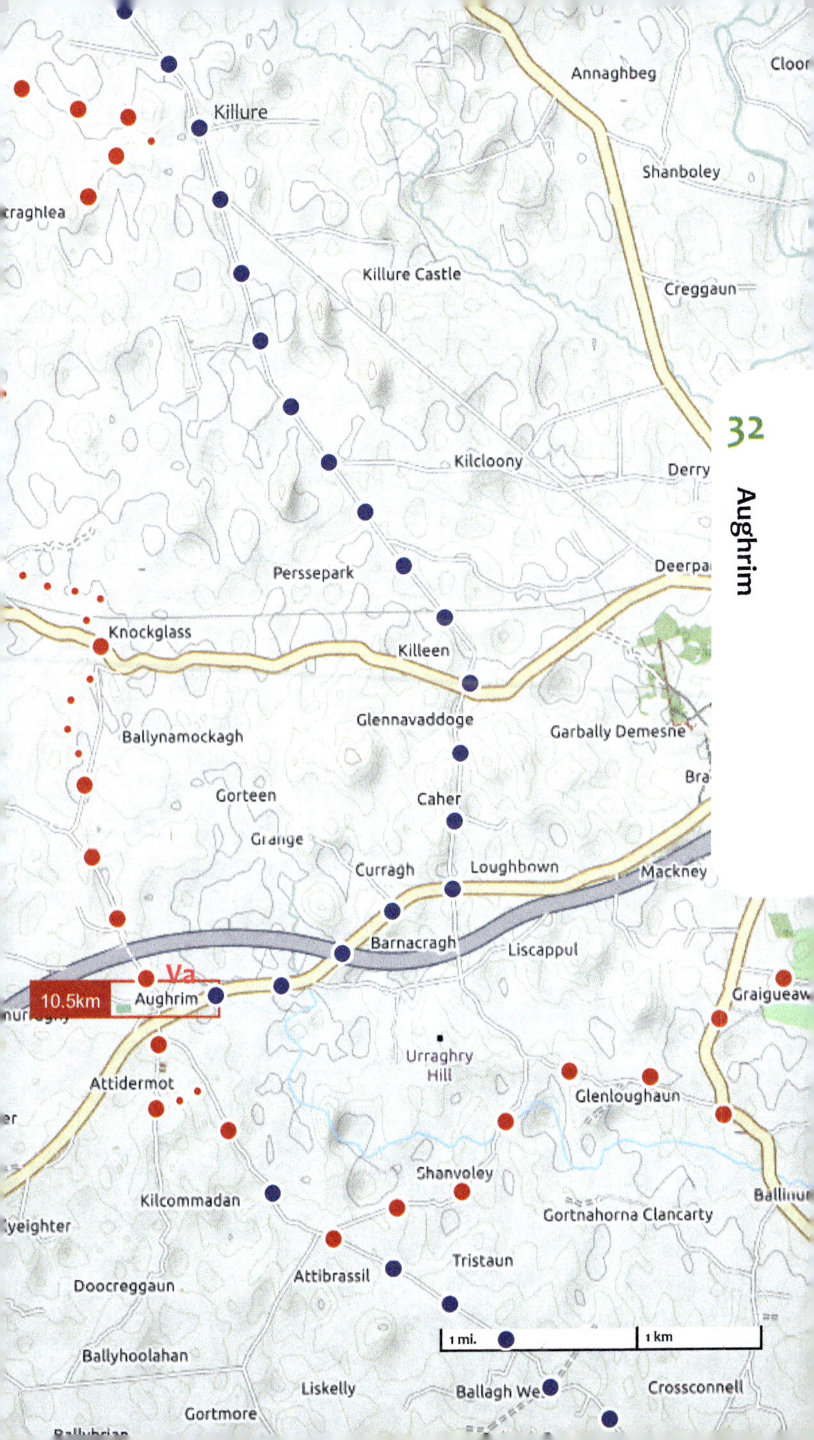
Killure
Annaghbeg
Shanboley
Killure Castle
Creggaun
Kilcloony
Derry
Perssepark
Deerpa
Knockglass
Killeen
Glennavaddoge
Garbally Demesne
Ballynamockagh
Gorteen
Caher
Grange
Curragh
Loughbown
Mackney
Barnacragh
Liscappul
10.5km
Aughrim
Graigueaw
Urraghry Hill
Attidermot
Glenloughaun
Shanvoley
Kilcommadan
Gortnahorna Clancarty
Tristaun
Attibrassil
Doocreggaun
1 mi.
1 km
Ballyhoolahan
Liskelly
Crossconnell
Gortmore

32

Aughrim

Hopper turf spread out to dry

stile. To exit this field keep straight and pass by the left of the house. However at time of writing it was fenced off and we went around the right of the house and were able to hop over the electric fence. Go left on the road and then turn right at the next road.

After 1.2km turn right down a boreen. Next is a stile on your left into a field with donkeys. Over in the field to your left on the hillock you can see a rounded mound which is the remains of a **ringfort**. Pass through a few more fields and then follow a rough track. The gorse bushes here are a vibrant yellow in spring and summer. The way-markers send you around the perimeter of this large field for some reason, but you will see some pieces of bog oak in the grass, likely from the bog the other side of the stream. Exit the field by crossing a stile near a fast-flowing stream.

The trail is on uneven ground with some hidden dips along the stream so watch your footing. Climb over a tree trunk to get into the next field. Keep to the left perimeter of the field as it is the only way to get

Bog Cotton at Crit Island West Bog

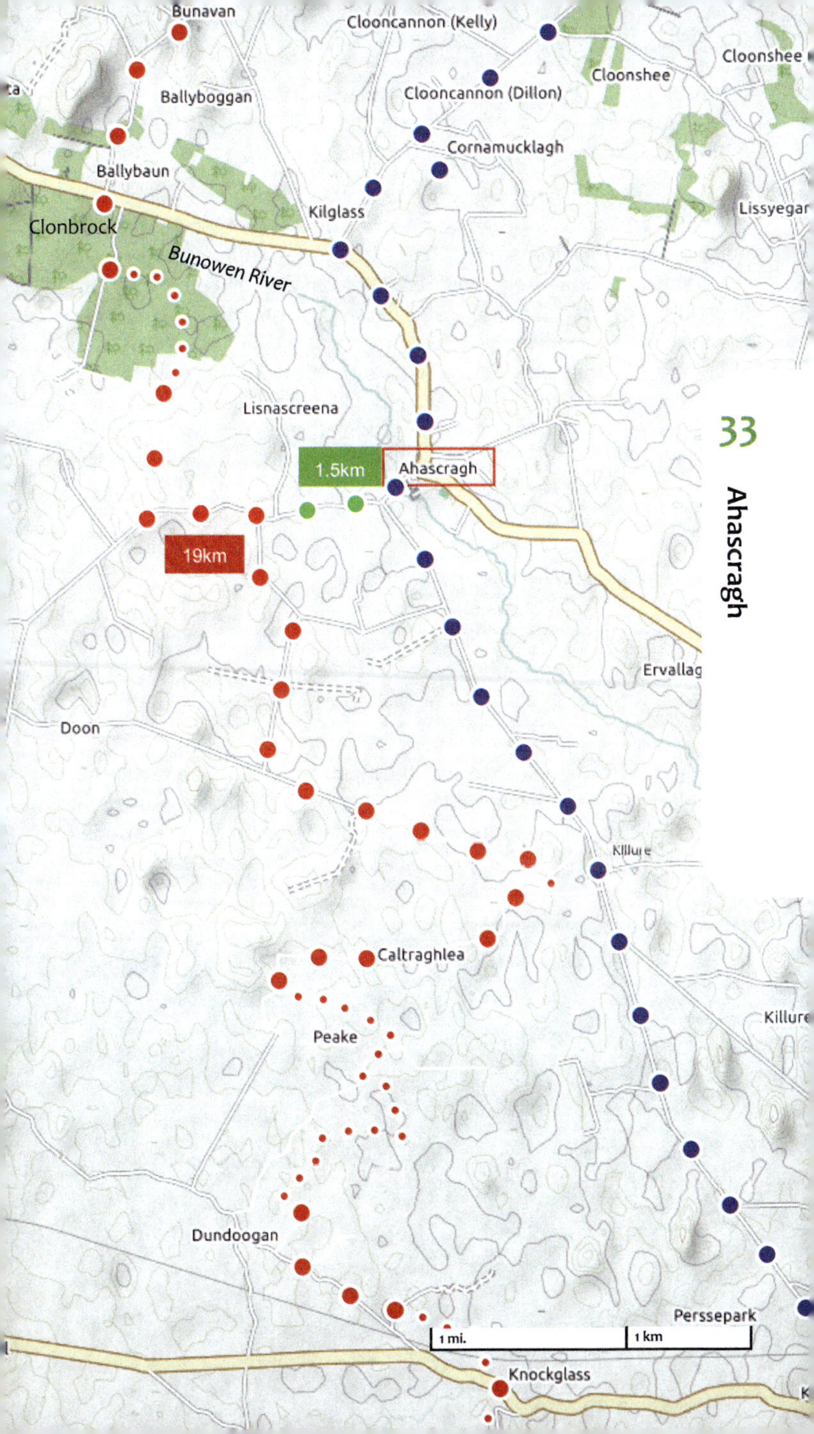
Bunavan
Clooncannon (Kelly)
Cloonshee
Cloonshee
Ballyboggan
Clooncannon (Dillon)
Cornamucklagh
Ballybaun
Kilglass
Lissyegar
Clonbrock
Bunowen River
Lisnascreena
1.5km
Ahascragh
19km
Ervallag
Doon
Killure
Caltraghlea
Killure
Peake
Dundoogan
Perssepark
1 mi.
1 km
Knockglass

to the next stile (don't cut across the field as there is barbed wire blocking the way). Cross over the concrete bridge and go left into the next field. Go through a couple more fields and onto a track.

At the next cattle farm the way-markers are a little confusing. Bear right at the yard rather than going into the next cattle field. You will need to go under the electric fence at the far end of the field, go through the gate and you will walk through a small copse of trees. Exit onto bog track and go left. Follow this track through the **Crit Island West Bog** where you may see turf laid out to dry and an abundance of bog cotton. After 3km, turn left to cross through three fields. Go left for a grass track, tree tunnel and rough road for 2.4km, then right on the tarmac road for 1.5km. Turn left at the bungalow with the yellow door and in 1km arrive at the road where you can take a 1.5km detour into Ahascragh village (no accommodation).

[19km(+1.5km)/11.8mi(+0.9mi)] Ahascragh

A S R PO D

Áth Eascrach - " Ford of the Esker/Ridge"

Ahascragh is on the cycle trail and is 1.5km off the walking trail. There are shops for food and several pubs. **Celtic Nest Holiday Apartments**, €€€, www.tripadvisor.com.

Following on from the left turn at the T-junction near Ahascragh, walk for 0.8km along this main road then right onto a narrow laneway for 1.4km and then over a stile and cross the field. Go over a wooden bridge and stile and veer right. Follow a grass track for 1.2km. Climb

Bunowen River

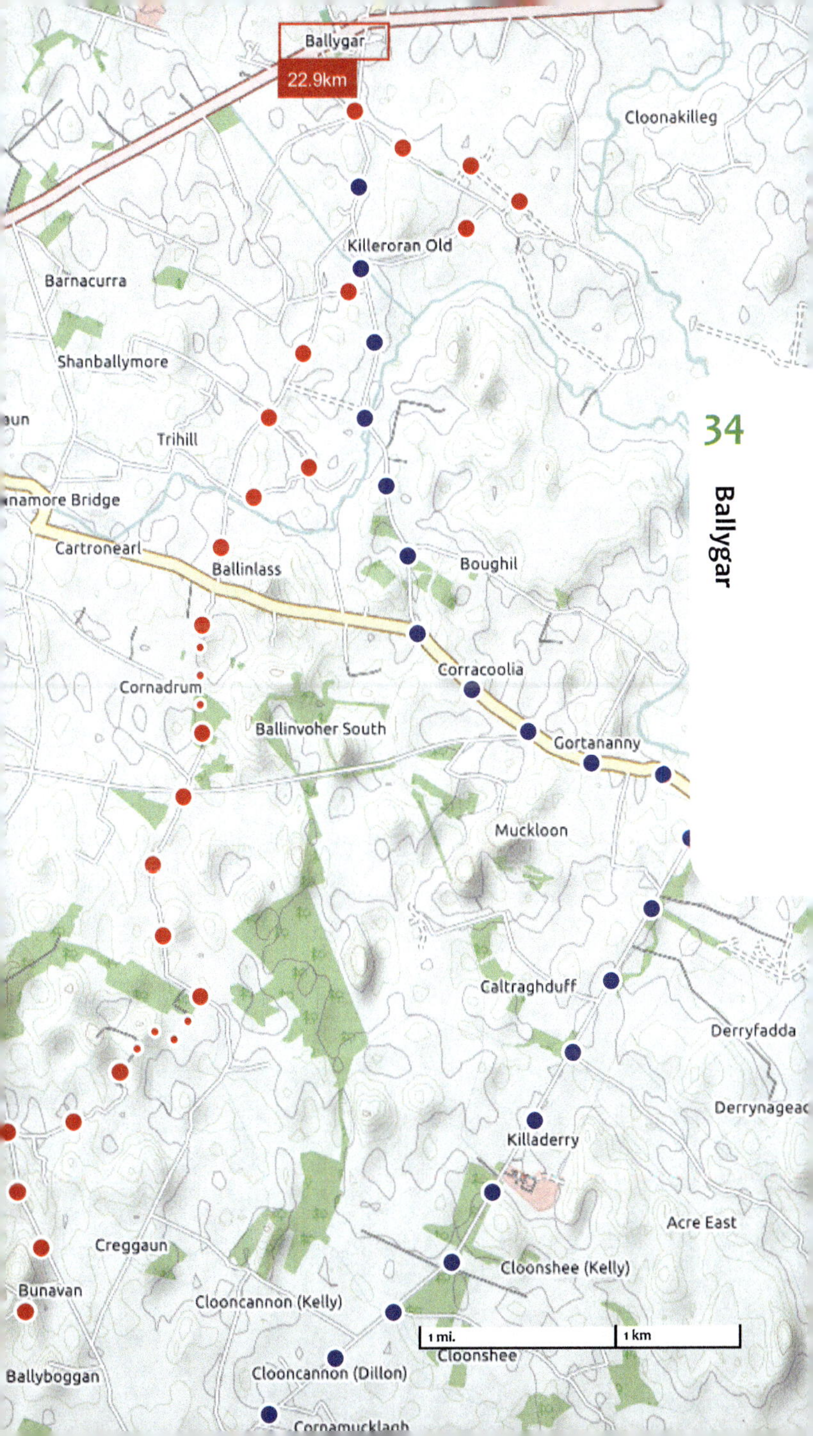
Ballygar
22.9km
Cloonakilleg
Killeroran Old
Barnacurra
Shanballymore
Trihill
Cartronearl
Ballinlass
Boughil
Corracoolia
Cornadrum
Ballinvoher South
Gortananny
Muckloon
Caltraghduff
Derryfadda
Killaderry
Acre East
Creggaun
Cloonshee (Kelly)
Bunavan
Clooncannon (Kelly)
1 mi.
1 km
Cloonshee
Ballyboggan
Clooncannon (Dillon)

Castle Ffrench West Bog

Hikers and tractor on the road

over a black and yellow barrier and go right on the boreen with a tunnel of beech trees, some of which are oak trees over 200 years old. Next is a bridge over the **Bunowen River**. Exit **Clonbrock** and go left on the busy R358 road for a short distance then right down a rough track for 1.7km where you will see bogland along your left. Exit straight onto a quiet tarmac road by an old white cottage and farm.

At the T-junction go left for 1.4km, passing by **Chapelfinnerty Graveyard**. Turn right down a boreen and pass by an old water pump and farm machinery followed by the **ruin of an old cottage**.

In 1.6km reach **Castle Ffrench West Bog** and take a right for the track through the wet bog. After the first way-marker on the mound to the right, the next way-marker is diagonally to the right. Enter into the trees and onto a stony track. Exit around a metal barrier and onto a boreen for 1.8km and you will soon have **Castle Ffrench East Bog** on your right. At the crossroads continue straight on past the house and

Bridge over the Shiven River

soon arrive at a grass track and veer left. After grass track you enter onto a forest track with spruce trees followed by wet bogland. Cross straight across the field and exit onto a track.

At the road go right and immediately left onto a quiet road. Cross the bridge over the **Shiven River**. Turn right after the bridge down a boreen and then track road through bog. Where the track splits veer left and on reaching the tarmac road go right. In 1km take the next right onto a track beside a bog. Go left on the busy road and then right onto a boreen.

Graveyard with round tower

At the next T-junction go right on the road. After a short walk turn left off the road and follow the grass track along bog, nettle track followed by a very muddy track, then join back on road and go right. Alternatively, take a shortcut by just turning left at the T-junction.

Pass by a graveyard with round tower and in 0.7km take the second right for another 0.7km into Ballygar village which has one B&B on the main street.

The Coffee Drop B&B, Ballygar

STAGE 8:

Suck Valley Way

Slí Ghleann an tSuca

Ballygar - **Creggs** - **Glinsk** - Ballymoe - Ballinlough - Loughglynn

Distance:	66.5 km / 41.3 miles
Difficulty:	Easy
Counties:	Galway, Roscommon
OSI Maps:	Discovery Series 40, 39, 32

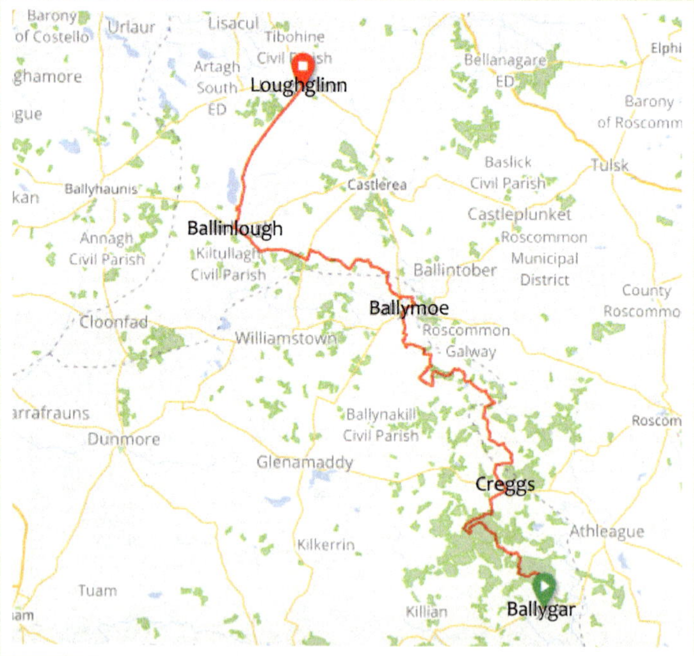

The Suck Valley Way is well way-marked, however, there is a shortage of accommodation. This trail was created by the River Suck Valley Development Co-operative and opened by Enda Kenny, Minister for Tourism and Trade, in 1997. The trail is a 105 km/65 mile circular route, but the Beara-Breifne Way only covers 66.5km of the western section. Watch out for the turn-off to continue on the Beara-Breifne Way as it is not clearly marked and many hikers miss it. Much of this trail is off-road or on quiet roads. The trail meanders along the **River Suck** (An tSuca). This callows area, being prone to flooding, is a haven for wildlife. Look out for fallow deer, grey squirrels and the rare pine marten. If flooded at the time of walking, follow the signs for the alternative route. You will pass through several cattle fields. As always, check for bulls and take an alternative route if necessary.

View on the way to Creggs

[22.9km/14mi] Ballygar

A S R PO € D P W

Béal Átha Ghártha - "Mouth of the Ford"

Laundry services in the town, ask at the accommodation.

The Coffee Drop B&B, +353 (0)87 3265922, email: patgreally @gmail.com.

Past Centra, take a left and pass by St Mary's College and a row of bungalows. Turn right into **Aughrane Forest** for 4km of off-road track. The trail has a mixture of deciduous trees followed by Sitka Spruce. After 2km, cross a unique wooden bridge and soon come to arrive at a clearing with a picnic bench. Veer left where the gravel path splits. Through the trees to your right is the ruin of a walled garden. Continue on to a wooden bridge over a stream and through more forest track. At the gravel track go right. At the next way-marker go right. Exit the forest through a black and yellow metal barrier and at the road take the next right down a boreen. You will be able to see **Aughrim Bog** through the trees.

At the road go right and then as the road veers right, go straight ahead into the forest for a 1.8km ascent up **Mount Mary**. Pass by the telecommunication masts followed by a gentle descent. Exit the forest track through a black and yellow metal barrier and go right on the narrow road to continue your descent. After half 0.5km turn right down a track.

Creggs Wildlife Park

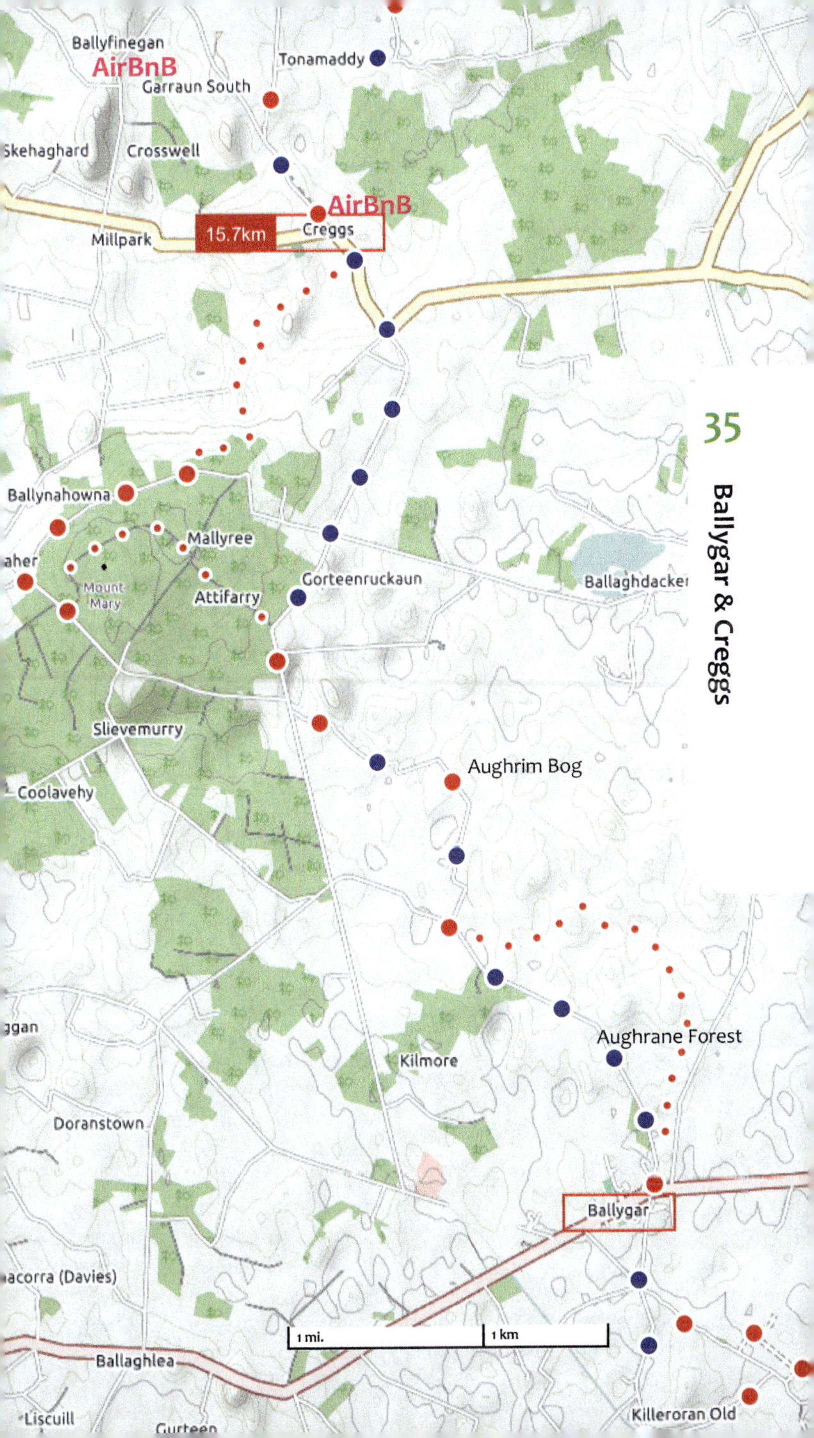
Ballyfinegan
AirBnB
Tonamaddy
Garraun South
Skehaghard
Crosswell
AirBnB
15.7km
Creggs
Millpark
Ballynahowna
Mallyree
Mount Mary
Attifarry
Gorteenruckaun
Ballaghdacker
Slievemurry
Coolavehy
Aughrim Bog
Aughrane Forest
Kilmore
Doranstown
Ballygar
1 mi.
1 km
Ballaghlea
Killeroran Old
Liscuill
Gurteen

Go left over a stile and follow the grass track. If the weather is very wet, you may prefer to stick to the road as the path, as after rain this track gets muddy. Some of the track here has a wooden walkway. Go through a gate and descend the grassy path, then through some fields, some of which have cattle. This is followed by forest track which can be muddy and then follow alongside a stream lined with Flag Iris which have beautiful yellow blooms in summer. Exit the forest track over a stile and cross a large field, keeping alongside the stream. After a few more fields (some with cattle) you will pass through the tiny **Wildlife Park** in Creggs, to arrive at the small village.

Camp at Mount Mary

O'Sullivan camped at Mount Mary on 10th January 1603 after an 80-km/50-mile trek to escape pursuit following their battle at Aughrim. Here they were met with snow and many of his men died from the cold and exhaustion. A few of them were sent down to Creggs to look for food, but the locals warded them off by throwing rocks at them. Some of his followers remained in the area; their descendants have surnames such as O'Connell, Cronin and Hurly.

[15.7km/9.7mi] Creggs

S R PO €

Na Creaga - "The Rocks"

Creggs is a small country village with pubs and a shop to stock up on food and water. In the village you will see a monument to Charles Stewart Parnell and an old church in ruin, Ballinakill Abbey.

AirBnB in Creggs.

Wooden Bridge passed Creggs

Leave Creggs passing by the church ruin on your left and a football pitch to your right. Follow roads for 10.5km. Leave the road to climb over a stile and cross the sheep field with yellow **Flag Iris** in summer months. Cross a wooden bridge and you will come to a lovely nature area with wild grasslands, bog, stream and lake. Cross the wooden bridge and enter a field of bracken and rough grassland with boggy patches. Look out for the small lilac **Bog Orchid** in sping/summer. You

Creggs & Glinsk

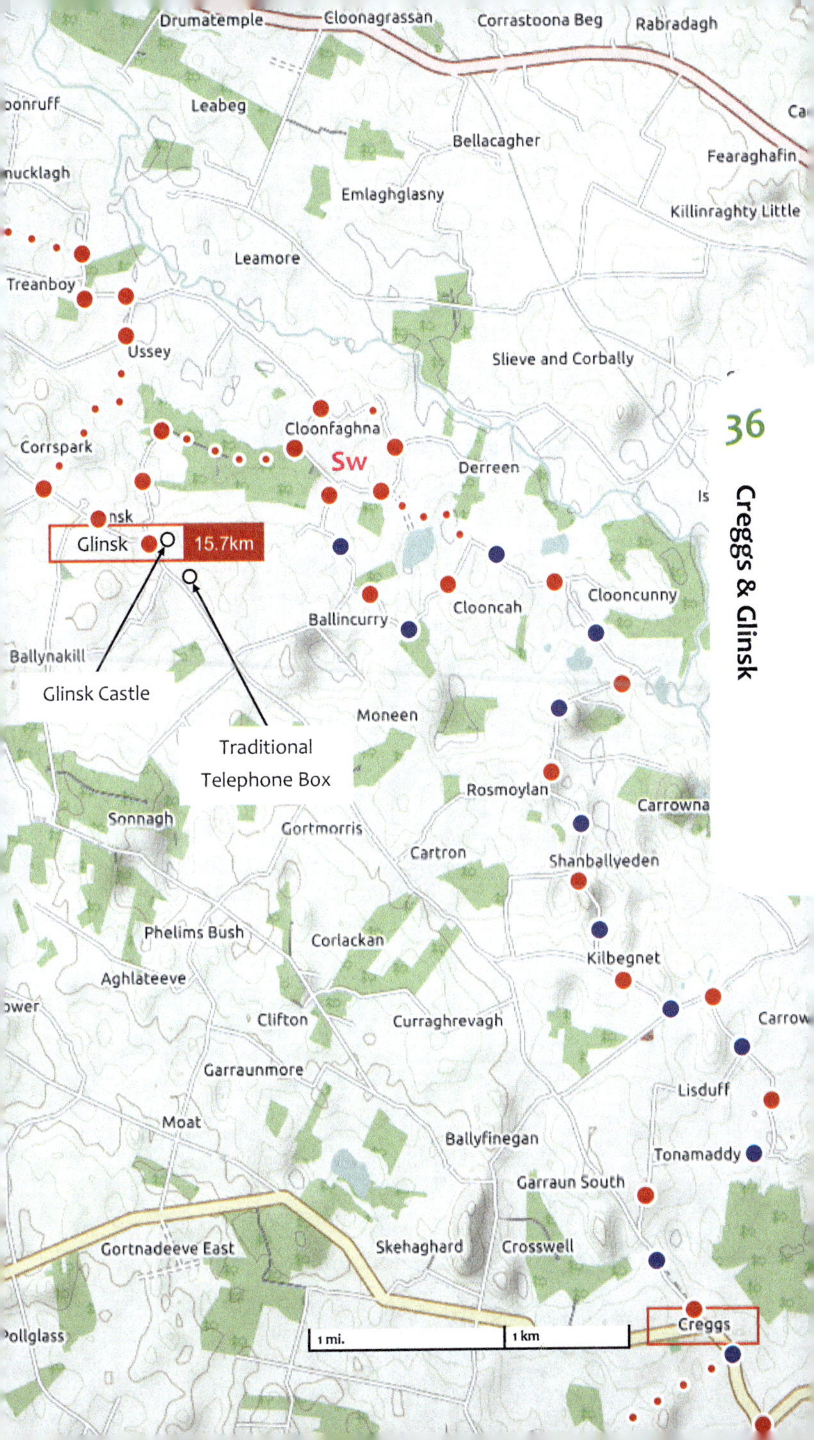

will see **Lough Loung** in the distance to your left. Cross a stile to a small wooded grass track. Next turn right on the road track (or take a detour of about 150 metres to the left for Lough Loung, a beautiful rest stop to dip your feet in the water).

Bog Orchid

Continue along the track road until you reach a gate. Pass through the gate and go right (or left if wet weather and risk of flooding). Walk on road for 0.8km then climb over an overgrown stile on the left of the laneway and into a field. Keep along the left and in the corner cross a metal stile. Go left into another corner where the stile is hidden in the bushes. Go straight across the next field to another metal stile and onto a small road where you go left and left again. This road is lined with alternating Ash and Oak trees. Go left at the slightly bigger tarmac road. Where the road veers left, continue straight onto a woodland track for 2.3km. As you get closer to Glinsk you will have a stream along your left and you can see **Glinsk Castle** on the far side through the trees. The castle is accessible by steps at the side of the road but there are cattle in this field so take care. From the end of the track turn right into Glinsk village.

Lough Loung Boardwalk

[15.7km/9.7mi] Glinsk

A PO

Gleann Uisce - "Glen of the Water"

Glinsk Castle was built in the mid 17th century. At this time, wealthy land owners were starting to build houses instead of castles; Glinsk Castle might be better described as a fortified house.

Before Glinsk is **The Swallows B&B**, 090 6621926.

Glinsk Castle

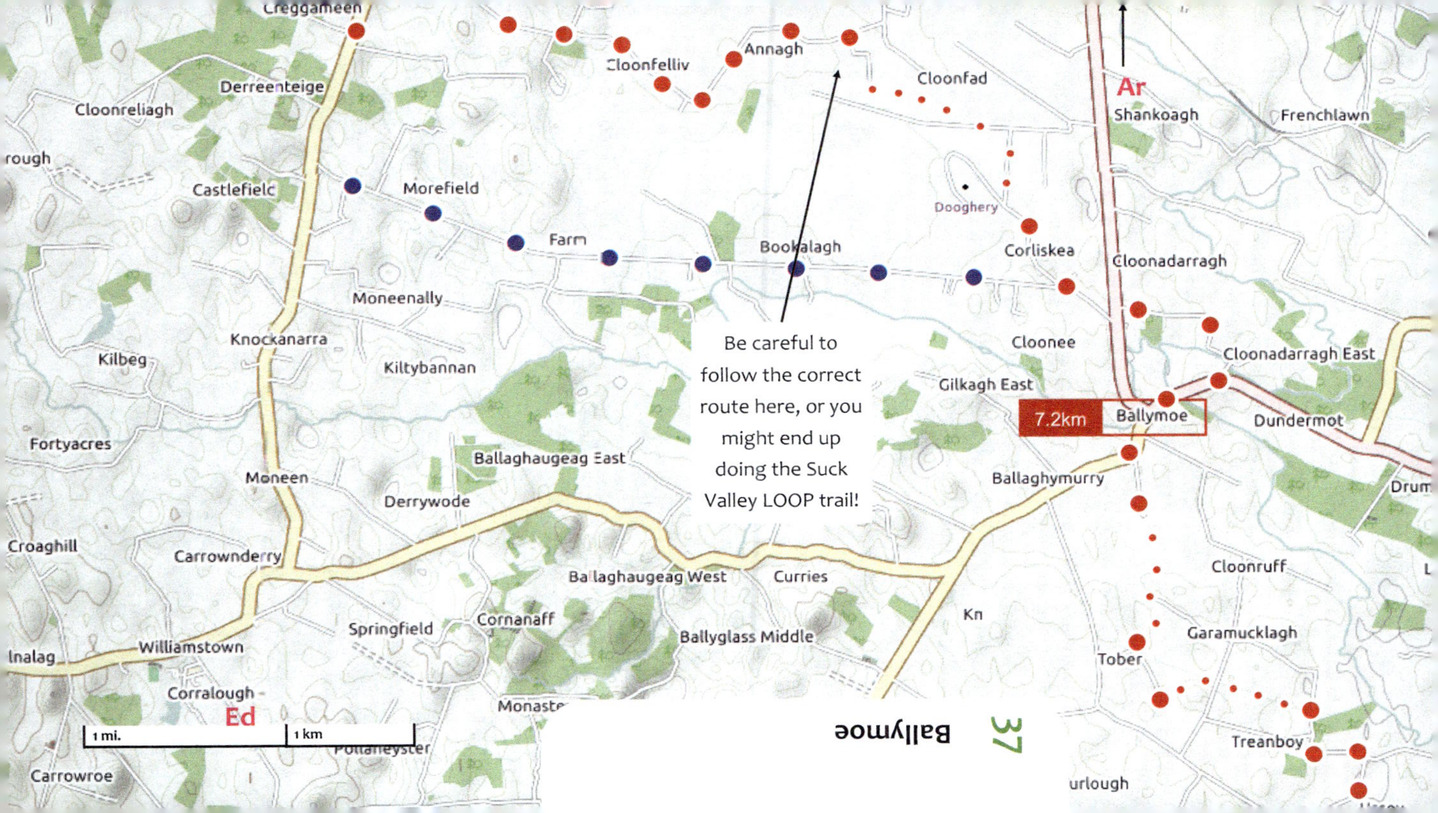

Creggameen
Annagh
Cloonfelliv
Cloonfad
Derreenteige
Cloonreliagh
Shankoagh
Frenchlawn
Ar
rough
Castlefielc
Morefield
Dooghery
Farm
Bookalagh
Corliskea
Cloonadarragh
Moneenally
Knockanarra
Kilbeg
Kiltybannan
Cloonee
Cloonadarragh East
Gilkagh East
7.2km
Ballymoe
Dundermot
Be careful to follow the correct route here, or you might end up doing the Suck Valley LOOP trail!
Fortyacres
Ballaghaugeag East
Moneen
Derrywode
Ballaghymurry
Drum
Croaghill
Carrownderry
Ballaghaugeag West
Curries
Cloonruff
Kn
Springfield
Cornanaff
Ballyglass Middle
Garamucklagh
Inalag
Williamstown
Tober
Corralough
Ed
Monaste
Treanboy
1 mi.
1 km
Pollaneyster
Carrowroe
urlough

Donal Cam and the Burkes

Glinsk Castle was owned by Ulick Burke. He had heard that O'Sullivan was on his way and ordered his people to hide their food and animals. Donal Cam and his followers, having not eaten or slept for thirty-six hours, marched on to Glinsk Castle disguised as "Royalists", wearing clothing and carrying flags they had taken from the English at Aughrim. They hoped to be welcomed and given food. Unfortunately the Burkes were not deceived.

That night, Donal Cam decided to light campfires in the woods nearby. The Burkes assumed they were camping there for the night and planned to attack them in the morning. However, Donal Cam and his men cleverly snuck away during the night. All that was found the next morning were the ashes from the fires.

In Glinsk you will pass by **St. Michael's Church** before coming to a small shop. Shortly after the shop, turn right through a gap in the wall, cross the small field and in the following larger field the next stile is diagonally to the left. Continue straight through the next few fields. You will enter a patch of wetland with reeds and go left.

Wooden stile on the way to Ballymoe

Traditional Craft Project: This is a good place to collect 10 or 12 reeds to make a traditional St. Brigid's Cross. You will find an instructional diagram at the end of this chapter.

Keep to the left and come to a grassy track alongside bogland. At the tarmac road go right. Along this road I saw a farmer with his family using a tractor and rope to rescue a cow from the drain running along the roadside. Take the next left down another grass and pebble track through bogland. At a small bridge go left over a wooden stile with a Beware of the Bull sign (after checking it is safe to do so!). There are several fields here; four of them with cattle and one with a bull who thankfully did not bother us.

Turf stacked to dry

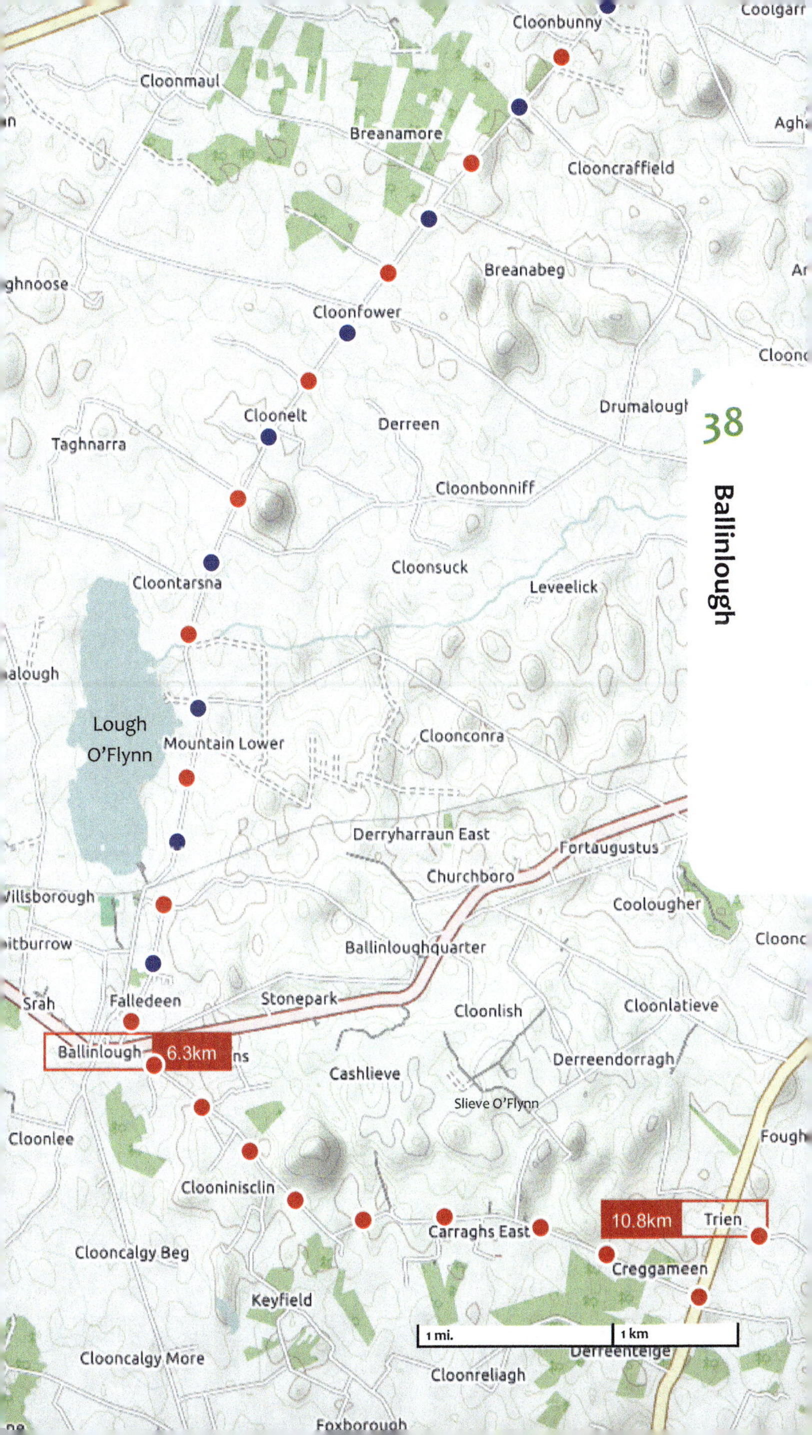
Cloonbunny
Coolgarr
Cloonmaul
Breanamore
Agha
Clooncraffield
Breanabeg
ghnoose
Cloonfower
Cloonc
Drumalough
Cloonelt
Derreen
Taghnarra
Cloonbonniff
Cloonsuck
Leveelick
Cloontarsna
alough
Lough O'Flynn
Mountain Lower
Clooncorra
Derryharraun East
Fortaugustus
Churchboro
Willsborough
Coolougher
itburrow
Ballinloughquarter
Srah
Falledeen
Stonepark
Cloonlish
Cloonlatieve
Ballinlough
6.3km
Cashlieve
Derreendorragh
Slieve O'Flynn
Cloonlee
Clooniniscin
Carraghs East
10.8km
Trien
Cooncalgy Beg
Creggameen
Keyfield
1 mi.
1 km
Derreenteige
Clooncalgy More
Cloonreliagh
Foxborough

Walkers on the Suck Valley Way

After these fields there is a wooden stile and grass track which eventually leads to a tarmac road where you go left for a short distance before going back onto a grass track. This joins onto a tarmac road and then at the main road turn right into Ballymore village.

Church Ruin, Ballymoe

[7.2km/4.5mi] Ballymoe S R PO

Béal Átha Mó - "Ford-Mouth of Mó"

The ruin of **St. John's church** is at the far end of the village.

The only accommodation nearby is 9.1 km off the trail: **Edmar B&B**, 1 Findale, Corralough, Williamstown, 094 964 3895; Or **Armcashel B&B**, Knock Road, Castlerea, 9km north of Ballymoe: 094 962 0117. Ballymoe local cab driver: Dara 086 8415523. **AirBnB** in Williamstown.

Continue through the village of Ballmoe, cross the Smalghrean river and take the next left. Cross the River Suck and go left and follow this road for 1.3km and you will come to the busy N60 road. Go left and then right, taking care crossing the road. After 0.5km turn right at the bungalow, from where the road will then take you through 3km of bogland. Exit the track onto a narrow road and go left following the road for 4.6km before arriving at Trien and the busy R631 road. Go right for Trien or left to continue on the trail.

[10.8km/6.7mi] Trien

No shops, food or accommodation in Trien.

Walk for 0.6km along the R631 road and turn right at the large blue shed. Follow this road for 5.6km to arrive at Ballinlough village.

COUNTY ROSCOMMON / CONTAE ROS COMÁIN

[6.3km/3.9mi] Ballinlough S R PO P

Baile an Locha - "Town of the Lake"

Black Donkey Brewing Ltd. is county Roscommon's only brewery. It is best known for the farmhouse ale Sheep Stealer. North of the town is **Lough O'Flynn which** is good for brown trout fishing and is also

Ballinlough Village

the source of the river Suck. The White House Hotel may be reopened some time.

From Ballinlough take the Falladeen road north for just over 1km. Go left at the T-junction and you will see Lough O'Flynn in the distance. At the end of this road turn right alongside the graveyard, towards the lough. Walk along this road for 5.4km with occasional glimpses of the lough to your left. At the junction go right and immediately left, following the sign for Loughglynn which you will reach in 4km.

Help from the O'Flynn Clan

The O'Flynns from Ballinlough Castle were the first clan to provide food and comfort to Donal Cam and his people along their journey.

How to Make a Traditional St. Brigid's Cross from Reeds

There are many fields on the trail where you can collect long reeds if you want to try this simple craft project.

Take 12-16 pieces of reed or straw, if very dry soak so they don't break. Hold one upright.

Turn 90? counter-clockwise, holding it at the centre.

Turn 90? counter-clockwise, holding it at the centre.

Turn 90? counter-clockwise, holding it at the centre.

Fold the second straw in the middle and wrap around the centre so that it opens to the right. Then pull it tight.

Take the third straw and wrap it around the second straw so that it is opens to your right. Then pull it tight.

Take a fourth straw and wrap it around the third straw so that it opens to your right. Then pull it tight.

Take a fifth straw and fold it around the fourth straw so that it opens to your right. Then pull it tight.

STAGE 9:

Lung/Lough Gara Way

Slí Lung/Lough Gara

Loughglynn 11km/7mi **Ballaghaderreen** 12km/7mi **Monasteraden** 20km/12mi **Ballinafad**

Distance: 44.6 km / 27.7 miles
Difficulty: Easy
County: Roscommon
OSI Maps: Discovery Series 32, 33

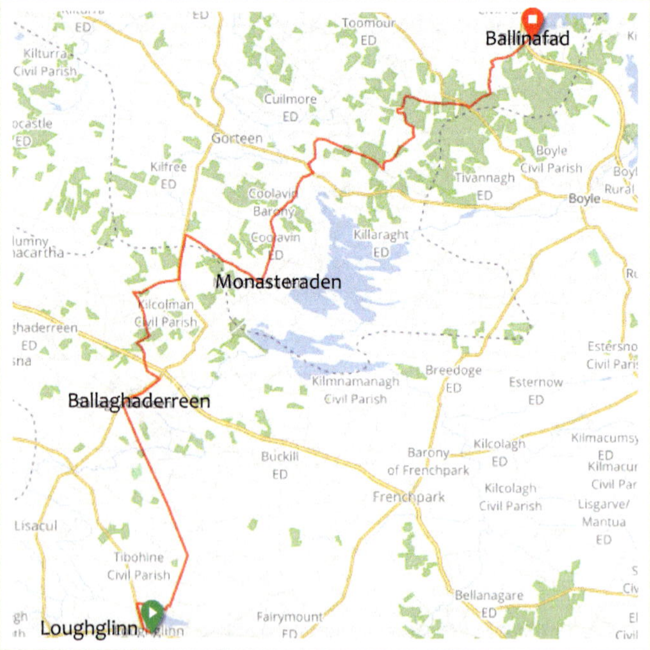

Hikers on the Lung/Lough Gara Way

There is a lack of signage on the Lung/Lough Gara Way so use a GPS along with maps to navigate the route.

The Light Guided the Way

Following their escape from the Burkes under the cover of darkness, Donal Cam arrived at a wood called "Diamhrach" (the Solitude). Here he had only twelve companions so he ordered a fire to be lit so that others could find their way to him. As they neared O'Rourke territory the locals became friendlier. By morning the locals had seen the fire and brought Donal Cam and his men food.

COUNTY ROSCOMMON / CONTAE ROS COMÁIN

[10.8km/6.7mi] Loughglynn/Loughglinn

S R PO

Loch Glinne - "Glinn lake"

Memorial Statue, Loughglynn

Loughglynn has a large church with a statue of St. Patrick holding a shamrock in front.

Go left as you arrive in Loughglynn and go through the village and continue straight on the R325 for 1.3km then turn right following the sign for Moyne. Walk alongside Lough Glinn and then through a tree-tunnel beside some woods. Take the next left and after 2km cross straight through the crossroads at Moyne, following the sign for Ballaghaderreen. You will arrive there in 6km and cross the Lung river on the way.

[11.2km/7mi] Ballaghaderreen

A S R PO € D P

Bealach an Doirín - "The Way of the Little Oak Wood"

Durkin's Bar, Restaurant & Guesthouse €€€, phone to book and ask for Ireland Way hiker's discount, 094 9860305, www.durkins.ie. **AirBnB - Teach Doirín B&B** €€, close to the town, www.airbnb.ie.

From Durkins, go over the road past the library and onto Pound Street, continuing for almost 1.8km before turning left down a narrow road. After 1.7km turn right at the T-junction and then left at the crossroads. Follow this road for 1.8km between forests and then turn right at the crossroads towards a windfarm. Take the next left at another forested area, still going towards the windfarm. After 1.6km and passing right by the windfarm turn left on the R293 road for 1.7km. Turn right between two houses, following the sign for Monasteraden which you will reach in just over 3km.

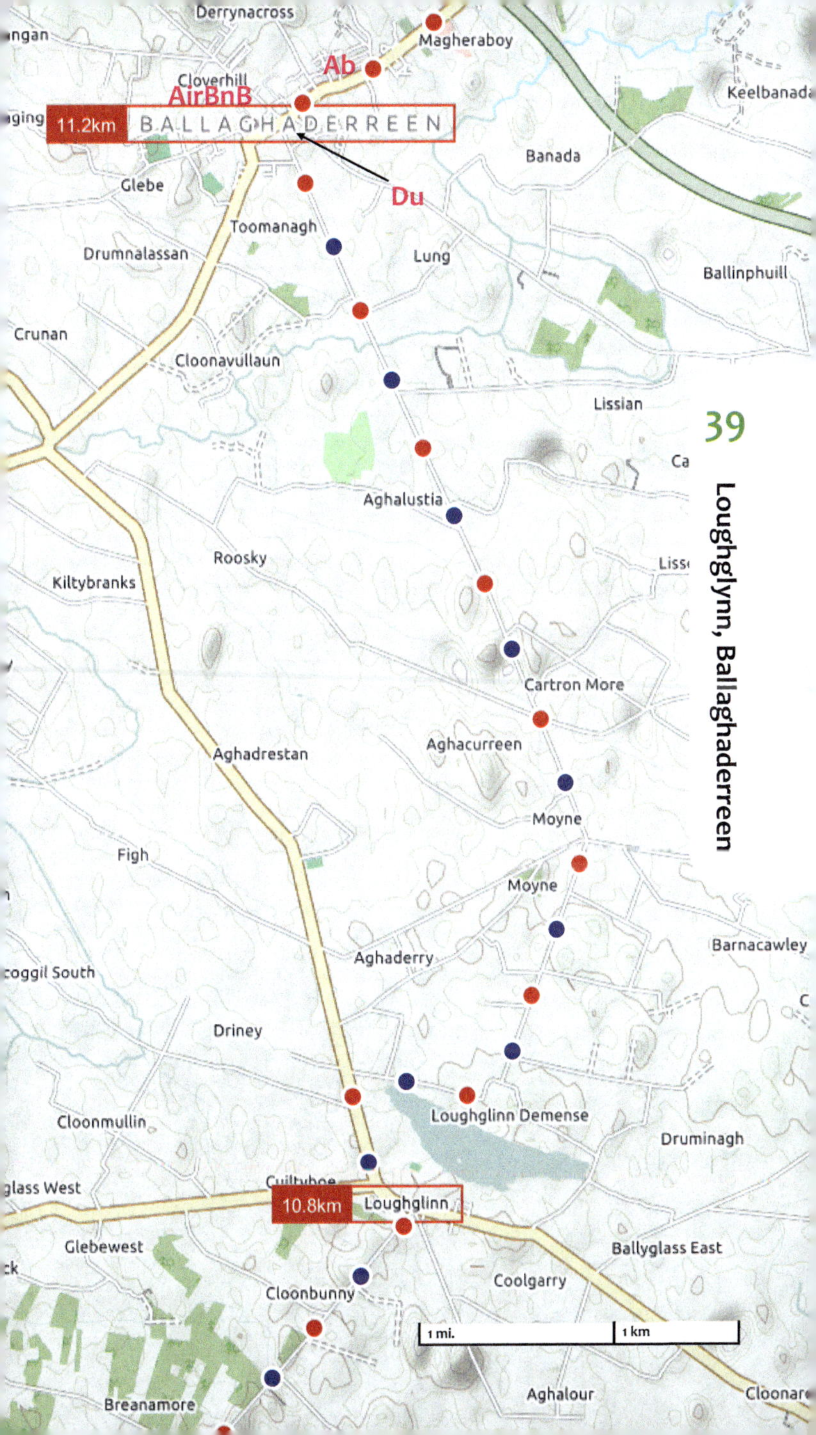

Loughglynn, Ballaghaderreen

[13km/8mi] Monasteraden

A S R PO

Bealach an Mainistir Eidín - "The Monastery of Aiden"

Lough Gara Lodge is to your left. An Irish cross monument stands in the village for the people who died for independence.

Monasteraden Church

Lough Gara Lodge, 083 108 4619, www.loughgaralodge.com. Other accommodation is 5.3 km off the trail in nearby village Gorteen (note that there are a few towns in Ireland of the same name but this one is in Co. Roscommon), see map 41. **The Hill Hotel**, Rathmadder, Gorteen, 071 918 2822.

Stay on the same road as Lough Gara Lodge for 5.2km with views of Lough Gara to your right. On this stretch of road you will pass by the ruin of **Moygara Castle** on your right which you can take a stroll around.

Ruin of Moygara Castle

40 Ballaghaderreen, Monasteraden

Cow & Calf at Ballinafad

Built around 1500AD, **Moygara Castle** was the main fortress of the O'Gara family who ruled the area and had two other castles nearby.

Continuing along onto the R294 road go left (there should be a small shortcut across the road here but at the time of hiking this part I couldn't spot any obvious way through the wooden fence) towards Ballina and take the next right towards Culfadda. At the next junction go right and follow for 3km, crossing a railway line on the way. Turn left and after 2km leaving views of Lough Gara behind you, turn left at the T-junction and left at the next T-junction. Take the next right and the next right again and follow for 3.1km. Turn right towards Boyle on the R295 road and the next left down a laneway. After 1km turn left and another 1km turn right at the T-junction and Corradoo Cottages. After 1.8km arrive in Ballinafad, having walked through the underpass of the N4 motorway and checked out the ruin of **Ballinafad Castle** on your right just before the village. The castle is in a field which may contain cattle or sheep. The first time I was here there were two cows and their two young calves and the mothers came running over to the wall to ensure I was not a threat to their young.

Doorway of Ballinafad Castle

41 Monasteraden, Moygara Castle

STAGE 10:

Miner's Way

Slí Miner

Ballinafad - **Castlebaldwin** - Highwood - **Ballyfarnon** - **Keadue** - Knockvicar - **Leitrim Village**

Distance:	53 km / 32.9 miles
Difficulty:	Moderate
Counties:	Sligo, Roscommon, Leitrim
OSI Maps:	Discovery Series 33, 25, 26

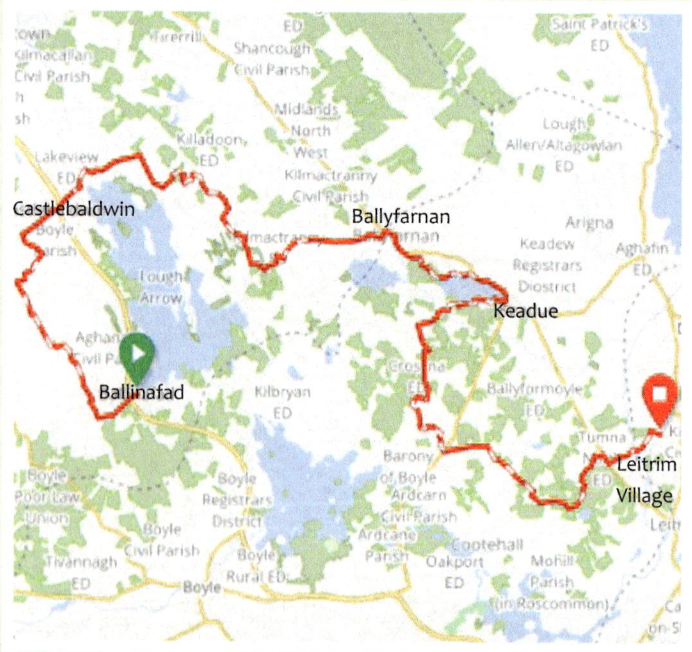

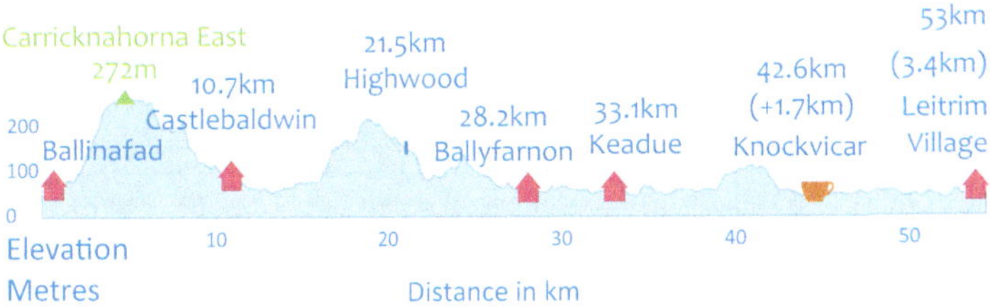

The Miner's Way & Historical Trail is very well way-marked. It consists of two large looped trails. From Ballinafad onwards the signposts will say 'Miner's Way' or 'Historical Trail'.

The trail goes around Lough Arrow and then south-east to Leitrim, because this is the way Donal Cam and his people went to avoid English troops in Boyle and this follows the original route. If you prefer to continue in a northerly direction you can do so from Keadue, saving you 8.7km only. Details for this detour are not included in this book but you can get free maps from www.irishtrails.ie.

1) Beara-Breifne Way Route:

   Keadue - Leitrim - Dowra = 21.3+25.7 = 47km

2) Alternative Miner's Way Route (Skips Stage 11, Cavan Way):

   Keadue - Arigna - Dowra = 38.3km

Knockranny Woods

Near the End of the O'Sullivan Bere Journey

As they neared the end of their journey, Donal Cam had his people kill their last two horses. They ate well that night and made shoes for the most lame of the group. Even though they were in safe territory, they skirted modern-day Boyle and headed north around Lough Arrow to avoid English patrols.

COUNTY SLIGO / CONTAE SLIGIGH

[20.4km/12.7mi] Ballinafad

A S PO

Béal an Átha Fada - "Mouth of the Long Ford"

Ballinafad is at the foot of the **Curlew Mountains** with stunning views over **Lough Arrow**. The lake has four islands: Anaghgonda, Inismore, Inisbeg and Much Island. **Ballinafad Castle** was built around 1590 but modelled on 13th-century castle design.

Ballinafad Castle

Arrow Rock Hostel, 071 966073, www.arrowrockhostel.com; **Gyreum Ecolodge**, 071 9165994, www.gyreum.com.

Valley at Carrowkeel

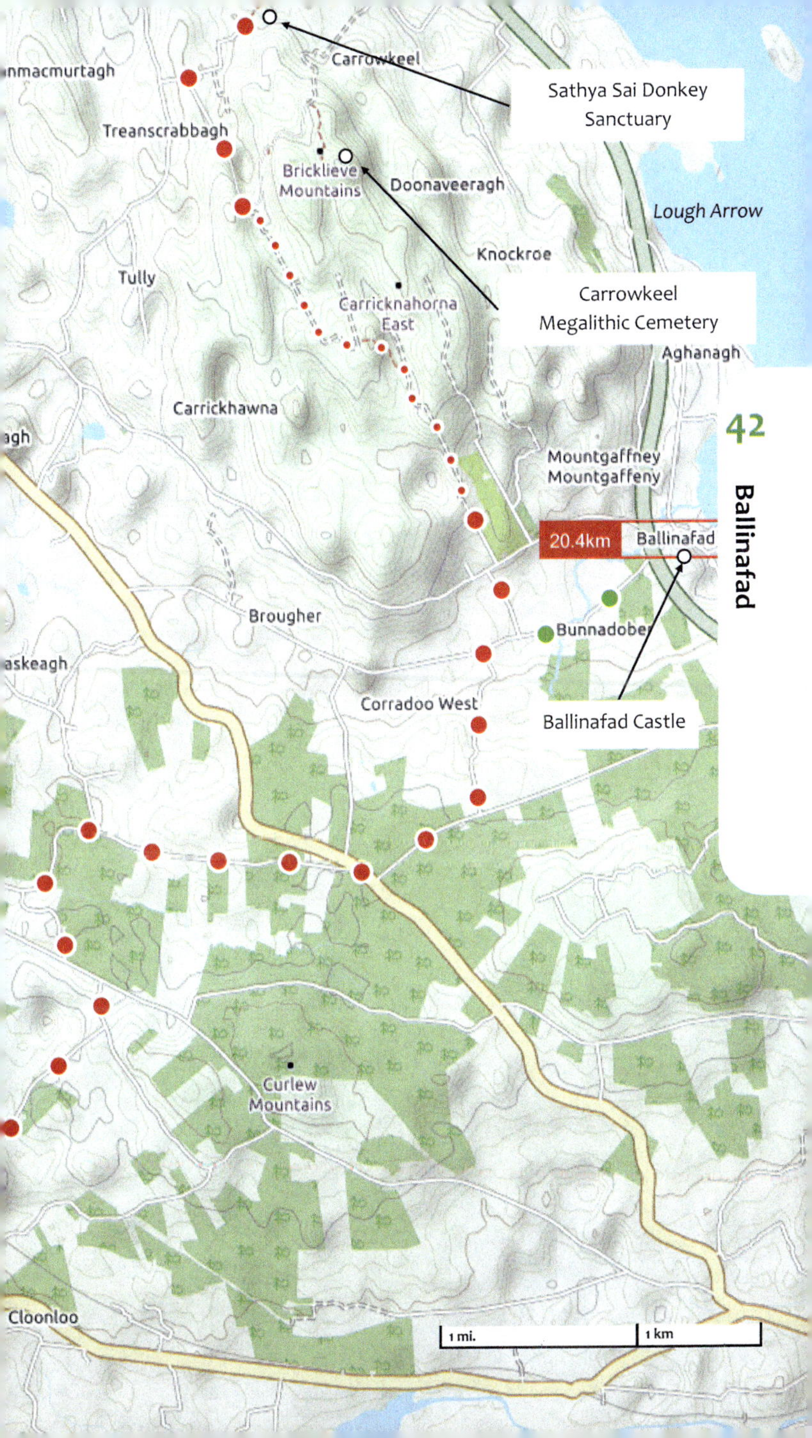
Carrowkeel
Sathya Sai Donkey Sanctuary
Treanscrabbagh
Bricklieve Mountains
Doonaveeragh
Lough Arrow
Knockroe
Tully
Carricknahorna East
Carrowkeel Megalithic Cemetery
Aghanagh
Carrickhawna
Mountgaffney
Mountgaffeny
20.4km
Ballinafad
Brougher
Bunnadober
Corradoo West
Ballinafad Castle
Curlew Mountains
Cloonloo
1 mi.
1 km

Leave Ballinafad the same way you came in, through the underpass and after 1.6km turn right. At the end of the road turn right and almost immediately, at the red shed, turn left up the laneway and follow for 2.3km as you ascend the hill along a grass track. Behind you are beautiful views of Lough Arrow. At the top there is a dip in the track, a little steep in parts, and then ascend up the other side. Next you will walk on raised track through bogland for 1.6km to an optional but highly recommended detour. There are some beautiful views as you descend into this valley with an escarpment rising up on both sides as you near Carrowkeel. You will soon climb the one on your right if you want to visit the Carrowkeel Megalithic Cemetary. Allow approximately 1 hour for this detour. Follow the track around and when you get to a small parking area there is no clear way-marker, but just start climbing upwards until you get to the top. The **Carrowkeel Neolithic Passage Tombs** have been carbon dated from 3400 to 3100BC - older than the pyramids at Giza in Egypt by 500-800 years. The tombs were excavated in 1911, uncovering animal bone, cremated human remains, human bone, pottery and tools all dated from the Neolithic period. There are fourteen of these tombs dotted all over this mountain top, some still in relatively good condition but most long collapsed in. You will see stunning views over Lough Arrow, its islands and the surrounding countryside from the top. Back to the detour point and continuing on the Historical Trail after 1km turn right onto a narrow road for 0.5km, following the signs for the

Carrowkeel Passage Tomb

43 Castlebaldwin, Highwood

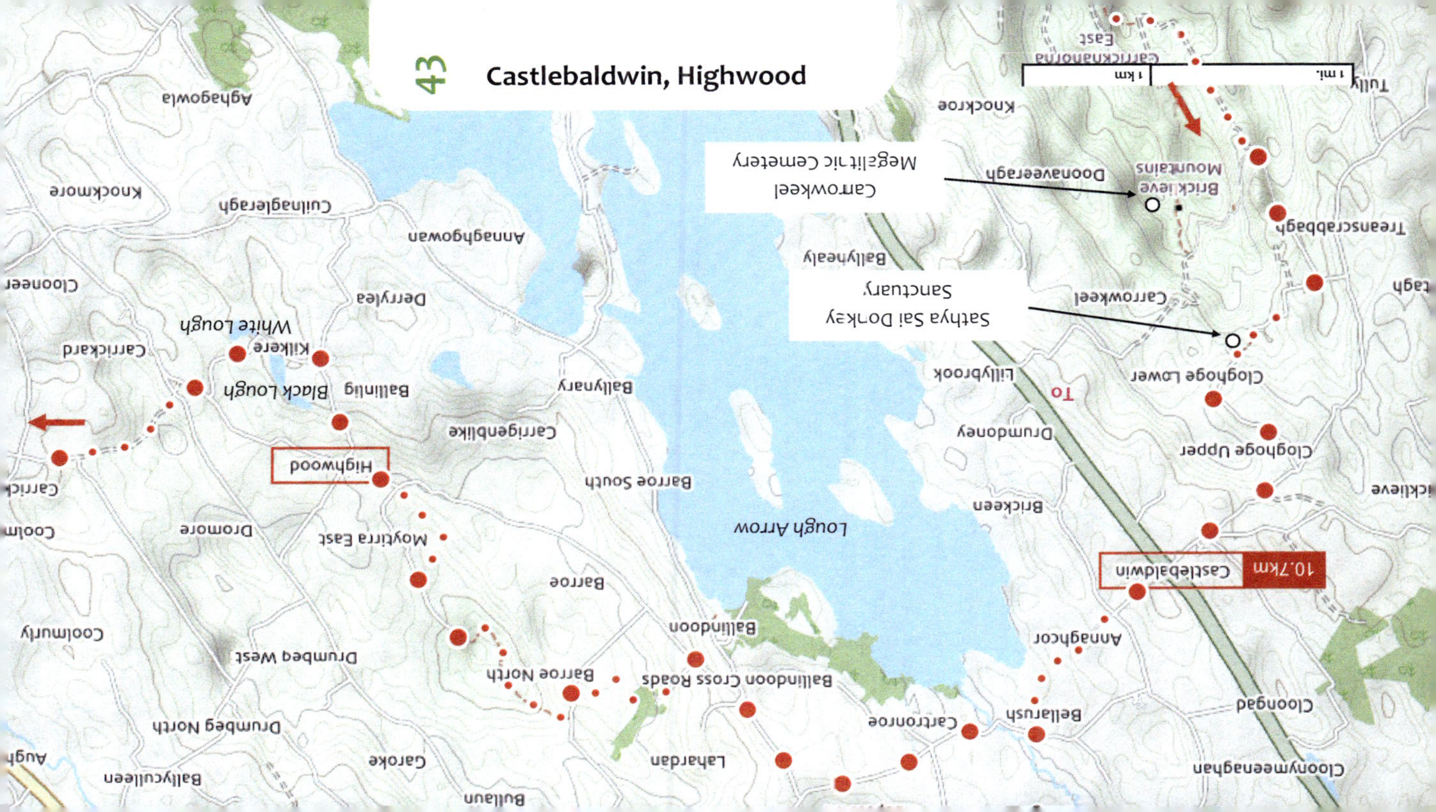

Sathya Sai Donkey Sanctuary

donkey sanctuary. **Sathya Sai Donkey Sanctuary**, open 1st April - 31st October at weekends and bank holiday Mondays from 10am - 4pm. I arrived here at 3.45pm and the lovely owner brought us out biscuits for the donkeys and about ten of them came over, along with two dogs, as soon as they heard the biscuit packet! A couple of local families arrived, one bringing carrots for the donkeys. A little girl was given a biscuit to feed to an eager donkey but proceeded to munch on it herself, not quite understanding it was meant for the donkey! There is a white donkey, I can't remember his name; he was quite bold and unfriendly with the other donkeys. His story is that he previously lived with two horses so would have had to be tough to stand up for himself! About sixty donkeys currently live at this sanctuary. Follow the road as it descends for 1.7km and turn right at the T-junction. Arrive in Castlebaldwin in 1.3km.

[10.7km/6.6mi] Castlebaldwin A S R

Béal Átha na gCarraigíní - "Mouth of the Ford of the Small Rocks"

McDermott's is recommended for great food!

Clevery Mill Guesthouse, 071 9127424, www.cleverymill.com; Tower Hill B&B, 1.6 km from town, 071 9666021; Hillcrest B&B, 071 9165559, www.hillcrestbandb.ie. Also accommodation on AirBnB.

Leaving Castlebaldwin take the road opposite McDermotts. Continue straight through a laneway. You can see Lough Arrow and Carrowkeel

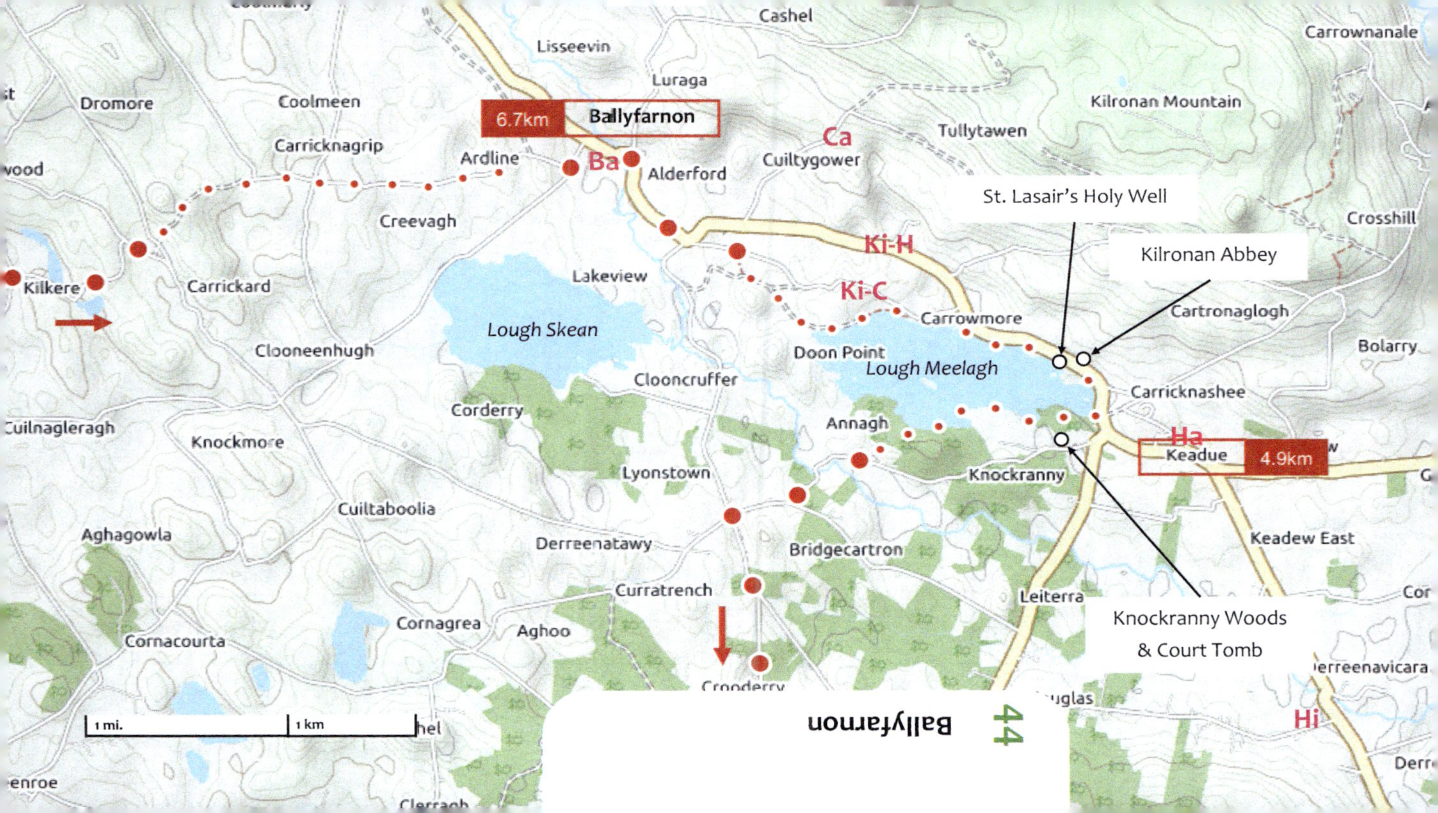

44

Ballyfarnon

Unshin River

to your right. At the stream go left over the stone stile and go through a field. Over the next stone stile go left and right to a metal gate, then right to a green stile. Continue straight through the next gate and stone stile.

Next is 3.3km of quiet road. At the road go right and soon cross the **River Unshin**. It is 0.9km to Heapstone Cross Roads where there is a small shop with limited opening hours. At Killadoon cross roads turn right and at Ballindoon Cross go left. On the ascent you will see **Lough Arrow** and **Carrowkeel** again on your right (Bricklieve Mountains).

Turn in to the left to enter a cattle field. Exit onto the driveway of Cromleach Lodge and go left towards the lodge. Past the lodge go left through a gate following the sign for **The Labby Walk**. There is a large **Portal tomb** known as **Labby Rock** at the bottom of the valley which dates from between 4,000 - 2,500BC. Pass through a few fields and at the road go left.

Labby Rock

The high point is called **Seeleewy** (Suigh Luadhaigh, Seat of Louis). From here you can see **Lough Arrow** and above it the **Bricklieve Mountains** (including Carrowkeel), and going right are the **Ox Mountains**, the single mound is **Knock na Rea** (passage tomb visible on top), and behind **Lough na Siúl** is **Ben Bulben**. To the left of Lough Arrow is **Lough Key**.

Leaving the summit follow the waymarkers through farmland and exit onto road for a while. Take the gate to the right for a few fields. Exit onto the road at Moytura and continue along the road to Highwood.

[10.8km/6.7mi] Highwood (No facilities)

Black Lough

At the crossroads turn left and follow this road for 0.4km with more views over the Lough, then turn left towards Cromleach Lodge. In 1.6km turn left at the T-junction and then the next right shortly after. You will go through some forest and then fields for 2.7km. Exit onto a narrow road at a farm and descend down the hill, soon turning right through a little metal gate into a field. Cross through a few fields and after 1km exit through a similar gate. There is a pretty rest area to your right. Go left for the trail and follow the road, turning right just past the church. Descend the hill for 1km, with Lough Arrow in the far distance, then turn left at the crossroads. You will soon pass **Black Lough**, and further on **White Lough**. At the T-junction turn right and then left shortly after. Take the next right up a laneway. Follow this track for 3.5km going straight through the

Country Laneway to Ballyfarnon

crossroads and with a view of **Lough Skean** to your right. Continue straight towards windmills in the distance and soon arrive in Ballyfarnon.

COUNTY ROSCOMMON / CONTAE ROS COMÁIN

[6.7km/4.1mi] Ballyfarnon

A S R PO

Béal Átha Fearnáin - "Ford-Mouth of the Alders"

Ballyfarnon House, 078 9647311; **Castle House B&B**, €€, Kilronan, 071 9647555, www.castlehousebnb.com; **Drumhierney Lodge**, 071 9623145, www.drumhierneylodge.com; **Amber B&B**, Corrigeenroe, 071 9666918, www.amberbnb.wordpress.com; **Radharc na Sleibhte**, 071 9667226; **Kilronan Castle** €€€, 071 9618000, www.kilronancastle.ie; **Kilronan House B&B**, 071 9647048.

Window to the World, Doon Point

St. Lasair's Holy Well

At the far end of the town keep to the right as you pass the shop on the R284 for 1.3km and going straight through the crossroads and in through the gates at **Kilronan Lodge**. Turn right for a forest track which will take you to the shores of **Lough Meelagh** (meaning *'Lake of the Marsh'*) and into the grounds of **Kilronan Castle**. Built in the 18th-century and with it's beautifully decorated interior, it is worth staying here if you would like the experience of staying in an Irish castle and have the budget for it. The name Kilronan comes from the Irish meaning *Church of St. Ronan*.

You have a 400m optional detour to the *'Window of the World'* at Doon Point which provides a view of the lake. Further along this beautiful forest trail there is a signpost

45 Knockvicar Bridge, Leitrim Town

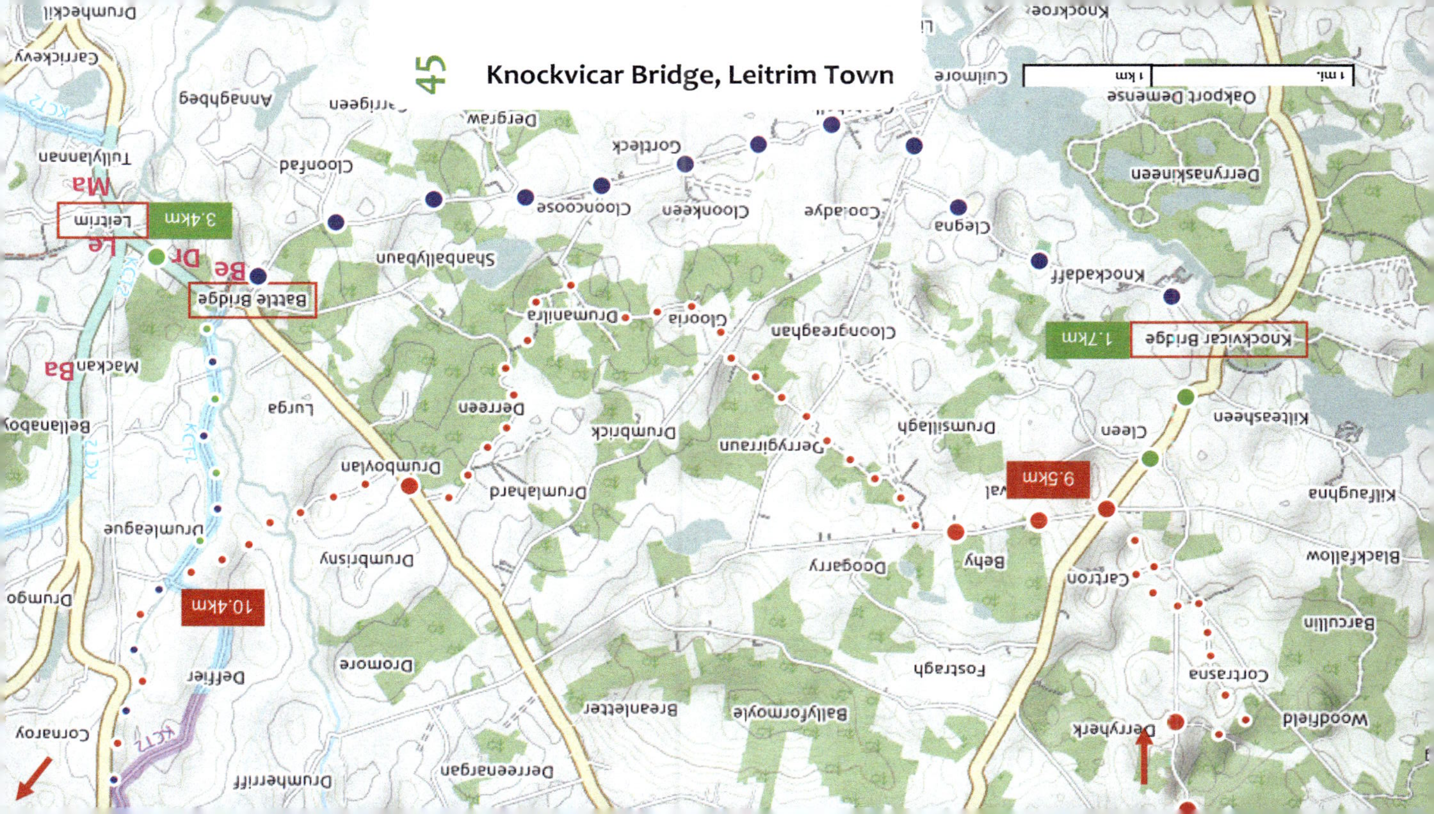

Lough Meelagh at Knockranny Woods

for a shortcut to Kilronan Castle. Take this shortcut to see the castle, otherwise continue along the trail which bypasses the castle. Back on the forest trail, exit onto the driveway of the castle and onto a road. The track runs parallel to the road. You will arrive at **St. Lasair's Holy Well.** St Lasair is thought to be the daughter of St. Ronan. Just past the well on the opposite side of the road is **Kilronan Abbey**. In the graveyard of the Abbey inside the walls of the ruin, you will find the **gravestone which commemorates Ireland's great harper Turlough O'Carolan**. Further along the roadside track the trail takes you into **Knockranny Woods** which contains the ruin of a **megalithic court tomb**. Detour just 0.5km from here into Keadue village.

Court Tomb dated c3500-2000BC

[4.9km/3mi] Keadue/Keadew

A S R PO

Céideadh

The Harp & Shamrock B&B, 071 964 7288, www.harpandshamrock.net; **McCabe's B&B**, 071 964 7223; **Hill House B&B**, 071 964 7240; **Kilronan Cottage**, 087 255 9269,

Keadue town holds an annual festival to commemorate the life and music of Turlough O'Carolan (www. ocarolanharpfestival.ie).

Back at Knockranny Woods there are some picnic benches for a rest stop. The trail stays close to the lakeshore. Walk through mature forest and then grass track by the lakeside and more forest, before finally leaving the lake behind. Walk through fields for a short distance, then onto a track and turn right upon reaching the road.

After a short distance cross a stone bridge over a small river and shortly after veer right at the T-junction and then left at the crossroads. **New way-markers in place. Keep right at the fork in the road.**

[11.2km/7mi] Knockvicar

S PO

Cnoc an Bhiocáire

The cycle trail still goes through Knockvicar, however the walking trail bypasses it. At the crossroads at Crossna, be sure to follow the maps for new routing. The trail mostly follows rough track and passes by a forest and over a stream before reaching the **Shannon Blueway** trail. Once you reach the canal trail you can go right to Leitrim village to see the endpoint of the journey of Donal Cam O'Sullivan Bere. There is plenty of accommodation and dining options in Leitrim village, however it is an optional detour.

At the canal the trail goes left to continue northbound to **Acres Lake** and Drumshanbo.

Rough track towards Shannon Blueway

The End of a Journey

Arriving at O'Rourke's Castle at noon on the fifteenth day were sixteen armed men, eighteen attendants and one woman. The O'Rourkes of Breifne welcomed them, marvelling at their courage and resourcefulness.

The majority of Donal Cam's followers had either died or settled in villages along the way. They knew they could never return home to Beara.

Donal Cam sought to join with the O'Neills in the north to fight against the English, only to find out when he arrived that O'Neill had surrendered to the crown. It was only a matter of time before English rule in Ireland was absolute. There was no point in fighting any longer. The new English monarch, James I, refused to accept Donal Cam's allegiance so he was forced to flee once again, this time to Spain.

He first arrived in A Coruña, Galicia, where some of his family had already settled along with other Irish refugees. His son and nephew has been sent there for their safety before the march of 1602.

A plaque commemorating the march of Donal Cam O'Sullivan Beare beside the one remaining wall of O'Rourke's Castle, Leitrim

Portrait of Donal Cam O'Sullivan Beare (1561 - 1618)

Image provided by St. Patrick's College, Maynooth

In Galicia Donal Cam established an Irish school for Irish children. He later lived in Madrid as leader of the Irish in Spain and soon became a Count of Berehaven and Knight of Santiago. In the portrait painting of Donal Cam he wears a gold scallop shell with a red cross of St. James, an emblem of the order of St. Iago Compostella.

Donal Cam's life ended in Madrid in 1618 when he was brought out of mass to break up a dispute between two Irishmen, Philip O'Sullivan (his nephew) and Dubliner John Bath. Bath thought that *he* should be representing the Irish in Spain and be given a large pension by the Spanish, rather than Donal Cam. Philip challenged Bath to a duel. Donal Cam's servants broke them up, however, Bath turned on Donal Cam, first stabbing him in the arm and then slashing his throat. Bath served two years in prison.

Philip took asylum at the French embassy and later joined the Spanish navy where he wrote an account of Irish history, including the great march of his uncle Donal Cam O'Sullivan Bere.

STAGE 11:

Leitrim Way

Slí Liatroma

Leitrim Village - **Drumshanbo** - **Ballinagleragh** - Dowra

Distance:	22.1 km / 13.7 miles
Difficulty:	Moderate
Counties:	Leitrim, Cavan
OSI Maps:	Discovery Series 26

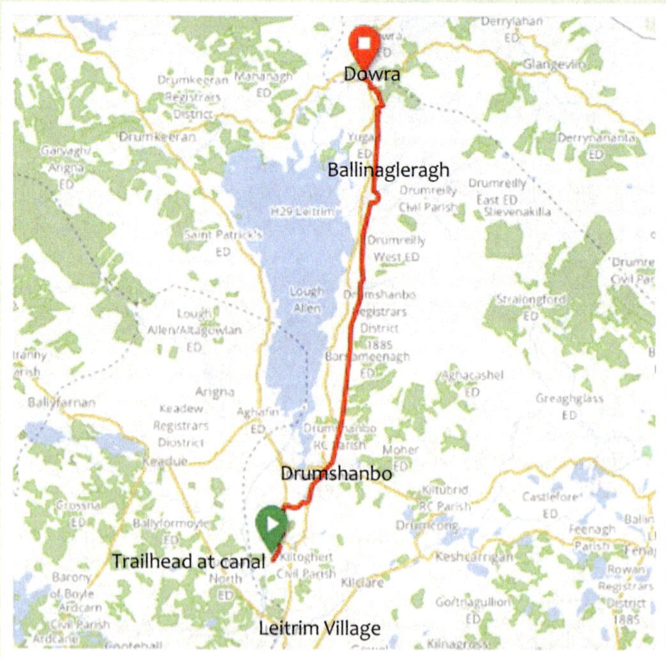

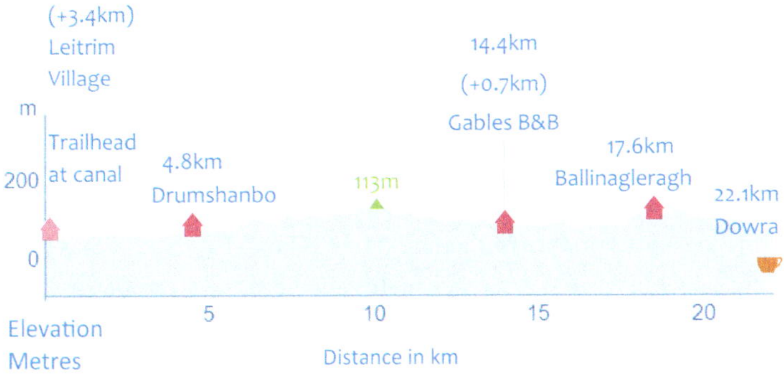

The Leitrim Way takes you along the **Lough Allen Canal** (also known as the **Shannon Blueway**) followed by a floating boardwalk over **Acres Lake**. From Drumshanbo the trail is mostly quiet laneways and farmland to Drumshanbo. It is optional to start from **Leitrim Village** if you need to stock up on food and water or stay the night in accommodation. **If starting from Leitrim Village, add 3.4km and follow the Shannon Blueway.**

Boardwalk on Acres Lake

COUNTY LEITRIM / CONTAE LIATROMA

[10.4km/6.4mi] Leitrim Village (+3.4km)

A S R PO €

Liatroim

In Leitrim Village you can visit the end point of Donal Cam's march at **O'Rourke's Castle**. It is located down a laneway in the centre of the village and sits on the river's edge. There is only one wall of the castle remaining as well as a memorial stone for the march of Donal Cam and his people.

Drumhierney Lodge B&B, €80, +353 (0)71 962 3145, +353 (0)86 8621920, www.drumhierneylodge.com; **Ballinaboy Lodge B&B**, +353 (0)86 897 1519. **Lough Bran House**, +353 (0)71 962 0707, www.loughbranhouse.com; **The Leitrim Lodge Hotel**, +353 (0)71 9621040, www.theleitriminn.com; **Leitrim Marina Hotel**, +353 (0)71 9623644, www.leitrimmarinahotel.com; **Shannon Key West Hotel**, +353 (0)71 9638800, www.shannonkeywesthotel.com; **Beirnes of Battlebridge Camping & Caravan Site**, +353 (0)71 9650724, www.battlebridgecaravanandcamping.ie.

If starting from Leitrim Village, take the road towards Battlebridge and after 1km turn right along the canal. You can walk on either side of the **Lough Allen Canal** and nearer to **Acres Lake** you must cross over to the east side. There are a couple of opportunities to switch sides if you desire. The **Shannon Blueway** is 5.7km to **Acres Lake**. At the lake you will walk on a **floating boardwalk** . The trail to Dowra follows a quiet narrow road and then crosses farm fields.

[4.8km/3mi] Drumshanbo

A S R PO € D P

Droim Sean Bhoth - "Ridge of the Old Huts"

Drumshanbo is on the southern shore of **Lough Allen**, at the foot of **Slieve Iarainn** (Iron Mountain) to the north and the **Arigna Mountains** to the west. Visit the town's heritage centre for local history and folklore. Drumshanbo used to be an iron and coal mining

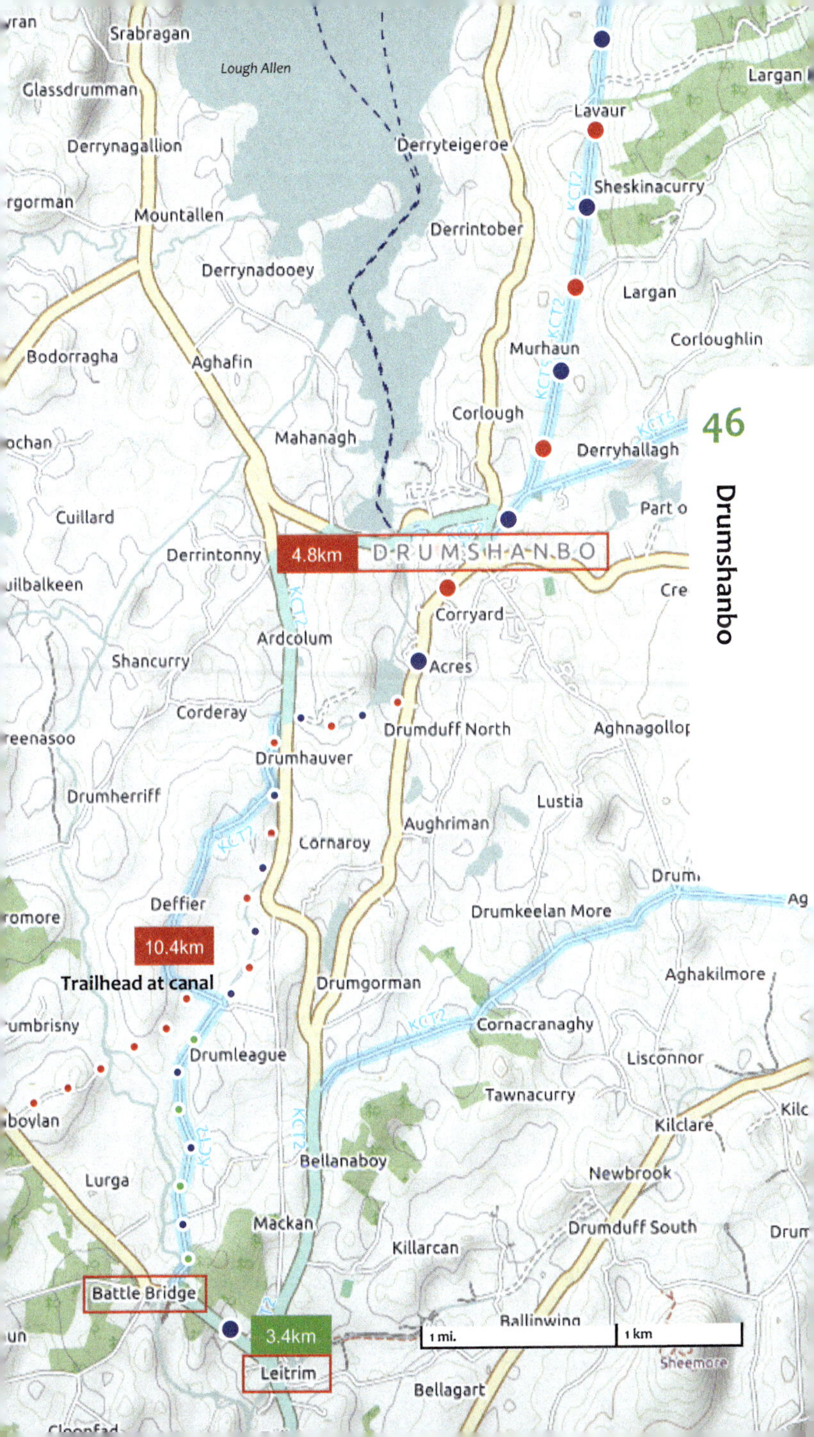
Srabragan
Lough Allen
Glassdrumman
Derrynagallion
Derryteigeroe
Largan
Lavaur
Sheskinacurry
Mountallen
Derrintober
Derrynadooey
Largan
Corloughlin
Bodorragha
Aghafin
Murhaun
Corlough
Mahanagh
Derryhallagh
Cuillard
Part o
Derrintonny
4.8km
DRUMSHANBO
Cre
Corryard
Ardcolum
Shancurry
Acres
Corderay
Drumduff North
Aghnagollop
Drumhauver
Drumherriff
Lustia
Aughriman
Cornaroy
Drum
Deffier
Drumkeelan More
Ag
10.4km
Trailhead at canal
Drumgorman
Aghakilmore
Cornacranaghy
Drumleague
Lisconnor
Tawnacurry
Kilclare
Kilc
Bellanaboy
Newbrook
Lurga
Mackan
Drumduff South
Killarcan
Battle Bridge
Ballinwing
3.4km
1 mi.
1 km
Leitrim
Sheemore
Bellagart
KCT2
KCT5

Drumshanbo Village

town and a producer of poitín (illicit alcohol). The town is popular for its live traditional music, with its **music festival** 'An Tóstal' held annually on the June bank holiday and the Joe Mooney Summer School Traditional Music and Dance Festival the third week of July every year. 1 km from Drumshanbo off the Leitrim Way is the **Lough Allen Centre** which provides a range of water-sports activities and a hostel.

Lough Allen Hotel & Spa, +353 (0)71 9640100, www.loughallenhotel.com. **Paddy Mac's B&B**, +353 (0)86 3898133, paddy.macs@hotmail.com. **Island View B&B**, +353 (0)71 9641434, loughallenview@gmail.com. **Forest View B&B**, +353 (0)71 9641106. **Berry's Tavern**, +353 (0)71 9641070, magscamp@hotmail.com; **Breeda McLoughlin B&B**, +353 (0)71 9641115; **Mooney's**, +353 (0)71 9641013.

[9.6km/6mi] Lough Allen (The Gables B&B +0.7km)

On the shore of Lough Allen before Ballinagleragh is **The Gables Restaurant & B&B** €€€, +353 (0)86 847 0766, www.thegablesleitrim.com; **The Lough Allen Centre** €, 48-bed hostel, +353 (0)71 9640588 or +353 (0)87 6312708, email: info@allen.ie, www.allen.ie; **AirBnB** nearby. Nearest shop is in Ballinagleragh.

[3.2km/2mi] Ballinagleragh

A S

There is one pub and a small shop near the church. **AirBnB** nearby.

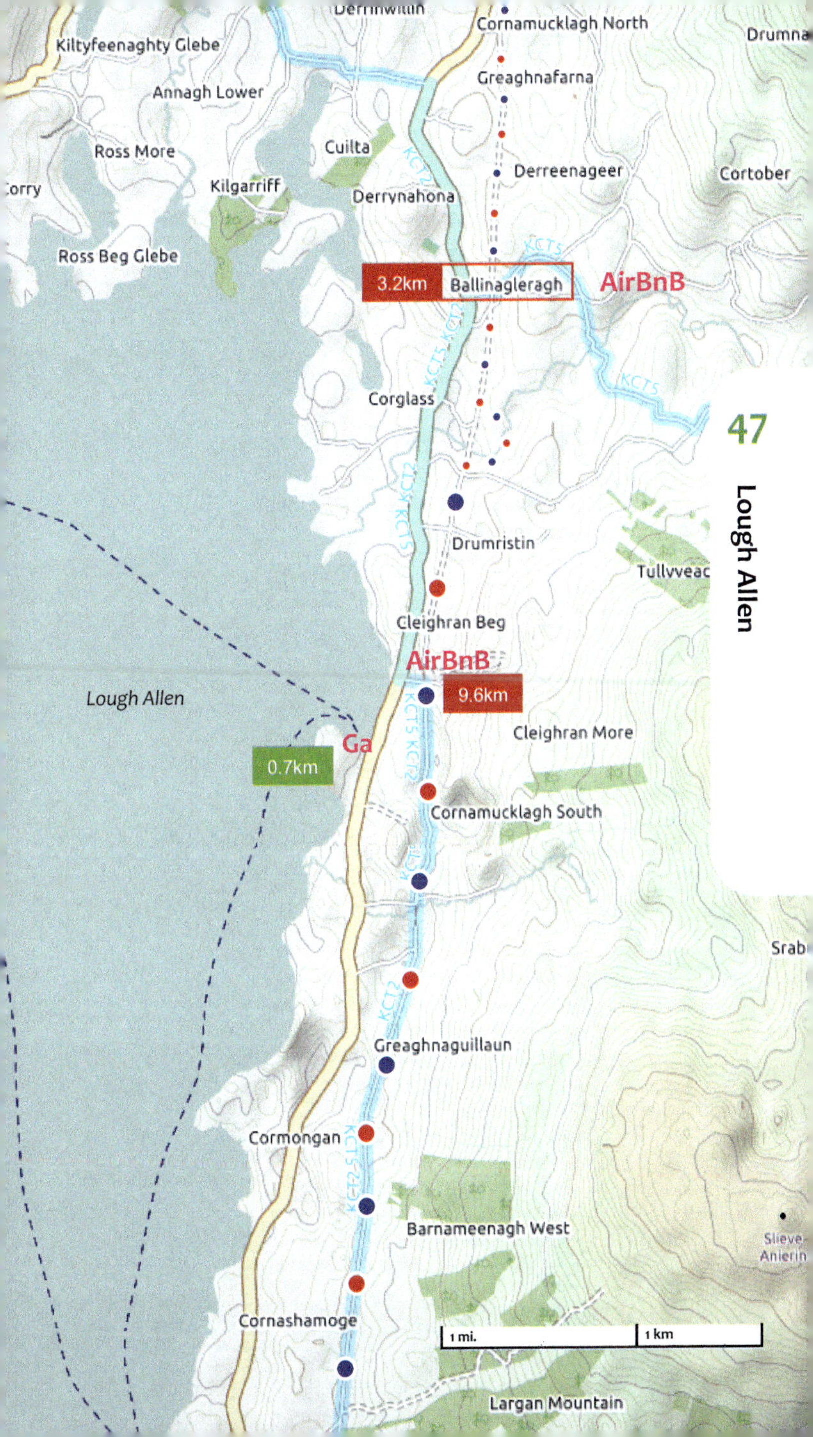
Cornamucklagh North
Drumna
Kiltyfeenaghty Glebe
Annagh Lower
Greaghnafarna
Ross More
Cuilta
Kilgarriff
Derreenageer
Cortober
Derrynahona
Ross Beg Glebe
KCT2
KCT5
3.2km
Ballinagleragh
AirBnB
Corglass
Drumristin
Tullyveac
Cleighran Beg
AirBnB
Lough Allen
9.6km
Cleighran More
Ga
0.7km
Cornamucklagh South
Srab
Greaghnaguillaun
Cormongan
KCT5 KCT2
Barnameenagh West
Slieve Anierin
Cornashamoge
1 mi.
1 km
Largan Mountain

STAGE 12:

Cavan Way

Slí Chabháin

Dowra - Blacklion - **Belcoo**

Distance: 22.3 km / 13.9 miles
Difficulty: Moderate
Counties: Cavan, Fermanagh
OSI Maps: Discovery Series 26

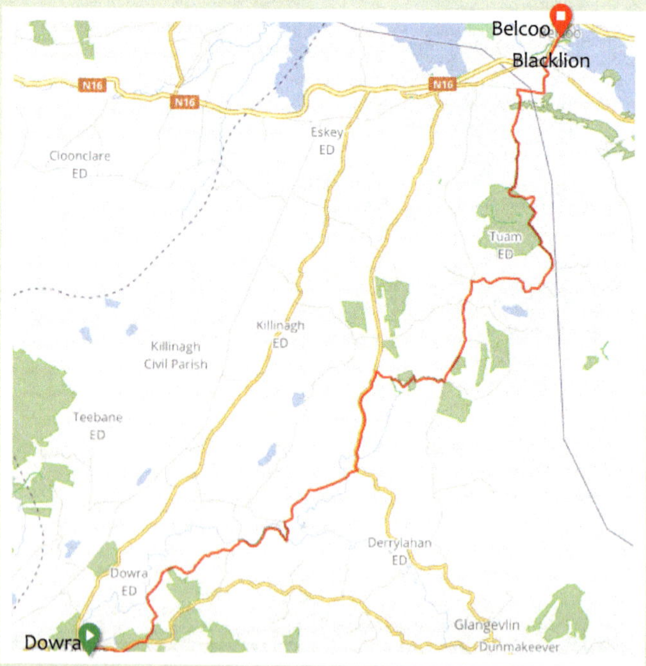

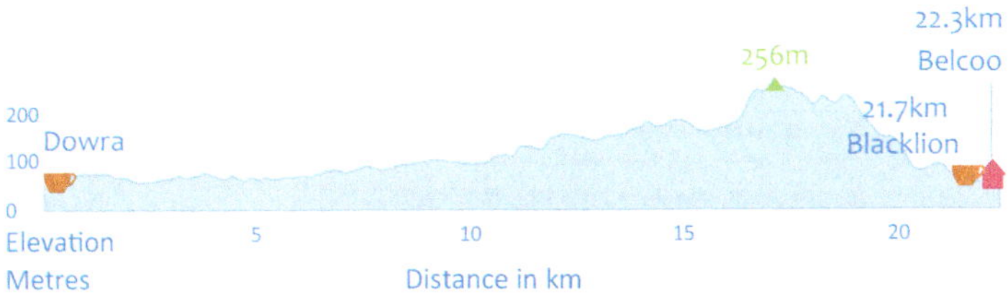

Bridge in Dowra Village

The Cavan Way is a gentle trail that brings you to the **Shannon Pot**, the source of the river Shannon and **Cavan Burren Park**. The trail is a mix of road (sometimes busy) and fields which can be quite boggy. Pass cattle with caution.

COUNTY CAVAN / CONTAE AN CHABHÁIN

S R PO

[4.5km/2.8mi] Dowra

An Damhshraith - "The Shrine of the Ox"

Dowra is the first village on the river Shannon. One side of the bridge is County Leitrim and on the other is County Cavan. Cross over the bridge for a shop and some pubs, but for the trail there is no need to cross to that side of the village. Instead, at the bridge, veer right alongside the river. **Don't get confused with signposts for the Miner's Way trail which goes back south as it is a looped trail.**

Shannon Pot

Follow the road for 1.3km and cross into County Cavan, then turn left onto the narrow road L5010 towards Cashelbane. This is a pleasant quiet country road for 3.1km. At the T-junction turn left for a short distance and then turn right. Just before the bridge over the River Shannon turn right over a stile to walk along the banks of the river for 1.2km, then cross a bridge over the river and follow the track to the road where you will turn right. Follow this road for 2km, crossing again over the Shannon and then turning left on the R206 road for a further 2km. This road is fairly busy. Turn right at the signpost for the **Shannon Pot**. This road will take you up to a carpark where you will go through a gate and follow a path through a field to the Shannon Pot. It is a 16-metre wide pool and at least 14 metres deep. The Shannon Pot is fed by underground streams from the surrounding mountains. Legend tells us the story of the Goddess, Síonnan, grand daughter of the Celtic God of the Sea (whose statue you will see on Stage 18). Síonnan came to this pool to meet the Salmon of Wisdom. The great salmon was angry and overflowed the pool to drown Síonnan, and in doing so created the longest river in Ireland which now bears her name, River Shannon.

Going back to the carpark, there is a way-marker for the trail beside the information board. Walk through fields, forest and more fields for 1.3km. On the road go left for 2km to Moneygashel where you will turn right for another 2km with views over **Lough Garvagh** to your right. Where the road bends to the right, continue straight for off-road track for 3.4km. Take care near cattle and watch out for bulls on

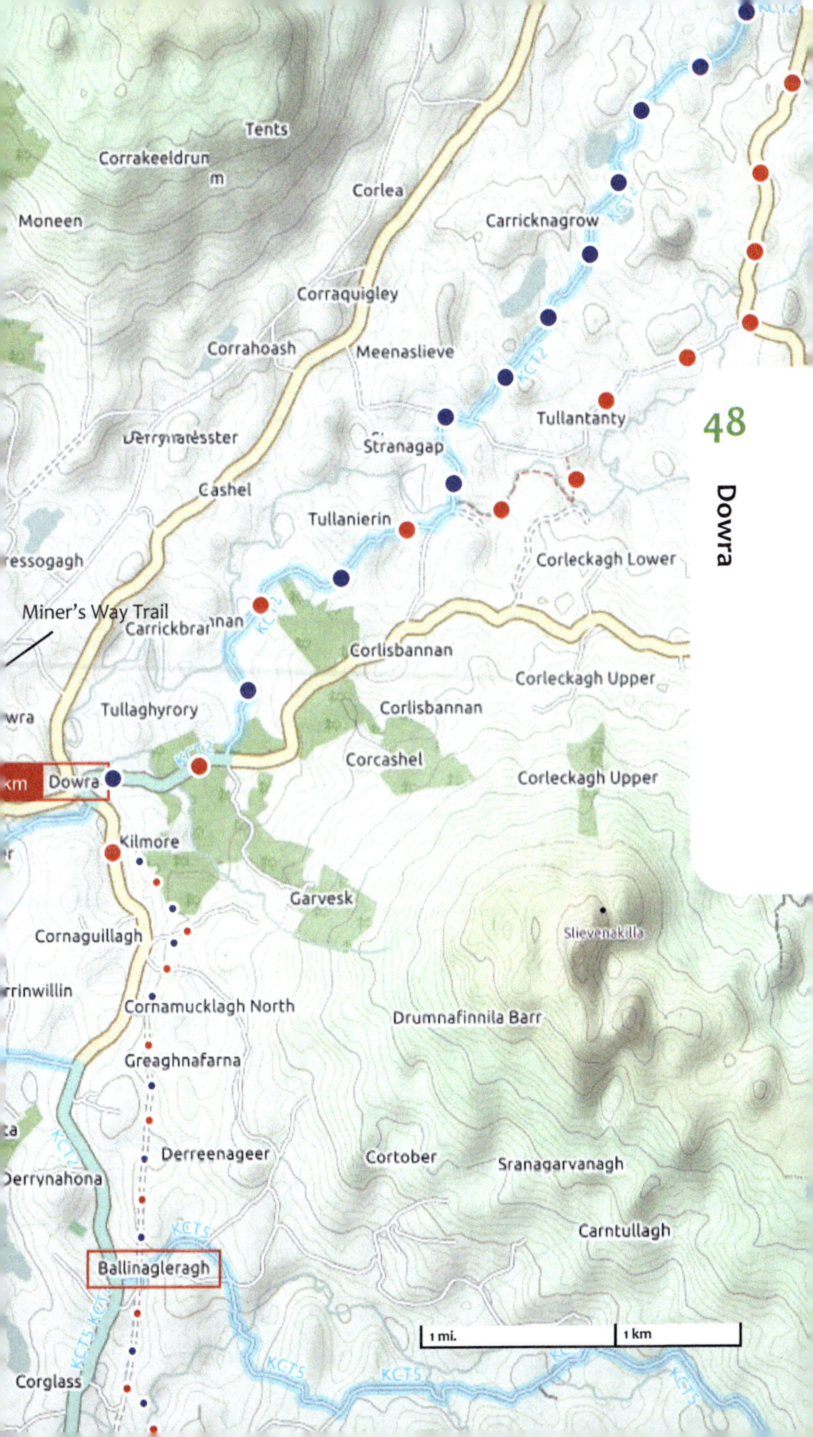
Tents
Corrakeeldrum
Moneen
Corlea
Carricknagrow
Corraquigley
Corrahoash
Meenaslieve
Tullantanty
Stranagap
Derrynatesster
Cashel
Tullanierin
Corleckagh Lower
essogagh
Miner's Way Trail
Carrickbrannan
Corlisbannan
Corleckagh Upper
Tullaghyrory
Corlisbannan
wra
Corcashel
Dowra
Corleckagh Upper
Kilmore
Garvesk
Slievenakilla
Cornaguillagh
rrinwillin
Cornamucklagh North
Drumnafinnila Barr
Greaghnafarna
Derreenageer
Cortober
Sranagarvanagh
Derrynahona
Carntullagh
Ballinagleragh
1 mi.
1 km
Corglass
KCT2
KCT5

this section. Pass through some beautiful forest track followed by the **Cavan Burren Park.** The park is a UNESCO Global Geopark due to its many archaeological and historical features. You will pass by a Neolithic tomb said to be the grave of a giant according to local legend. Two giant's were competing for the love of a female giant and challenged each other to jump over a chasm, now known as the **Giant's Leap**. They both succeeded in making the leap across but one of the giant's then attempted the jump backwards and being unsuccessful in his attempt was buried here in the **Giant's Grave**. The Burren Park is worth exploring for it's many large rocks and ancient rock structures such as the **Calf's House Dolmen**, also known as the Druid's Altar; the glacial erratic known as **Fionn's Fist** (named after legendary warrior Finn McCool), and **Tullygoban Tomb**. The Visitor Centre provides information about all of the structures in the park as well as maps for the five walking trails within the park.

Continuing along the trail and the Burren limestone landscape for 1.5km and then onto narrow laneway for another 1.5km. You will have stunning views over **Lough Macnean Upper and Lower** to the north and the **Cuilcagh Mountains** to the south. At the T-junction turn right and after 1km you will arrive in Blacklion.

[21.7km/13.5mi] Blacklion

A S R PO D

An Blaic

Blacklion marks the end of the Cavan Way. From Blacklion cross the bridge and the Belcoo River to Belcoo village where you will follow the Ulster Way trail for the rest of your journey.

The Market House, Blacklion

Olive Grove B&B, Main Street, +353 (0)71 985 3443. **Killinagh House**, +353 (0)86 666 3226, www.killinaghhouse.com. It is 2 km off the trail. There are more accommodation options across the bridge in Belcoo.

Corraglass West
Ballysroonagh
KCT1
91
Braneen
Cavanmore
Carrickalou
Holywell
Carrickadrantar
Lough Macnean Upper
Lough Macnean Lower
0.6km
Belcoo
Leck
21.7km
Blacklion
Gortaquill
Killinagh Glebe
NWT
KCT2
Gortahill
Killycarney
Kiltaglassan
Ture
Corratirrim
Cornagee
Gortnaleg
Barran
Cavan Burren Park
Visitor Centre
Burren
Legalough
Legeelan
Manragh Upper
Moneygashel
Garvagh Lough
Duckfield
Stranamart
Cornahaw
Gowlan
Skeagh
Garvagh
Shannon Pot
River Shannon
Edenmore
1 mi.
1 km

PART 2:

The Ulster Way

Northern Ireland

Belcoo to Ballycastle

Stages:	13 - 20
Distance:	332 km / 206 miles
Counties:	Fermanagh, Tyrone, Derry, Antrim

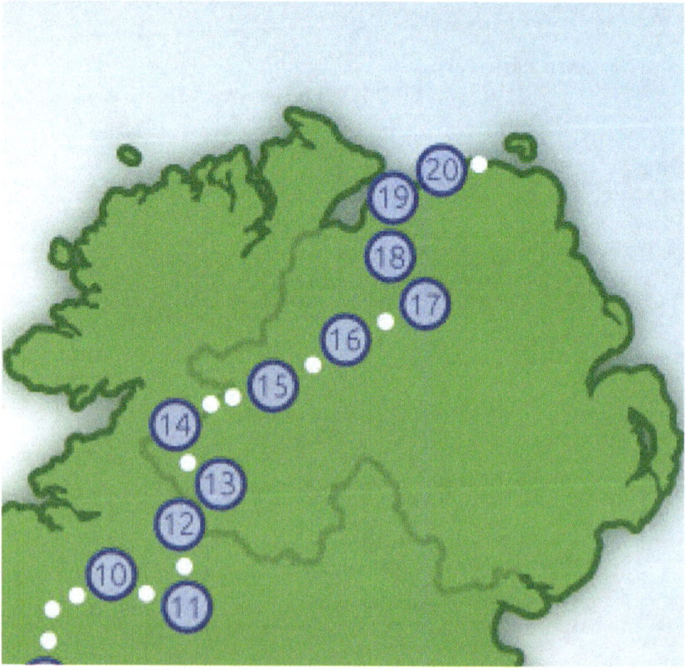

Runkerry Beach. Photo by F. Richichi.

The Ulster Way is a looped walk around the province of Ulster in Northern Ireland. The Ireland Way includes about 330 km of the 1,000 km loop, finishing your journey at Ballycastle.

The Ulster Way was first opened by Wilfrid Capper in 1974. He was inspired by the success of the Pennine Way in England which he walked in 1946. Capper protected White Park Bay from development by raising money to purchase and present it to the National Trust to preserve the area.

For bus and train times in Northern Ireland check www.translink.co.uk and make sure you have pound sterling (UK) currency for the remainder of your journey. There is a shortage of accommodation for stages 14 to 18 inclusive so unless you have a tent, be prepared to go off trail and/or use local taxi services.

If you wish to skip these stages you can take public transport. As stage 19 is a link section you can skip this also and go straight to Portstewart and continue walking from there along the stunning northern coastline. To take buses/trains to bypass these stages takes at least five hours.

STAGE 13:
Belcoo - Belleek

Belcoo - Lough Navar Forest - **Belleek**

Distance: 45.9 km / 28.5 miles
Difficulty: Moderate
County: Fermanagh
OSI Maps: Discovery Series 26
OSNI Maps: Discoverer Series 17

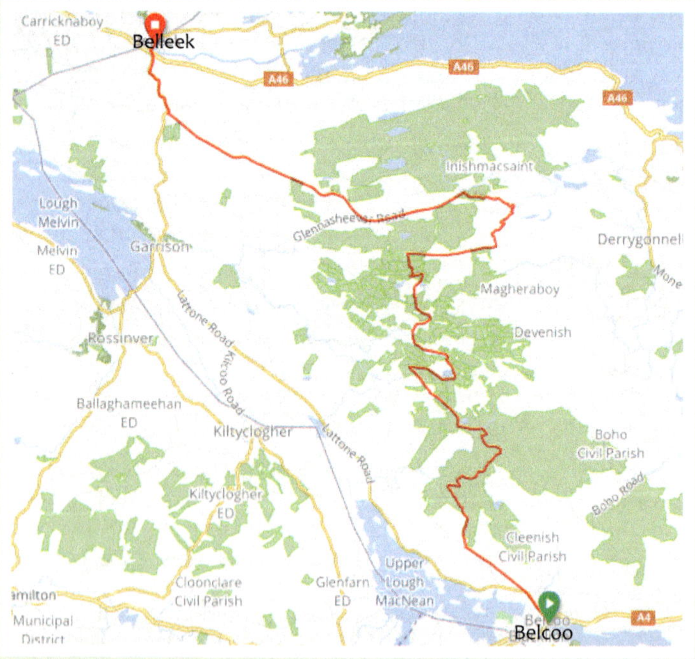

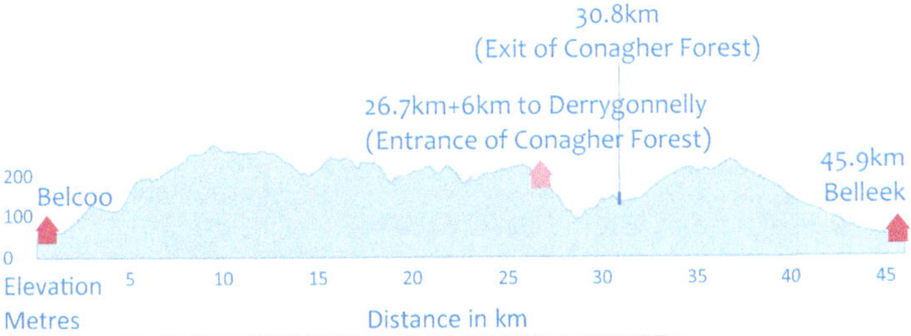

Belcoo

This Stage is entirely on road or gravel path and the forests are well way-marked. Most of the forest roads are closed off to vehicles which makes them pleasant for walking and cycling. The forests are mostly commercial and are dotted with some nice views and lakes.

COUNTY FERMANAGH / CONTAE FHEAR MANACH

[0.6km/0.4mi] Belcoo A S R PO D P

Béal Cú - "Mouth of the Narrow Stretch of Water"

You may need to withdraw pounds sterling from the ATM here and note that your phone operator may charge you for roaming for the rest of your journey through Northern Ireland.

Bella Vista B&B, Cottage Drive, Belcoo, BT93 5EZ., +44 (0)28 6638 6469, www.bellavista-belcoo.co.uk; **Woodford B&B**, Lattone Road, Belcoo, BT93 5ER, +44 (0)28 6638 6576, www.woodfordbedandbreakfast.com; **Customs House Inn Guesthouse**, 25-27 Main Street, Belcoo, BT93 5FB. +44 (0)28 6638 6285, email: info@customshouseinn.com, www.customshouseinn.com; **Rockview House B&B**, +44 (0)2866 386534; **Rushin House Caravan Park & Campsite**, Holywell, Belcoo, BT93 5DU, +44 (0)28 6638 6519, www.rushinhousecaravanpark.com.

Entrance to Ballintempo Forest

Walkers:

If you are unable to walk the entire trail from Belcoo to Belleek in one day, make arrangements to be collected along the way. The owner of **Tir Navar Hostel** in **Derrygonnelly** (6km off trail, 8mins drive) *may* be willing to collect you from the *entrance of Conagher Forest on the Doagh road*. There are no Taxis in Derrygonnelly. You may not get a phone signal at the pick-up point so try to make arrangements earlier in the day. Alternatively, call a taxi from Belleek to collect you at the *exit of Conagher Forest on Glennasheevar Road*. Taxi in Belleek: Mac's Taxis, +44 (0)785 170 5822. It is roughly a 20-minute drive.

View back over Cuilcagh Mountains

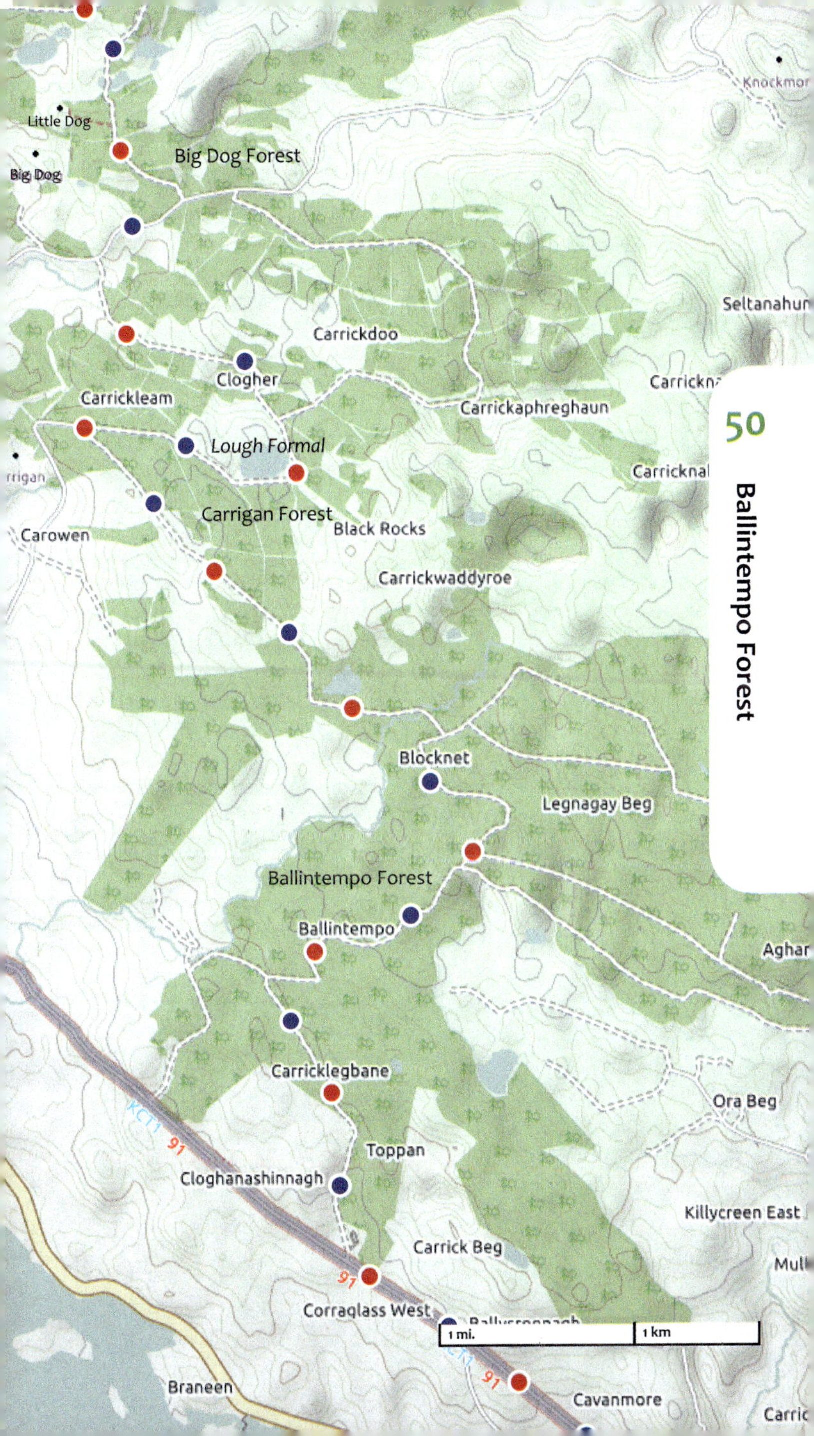
Little Dog
Big Dog Forest
Big Dog
Knockmor
Seltanahun
Carrickdoo
Clogher
Carrickleam
Carrickn
Carrickaphreghaun
Lough Formal
Carricknal
rrigan
Carrigan Forest
Carowen
Black Rocks
Carrickwaddyroe
Blocknet
Legnagay Beg
Ballintempo Forest
Ballintempo
Aghar
Carricklegbane
Ora Beg
Toppan
Cloghanashinnagh
Killycreen East
Carrick Beg
Mull
Corraglass West
1 mi.
1 km
Braneen
Cavanmore
Carric
KC11
91

BIG DOG

IRISH MYTHS & LEGENDS

Legendary giant Finn McCool was out hunting one day with his two dogs. They picked up the scent of a witch and began to chase her. The witch turned herself into a deer so as to outrun them but the dogs caught up with her. To save her own life she turned them into solid rock. They are now known as the hills 'Little Dog' and 'Big Dog.

Leave Belcoo on Railway Street and Lattone Road for 1.3km and arrive at Holywell where you will take the second right turn towards Ballintempo. For 2km follow along the Ballintempo road passing by St. Patrick's Well and St. Patrick's Church and turn right at the large wooden signpost for **Ballintempo Forest**. There are sufficient way-markers for the Ulster Way in the forest. The trail ascends to reveal views behind you of **Lough Macnean** and the **Cuilcagh Mountains** in the far distance. After 4km through this commercial forest you will cross a small bridge over **Black River** and 0.7km later you will see Lough Namanfin to your right. After 3km you will arrive at a T-junction in **Carrigan Forest** where you will turn right and in 1.5km pass by **Lough Formal**. The two hills on the western side of the lake are called **Formal Beg** and **Formal More**. Walk around the lake and in 2.5km exit Carrigan Forest and turn right onto Knockmore road. After 1km turn left into **Big Dog Forest**. Look out for the two hills of **Big Dog** and **Little Dog**. In 1 km you will arrive at **Lough Nabrickboy** which lies on either side of the road. In 2.3km exit Big Dog Forest and turn right onto Doagh road for 3.3km. Turn left into Conagher Forest and exit the forest in 4.3km.

Ballintempo Forest

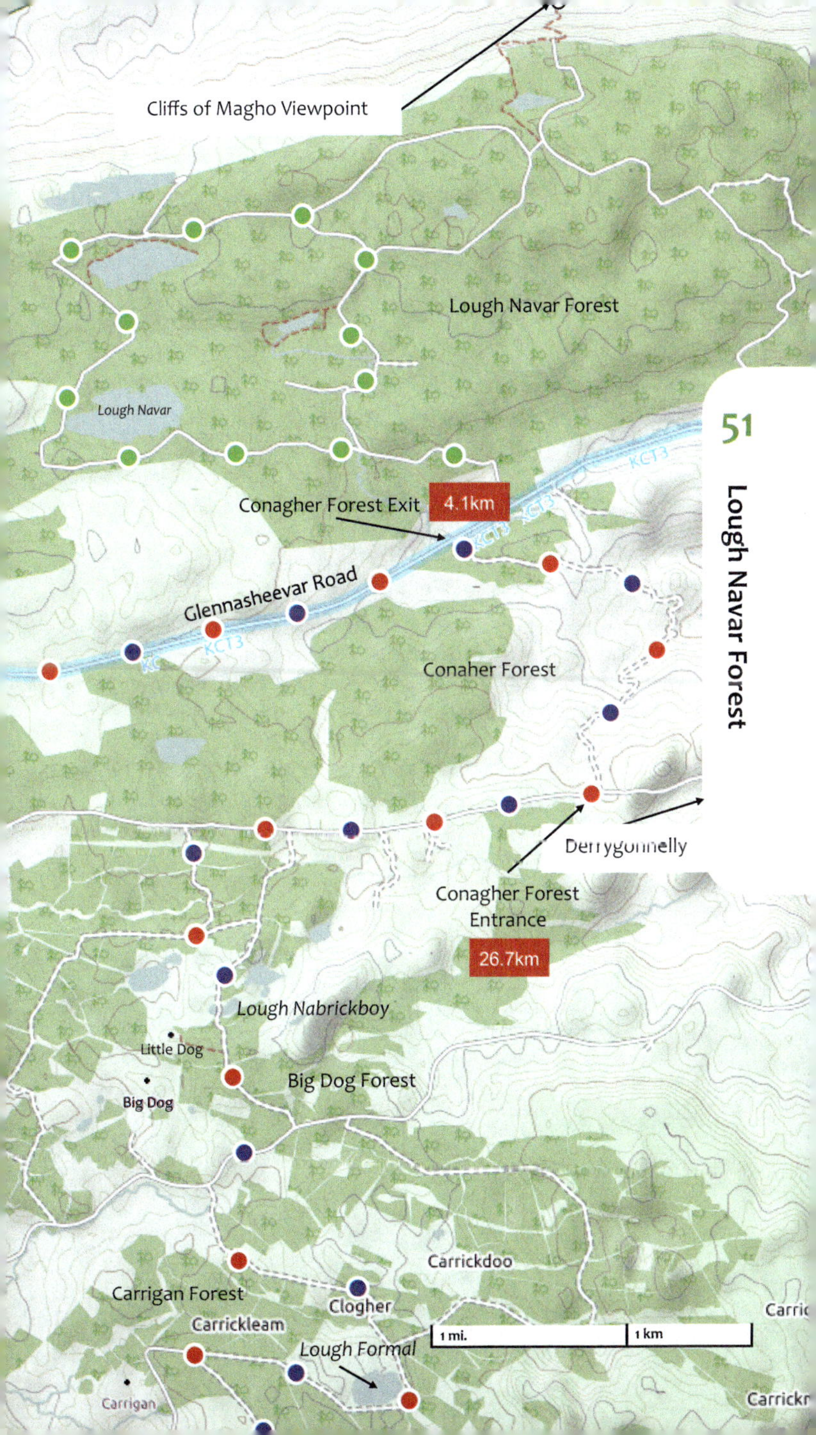
Cliffs of Magho Viewpoint
Lough Navar Forest
Lough Navar
Conagher Forest Exit
4.1km
KCT3
Glennasheevar Road
Conaher Forest
Derrygonnelly
Conagher Forest Entrance
26.7km
Lough Nabrickboy
Little Dog
Big Dog
Big Dog Forest
Carrickdoo
Carrigan Forest
Clogher
Carrickleam
Lough Formal
1 mi.
1 km
Carrigan

[26.7km/16.6mi] Entrance of Conagher Forest

Derrygonnelly (6 km/3.7 miles off trail) A S

From the entrance of Conagher Forest, Derrygonnelly is roughly 6 km off the trail, south-east of Lough Navar Forest.

Tir Navar Hostel, Main Street, Derrygonnelly, BT93 6HW, +44 (0)28 6864 1443. The hostel serves breakfast and lunch.

COUNTY FERMANAGH / CONTAE FHEAR MANACH

Lough Navar Forest offers an optional looped walk 11km / 7 miles which takes you by the lakes on forest tracks and quiet roads. There is also a Scenic Drive which you can cycle to get to the **Cliffs of Magho** viewpoint. I recommend it to cyclists if you have time to spare, but it is too long of a detour for walkers.

[4.1km/2.5mi] Exit of Conagher Forest

Exiting Conagher Forest it is 15.1km/9.4mi to Belleek. Turn left onto Glennasheevar road for 3.8km and you will see views ahead of **Benbulben** and the **Dartry Mountains** just before veering right onto the Cornahaltie road towards Belleek. Pass by **Callagheen Windfarm** to your right with views of **Lough Melvin** and **Benbulben** in the distance ahead. After 8.3km on Cornahaltie road, at the crossroads take the second right onto the B52 to Belleek for 2.5km. At the N3 road go left and then right, taking care crossing the busy road. Cross the **River Erne** into Belleek town and you will see **Belleek Pottery** which is just beside the river.

Lough Nabrickboy

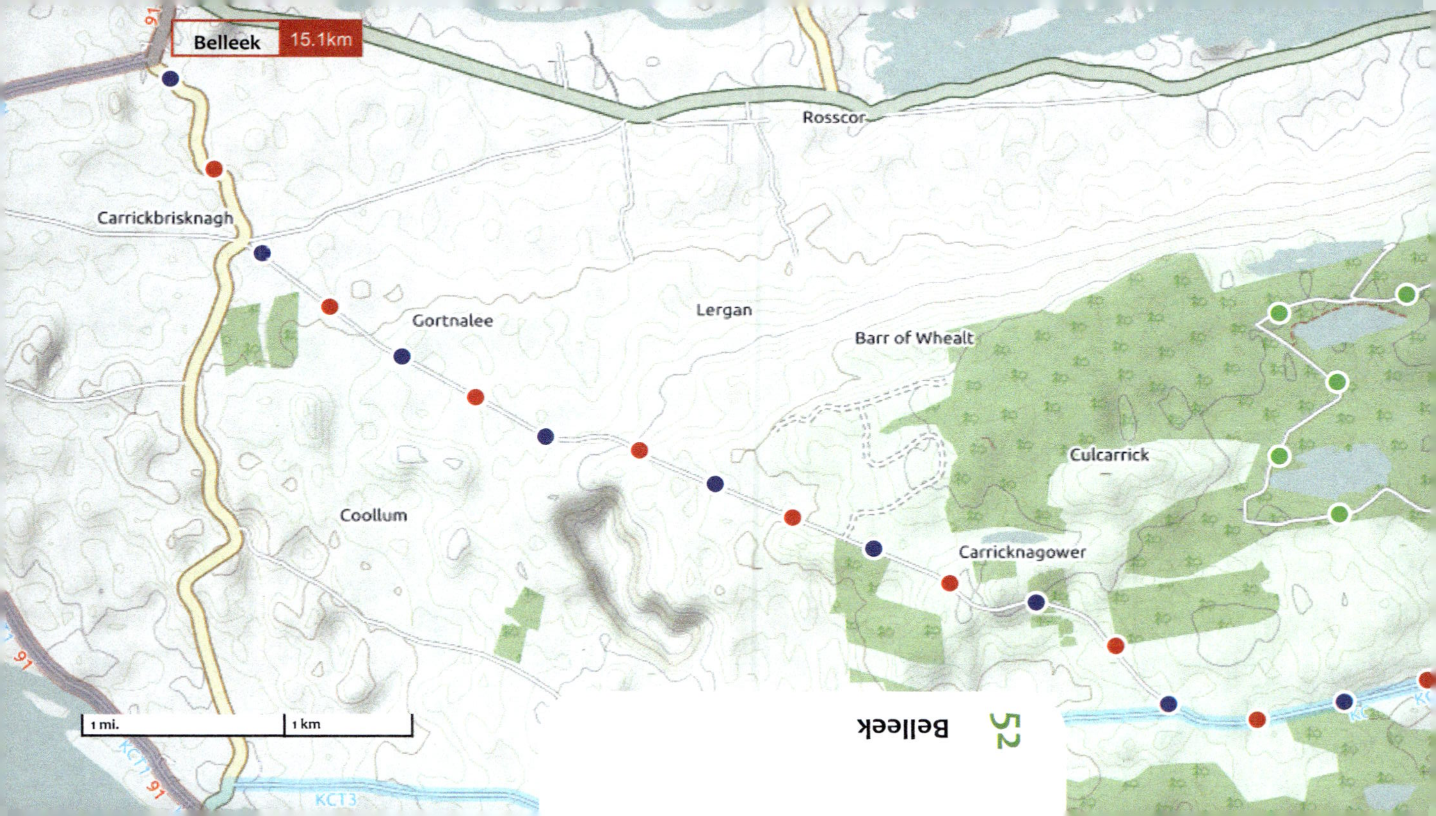
Belleek
15.1km
91
Rosscor
Carrickbrisknagh
Gortnalee
Lergan
Barr of Whealt
Culcarrick
Coollum
Carricknagower
1 mi.
1 km
KCT1
KCT3
52
Belleek

STAGE 14:

Belleek - Lough Bradan Forest

Belleek - **Pettigo** - Lough Bradan Forest

Distance:	50.6 km / 31.4 miles
Difficulty:	Link section, not for walking
County:	Fermanagh
OSNI Maps:	Discoverer Series 17, 12

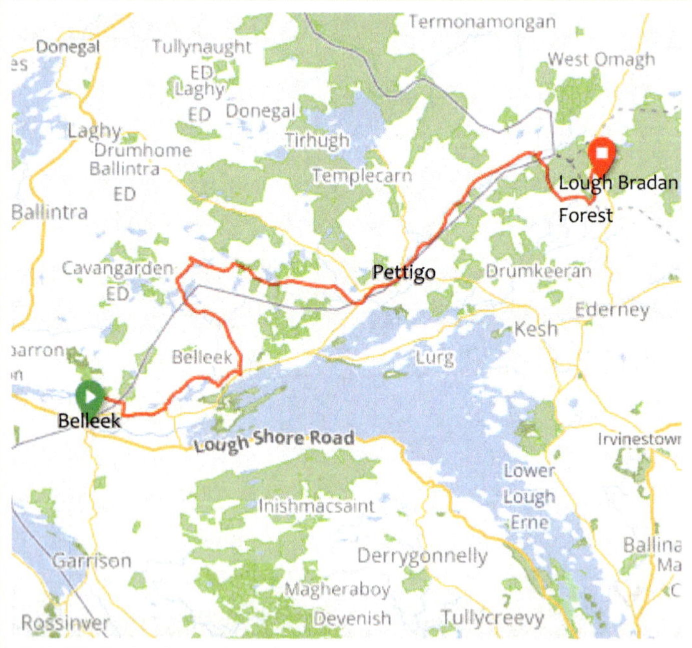

Drumskinny Stone Circle

This is an Ulster Way 'Link Section' and it is recommended to use public transport. This stage is marked as a cycle route on the maps but thru-hikers usually choose to walk. The trail consists mainly of quiet rural roads with only short sections on forest track and passes though the Fermanagh lakelands.

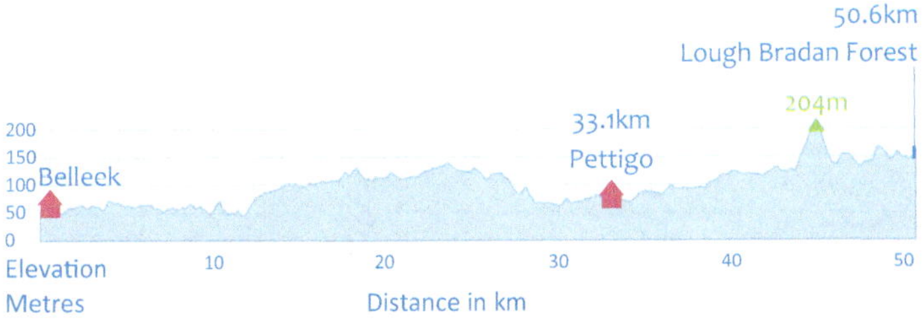

[15.1km/9.4mi] Belleek

A S R PO £ D P

Béal Leice - "Mouth of the Flagstones"

Visit Belleek Pottery Visitor Centre. It is free into the shop and £5 (adult fee) for a guided tour which runs every twenty minutes. They close at 5pm or 6pm depending on day and time of year.

Belleek Pottery

Belleek Hostel £, 1 Commons Road, BT93 3AP, +44 (0)7923 400096 or book on Booking.com; **The Fiddlestone Guesthouse** ££, 15 Main Street Belleek, BT93 3FY, +44 (0)28 6865 8008; **Glen Eden Hotel** £££, Main Street, Belleek, BT93 3FY, Hotels.com.

Belleek Pottery Visitor Centre

53 Lough Scolban

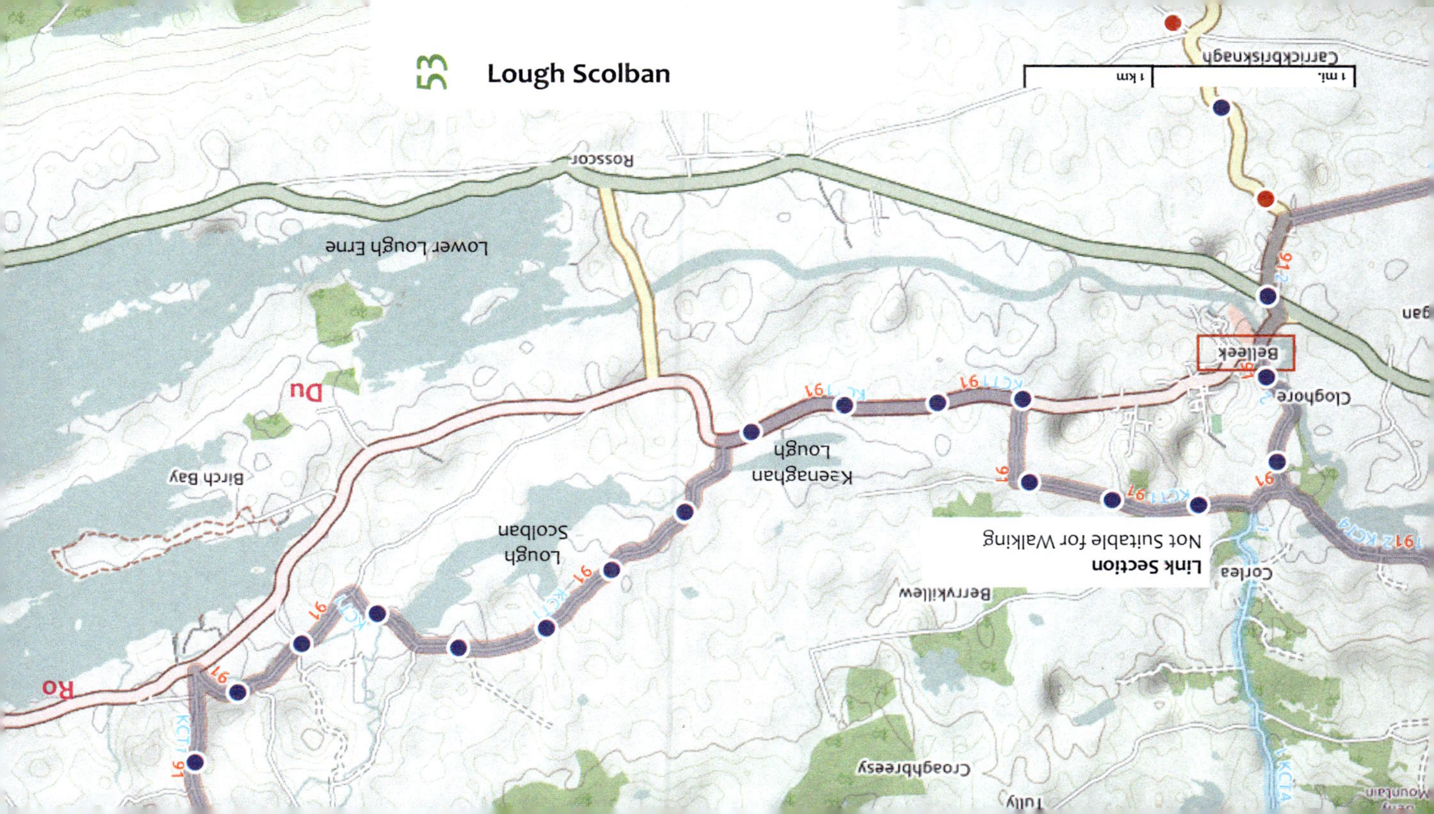

There are two accommodation options past Belleek but both are off trail so may suit cyclists (see map 53). **Dulrush Fishing Lodge & Guesthouse** (off trail), Leggs, Belleek, BT93 2AF, +44 (0)7540 418223, www.booking.com.

Rossharbour (off trail), glamping ££, bedding, towels and cutlery are not provided, 435 Boa Island Road, Leggs, BT93 2AL, +44 (0)28 66 381168, email: info@rossharbour.co.uk, www.rossharbour.co.uk.

Rossharbour Glamping photos provided by Rossharbour

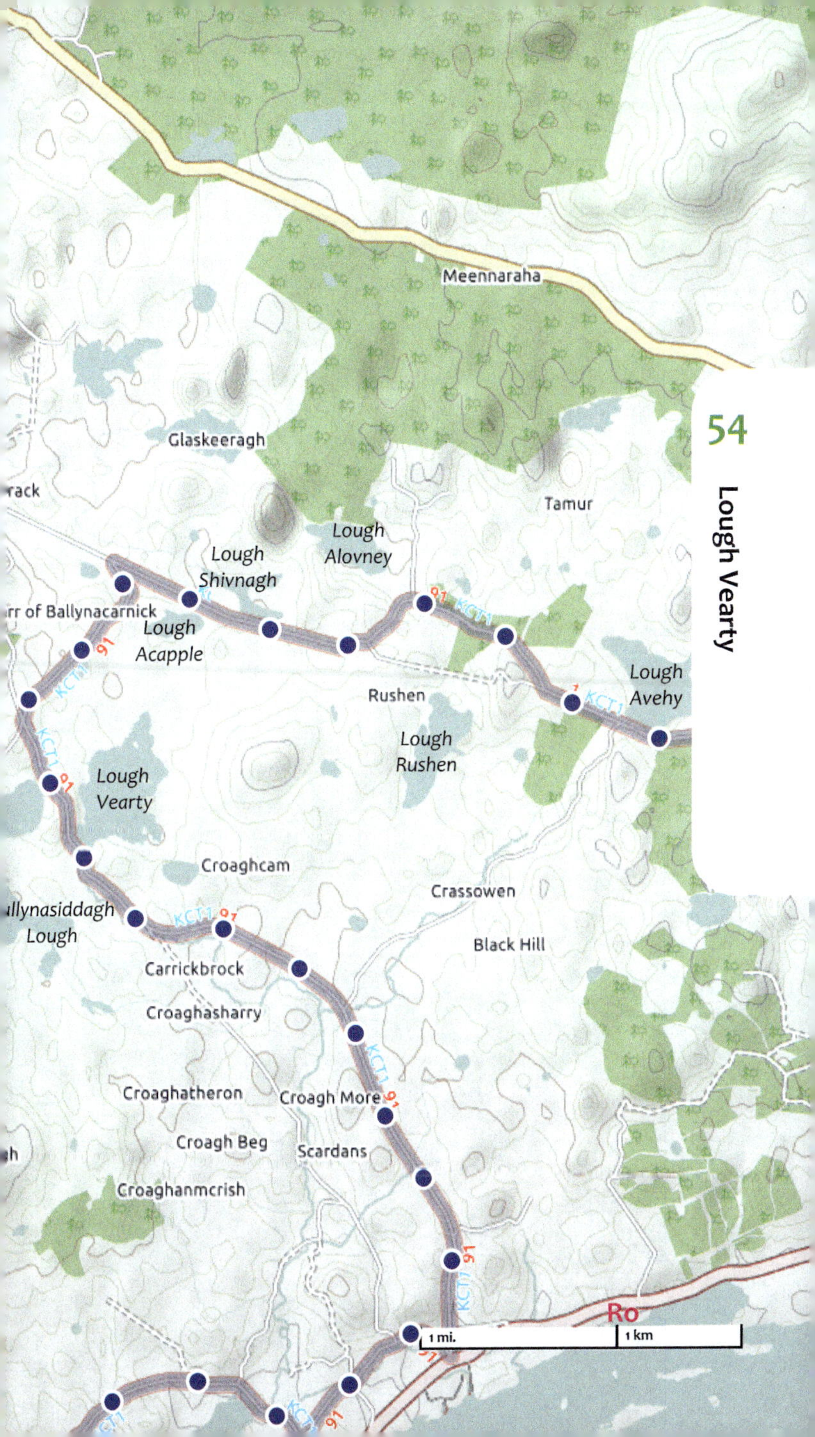
Meennaraha
Glaskeeragh
rack
Tamur
Lough Alovney
Lough Shivnagh
rr of Ballynacarnick
Lough Acapple
KCT1
91
Rushen
Lough Avehy
Lough Rushen
Lough Vearty
Croaghcam
Crassowen
llynasiddagh Lough
Black Hill
Carrickbrock
Croaghasharry
Croaghatheron
Croagh More
Croagh Beg
Scardans
Croaghanmcrish
Ro
1 mi.
1 km

[33.1km/20.5mi] Pettigo

A S R PO

Paiteagó

Pettigo is a small village which sits on the border of counties Donegal and Fermanagh. Its name derives from the Latin 'protectio' (protection). The Termon River marks the border.

Pettigo was traditionally known as the 'gateway' to St. Patrick's Purgatory, a Christian pilgrimage site located on Station Island in Lough Derg, Co. Donegal, 7.3 km north-west of Pettigo.

The Cross B&B, Pettigo, +353 (0)71 9861537; **Hilltop View B&B**, Billary, Pettigo, +353 (0)71 986 1535; **Avondale Farmhouse B&B**, 1 km off-trail north of Pettigo, +353 (0)71 9861520, www.avondalefarmhouse.com.

Gortinessy School B&B, Pettigo, 0.6 km off the trail, use AirBnB to book.

Pettigo Inn

55 Pettigo

33.1km
Pettigo
Ardnaglass
Bircog
Av
Hi
Cr
Go
Gortinessy
Tullycarn
Aghalough
Aghalough
Carn
Lemacraig
Carrickrory
Corlea
Loughultan
Kimmid
Aghafoy
Drumharriff
Aghnahoo Glebe
Long Rock
Fincashel
Carnressy
Bannus
Knocknamona
Belalt
Belalt South
Belalt North
Lough Avehy
Tamur
Black Hill
Crassowen
KCT1
91
95
1 km
1 mi.

Crisscross the Termon River and then leave it to walk towards **Drumskinny Stone Circle.** It is a small well-kept circle of stones dating from between 1600 and 1200 BC.

"You will never plough a field by turning it over in your mind."
- Irish Proverb

Termon River

56 Drumskinny

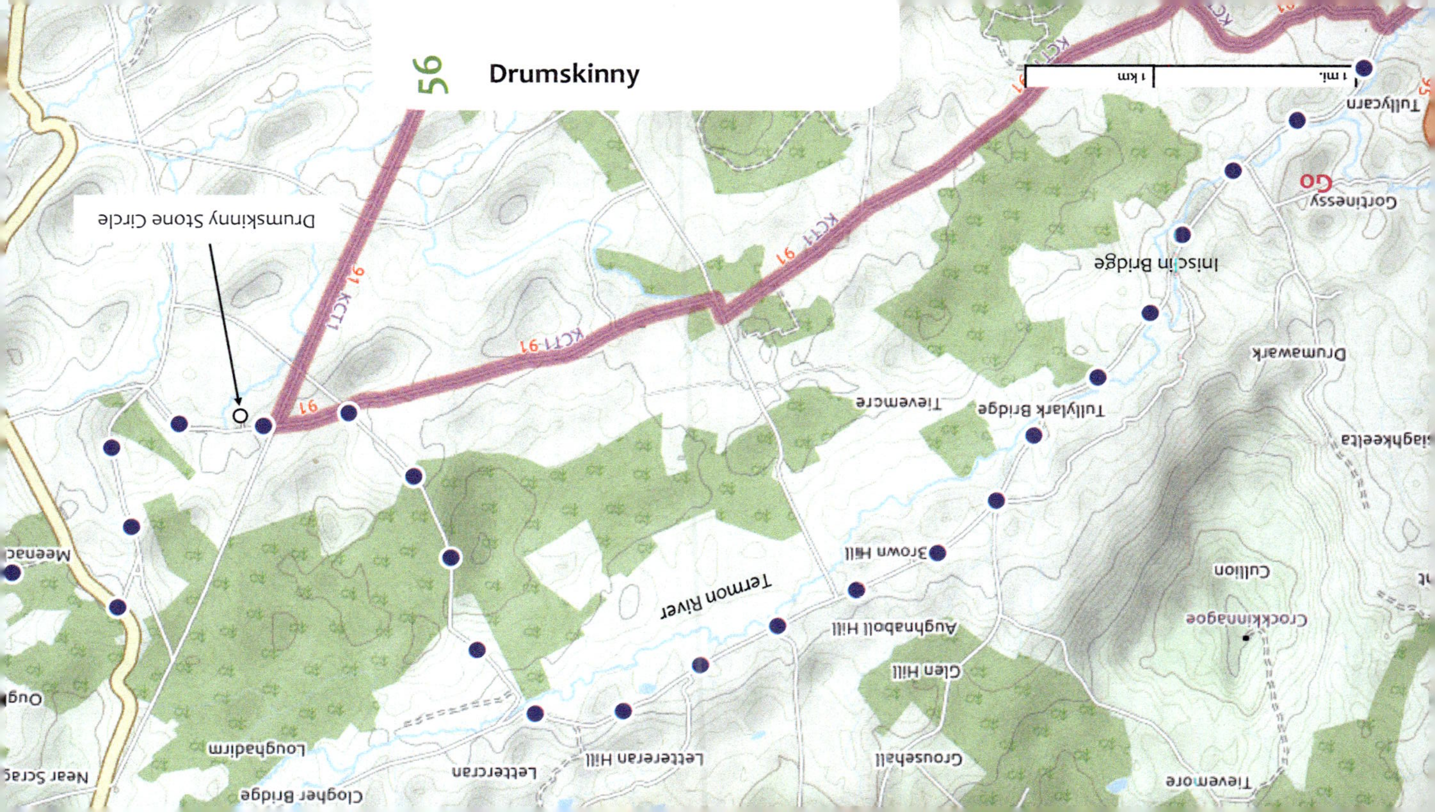

STAGE 15: Lough Bradan to Gortin

Lough Bradan Forest - Drumlegagh -
Mellon Country Hotel - Gortin

Distance: 56.2 km / 34.9 miles
Difficulty: Strenuous, remote
County: Tyrone
OSNI Maps: Discoverer Series 12 & 13

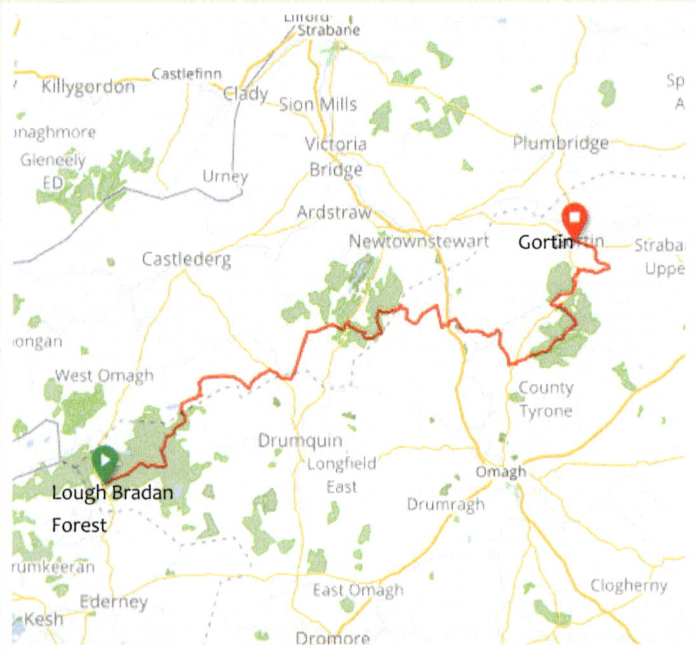

[17.5km/10.9mi] Lough Bradan Forest

The terrain consists of forest tracks, rural roads and open mountain. The trail takes you along roads through **Lough Bradan Forest** for 8km, passing over the small rivers of Meenbog and Soughan. Exit the forest to the view of **Bin Mountain windfarm** surrounding **Lough Lee**. There are spectacular views of Ulster from **Bolaght Mountain**. Next is a 1.3km off-road grassy track until you arrive at a metal gate. Turn left and descend down the narrow road with more views over the Tyrone countryside. After 0.8km at the crossroads turn right and follow Kirlish Road for 3.3km. Turn left following the sign for 'South Sperrins Scenic Route'. Follow this gently winding road as you descend further for 1.8km, passing straight across the cross-roads and arrive at the B50 Drumquin Road. Take a right on the B50 towards Drumquin but divert to the left after 0.8km. After 0.6km turn left at the T-junction. Follow the Drumlegagh Road for 2.5km, crossing over the **River Fairy Water** and finally arriving at Drumlegagh village.

Way-marker on the Ulster Way

[19.7km/12.2mi] Drumlegagh

S PO

Continue on past Drumlegagh to the crossroads and go right towards Omagh. After 1km take a sharp right and follow the road around, keeping to the left and passing by **Baronscourt Parish Church** and graveyard. Follow the Cloonty Road through forest as it veers left and begins your gradual ascent up **Bessy Bell**. Take a sharp right around a cottage on the corner onto Baronscourt Road for a short stretch and then left onto a rough road through forest, following the Ulster Way way-marker. Exit the forest onto Cashty Road, taking the next left towards the forest and **Ballyrenan Windfarm**. Continue your climb, taking a right at the crossroads and following the windy path to the summit of Bessy Bell and admire the view from the top.

Descent on the south-east side of Bessy Bell on grassy track and through the wind farm to meet the Gortgranagh Road. Turn right onto Castletown road and follow for just over 1 km before sliding left down a narrow road as you descend further into the valley. Arriving onto the busy A5 Beltany road with the Mellon Country Hotel located on the left.

[14.7km/9.1mi] Mellon Country Hotel

A R

134 Beltany Road, Omagh, BT78 5RA, +44 (0)28 816 61224 or +44 (0) 28 816 61702, email: info@melloncountryhotel.com, www.melloncountryhotel.com. There is alternative accommodation in Newtownstewart, 2.4 km/1.5 miles further up the road at the Castle Inn, 3 Townhall St., BT78 4AX+44 28 8166 2266, www.booking.com. Taxi: Jet Taxi, based in Newtownstewart, +44 7761 117747.

Fuchsia magellanica 'Fuchsia'

57 Lough Bradan Forest

Dunmullan Church & Graveyard

County Fermanagh

Going back to the previous junction, take the slip road down to the **Strule River** and the bridge across it. At the next T-junction turn right towards Omagh. Take the third left turn after about 1km and then veer right when the road splits. After 1km arrive at Tattynure road and take a right, then first left. Follow Golan road for 1.2km then right onto Dunmullan road. Follow the winding road then cross the bridge over a small river. You will pass by **Dunmullan Old Church and Graveyard** on your left. The ruin dates from the sixteenth century.

As I walked up the small slope to the graveyard gates I stopped suddenly when I saw something unexpected right on my path; a grey and white tabby kitten not much more than three weeks old curled up in a ball. It did a baby hiss at me when I went near it so I left it alone in case it's mother was nearby. I went on to explore the little graveyard and the church ruin while the kitten called for it's mother. Leaving the graveyard I saw that it hadn't moved and I noticed it's sibling lying at the side of the road, most

On the Way to Gortin

58 Drumlegagh

likely hit by a car a day or two previously. Not wanting the same fate for the little kitten I walked up the road to the nearest house but no one was home. Back at the graveyard and the kitten was still there calling for it's mother who was nowhere to be seen. Luckily a family with three dogs (obviously animal lovers!) were out for a walk. The little boy was delighted as he took the kitten from my hands and they took it home, promising to look after the kitten until they found it a home. It was the kitten's lucky day!

At the next junction cross the road and take the road to the right, continuing on Dunmullan road for another 1.4km. At the next junction follow the Ulster Way way-marker to the left onto Knockmoyle road. At the next junction turn left towards Gortin and then the first right. This road takes you up the gradual ascent of **Timurty Hill** and into **Gortin Glen Forest Park**. This is a beautiful forest with a pretty waterfall. Upon exiting the park go left along the main road and then take the first right onto Lisnaharney road, passing by the Sperrin Caravan Park & Campsite, and take the next right, entering another part of Gortin Glen Forest Park. Exiting the park for the final time go left on the busy road and take the next right onto the quiet Lenamore road for 3.7km with the beautiful scenic **Gortin Glen Lakes** just over the first hump in the road. These lakes are part of the **Boorin National Nature Reserve** which consists of small pointed hills formed from the last Ice Age when the melting ice left behind large amounts of sand and gravel. The area is now mostly covered in heather and surrounded by bog. The lakes are deep and known as kettle-hole lakes. There is a path around the lake to your left if you want to explore, which joins back up with the road a little further on. Ascend up the hill and admire the views behind you of the lakes and forest. Continue on to a scenic viewpoint over the valley and take a rest on the picnic benches there. Then begins your final descent into Gortin. Take a left on Crockanboy road to shortly arrive into Gortin village.

Hills of Boorin National Nature Reserve

Stream in Gortin Village

59
Melon County Hotel
More accommodation in Newtownstewart 2.4 km / 1.5 miles north from here
Me
14.7km
Lislap West
Ballykeel
Eskeradooey
skeradooay
Castleroddy Glebe
Castleroddy
Gortgranagh
Lurganboy
allyrenan
Bessy Bell
420m
Legacurry
Deers Leap
Aghafad
Beltany
Carrigans
Corlea
Dunbreen
Hill Head
Wind Farm
Golan
Tircur
Lislap
Gortinagin
ans Hill
Castletown
Dunmullan
Kingarrow
Tattynagole
Farrest
Rosnamuck
Beragh
Gortnacreagh
Killinure
Glasmullagh
Rylagh
Dunteige
Carnony
1 mi.
1 km
Broghan
Erganagh Glebe
NWT
92
3

STAGE 16: Gortin to Moneyneany

Gortin - Moneyneany

Distance:	36.6 km / 22.7 miles
Difficulty:	Moderate
County:	Derry
OSNI Maps:	Discoverer Series 13

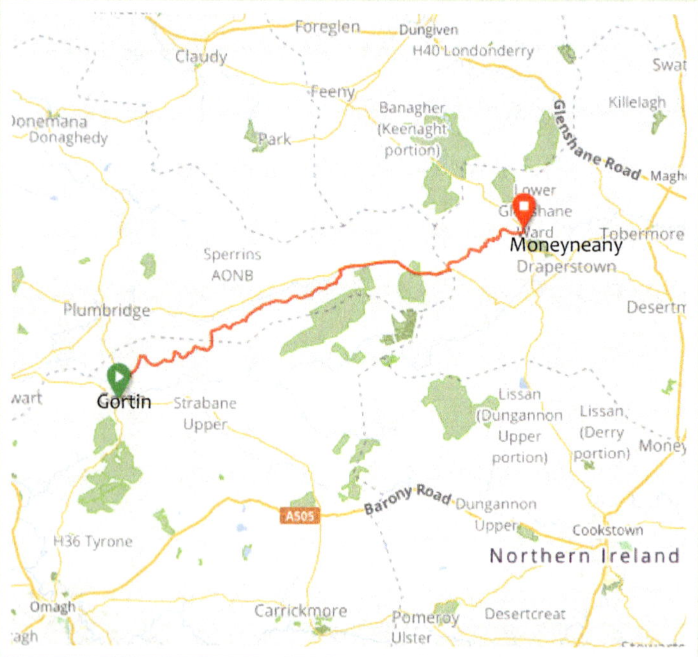

Glenelly Valley

This trail takes you through the **Sperrin Mountains.** However, there is very little ascent and descent due to the trail following the contours of the valleys. You will walk mainly in farmland and moorland. As you admire the views of **Glenelly Valley** look out for the many **ring forts.**

COUNTY TYRONE / CONTAE TÍR EOGHAIN

[21.8km/13.5mi] Gortin A S R PO £ D P

Goirtín - "Small Enclosed Field"

Sperrin Mountains Caravan & Campsite, 1 Lisnaharney Road, Omagh, BT79 7UG. +44 (0)28 8166 2288, email: mail@sperrincottages.com, www.sperrincottages.com. **Gortin Hostel**, 62 Main Street, Gortin, Omagh, BT79 8NH, +44 (0)28 8164 8346, email: info@gortin.net.

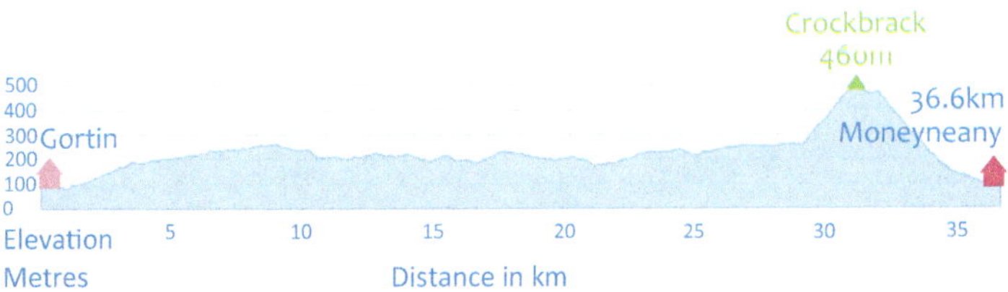

Hebe x franciscana 'Blue Gem'

From Gortin village head north in the direction of Plumbridge on the Culvacullion Road for 1.2km. Just after crossing the **Owenkillew River,** turn right onto Gorticashel Road followed by left onto Trinamadan Road for 2.2km. Turn right onto Meenadoo Road for 6.1km which eventually merges with the other end of Gorticashel Road.

Way-marker

Culvacullion
Trinamadan
Garvagh
Meenadoo
Drummagh
Owenkillew River
Bloody Oak
21.8km
Gortin
Go
Freaghdoo
Rylands
Robinsons Hill
Gortin
Lenamore
Glenma
Curraghchosaly Mountain
Lislap East
Caravan & Campsite
Cullion
Cullion
Head
Mullaghcarn
Stradowan
Tirmurty Hill
Glengawna
Crocknakeeferty
1 mi.
1 km
Rylagh

After 0.3km you will come to cross-roads. Take the road directly in front with 'STOP' printed on it. This scenic glacial valley is known as **Barnes Gap**. After Barnes Gap the road veers right onto Magherabrack Road and then take the next right towards Draperstown onto Corramore Road. This road stretches along **Glenelly Valley** for 10km, then crosses over to the other side for a further 7.6km on the busier Glenelly Road. See if you can spot one of the many ringforts close to the Glenelly River.

Near Barnes Gap

The Way to Moneyneany

61 Glenelly Valley

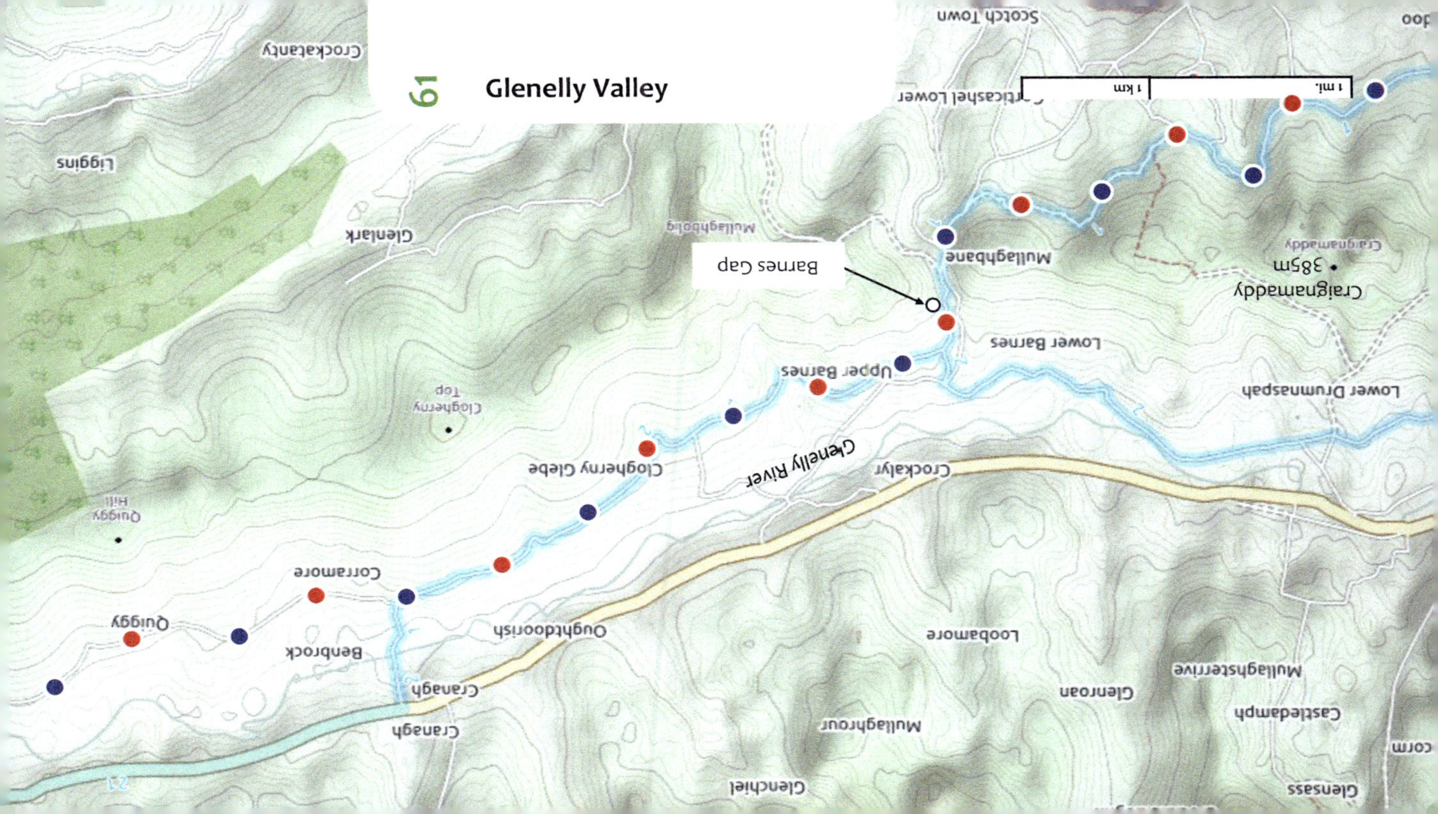

"If you have the words, there's always a chance that you'll find the way."

- Seamus Heaney

Take a left through an open gate for the big climb of this section; **Crockbrack Mountain.** It is a 5.9km over and down the mountain. A steep, rough and boggy track takes you up Crockbrack. Follow along the fences to the summit and continue across rough boggy terrain from Crockbrack over to the lower peak of **Crockmore**. On the descent follow track and then walk 1.5km on the Drumderg road. Turn left for a short stretch on the Magherafelt Road into Moneyneany. There is a footpath along most, but not all, of this busy road so take care here.

"Walking is man's best medicine"

- Hippocrates

The Way to Moneyneany

62 Crockbrack Mountain

STAGE 17:

Moneyneany to Dungiven

Moneyneany - Dungiven

Distance:	21.3 km / 12.9 miles
Difficulty:	Moderate
County:	Derry
OSNI Maps:	Discoverer Series 13, 8, 7

[36.6km/22.7mi] Moneyneany

A S PO

Móin na nIonadh - Bog of Wonders

Luxury Glamping in Sperrins @ Pod (4 km / 2 miles off trail) at the same location as camping and caravan park, book on www.airbnb.ie. **The Shepherd's Rest Camping & Caravan Park**, 220 Sixtowns Road, Draperstown, Magherafelt, BT457BH. +44 (0)28 7962 8517, email: info@shepherdsrestpub.com, www.shepherdsrestpub.com.

Leaving Moneyneany, pass by Devlin's shop and St. Eugene's Church on your left. The first kilometre has a footpath; as far as the school. From there you must walk on the main road for 0.4km which then turns into a quiet country road for another 0.7km. Cross the small stone bridge over the **Altalacky River** and immediately right into **Moydamlaght Forest**. The trail through the forest is 3km.

St. Eugene's Church, Moneyneany

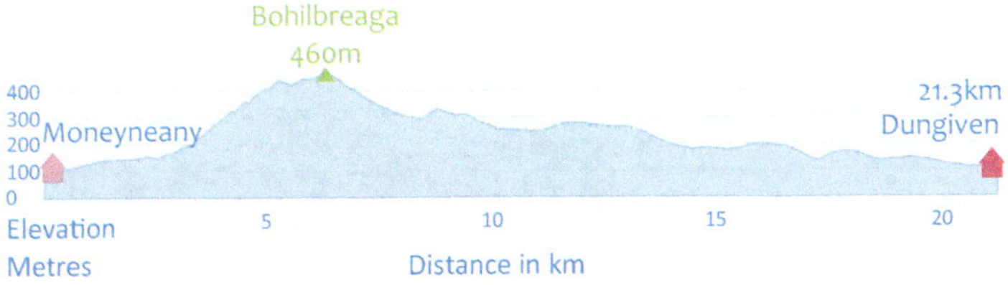

The gradual ascent becomes more steep as you exit the forest to climb the grassy track up to **Eagle's Rock**; a basalt escarpment rising over scree-filled slopes. Also known as *Creag-na-Shoke* the name translates to 'rock of the falcon or hawks'. It is an ideal location for birds of prey due to Moydamlaght Forest and agricultural lands surrounding it. From the top make your way across boggy terrain for 1.3km to **Glenshane Forest**. The hill between the two forests is called **Bohilbreaga** from the Irish *Buachaill Bréige* or 'lying boy'. The name comes from a story from The Penal Times of the 17th or 18th century which tells of a boy who was a lookout atop of the hill. He was questioned by soldiers as to the location of 'Mass Rock' and a priest they were looking for. The boy told the soldiers that he knew where the priest was and sent them in the wrong direction; thus saving the priest from capture. Mass Rock, also known as 'Priest's Chair' is a chair-shaped rock located in Glenshane Forest. Walk through Glenshane Forest, which is the source of the **River Roe**, for 4.7km and exit the forest soon after crossing the river.

The River Roe is designated an Area of Special Scientific Interest and is popular for fishing sea trout and salmon. The trail descends into Roe Valley along a quiet country road and then at a white bungalow turn left onto Corick Road for 4.9km.

There is a footpath on the far side of the busy Glenshane Road. Take care when crossing over at this junction. Walk along this narrow footpath for 1.6km where you will reach a shop and Edenroe B&B (see next chapter) just past it. It is 0.5km off trail if you want to explore Dungiven which has plenty of shops.

Purple Grass

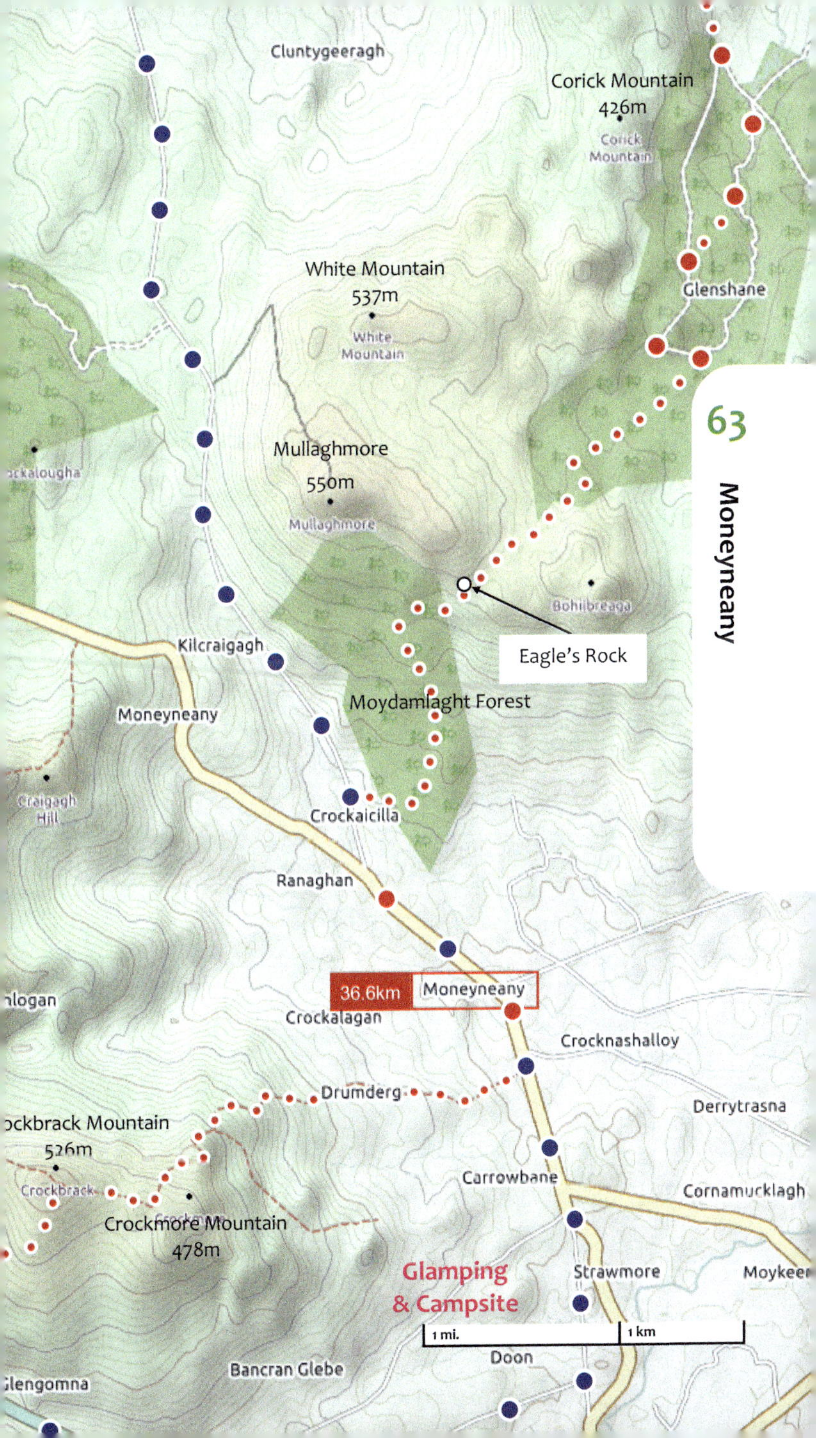
Cluntygeeragh
Corick Mountain
426m
Corick Mountain
Glenshane
White Mountain
537m
White Mountain
Mullaghmore
550m
Mullaghmore
Bohilbreaga
Eagle's Rock
Kilcraigagh
Moneyneany
Moydamlaght Forest
Craigagh Hill
Crockaicilla
Ranaghan
36.6km
Moneyneany
Crockalagan
Crocknashalloy
Drumderg
Derrytrasna
Crockbrack Mountain
526m
Crockbrack
Crockmore Mountain
478m
Carrowbane
Cornamucklagh
Glamping & Campsite
Strawmore
Moykeel
1 mi.
1 km
Doon
Bancran Glebe
Glengomna

STAGE 18:

Dungiven to Castlerock

Dungiven - **Limavady** (via taxi) - **Castlerock**

Distance:	56.1 km / 34.9 miles
Difficulty:	Strenuous
County:	Derry
OSNI Maps:	Discoverer Series 7, 8, 4

The stretch from Dungiven to Binevenagh is called the **North Sperrins Way** which follows along the broad ridge of the Sperrin Mountains. The rolling uplands are often shrouded in fog, particularly outside of the summer months. The trail starts off with roads that are often busy followed by a tough climb up **Donald's Hill**. From the top you cross open moorland, forest trails and finally along quiet roads as you approach the northern coastline and the village of Castlerock.

COUNTY DERRY / CONTAE DHOIRE

[21.3km/13.2mi] Dungiven A S R PO £ D P

Dún Geimhin - "Gevin's Fort"

The trail passes by the outskirts of Dungiven. There is a small shop beside Edenroe B&B, or else take a 10-minute walk to the shops and restaurants in Dungiven town.

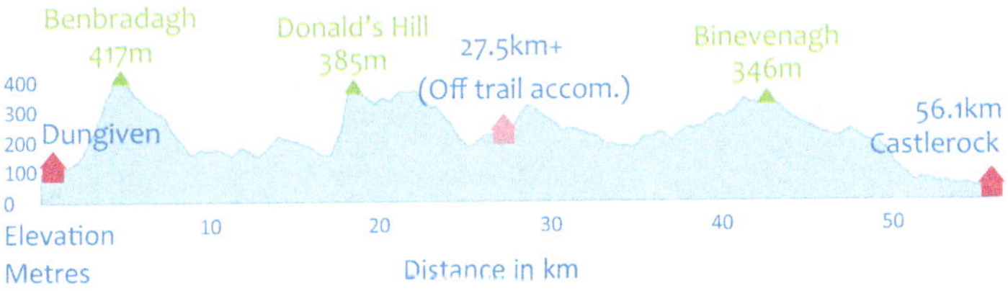

North Sperrins Way

Dungiven Castle is seen from the rear from the main street. Go through the carpark to the left of the castle to view it from the front (albeit from behind a fence as it is not accessible to the public). The castle dates from the 17th century although much of the current building is from the 1830s. During World War II it housed the US Army, and in the 1950s and 1960s it was used as a dance hall. It is now an Irish language secondary school.

Cashel Lake View B&B, 17 Birren Road, Dungiven, Derry, BT47 4SH, +44 (0)28 7774 2159, email: casheltrout@hotmail.com, www.cashel-lake-view.com. **Edenroe B&B**, 32 Chapel Road, Dungiven, Derry, BT47 4RT, +44 (0)28 7774 2029, email: edenroe@aol.com, www.bedandbreakfastni.com.

Starting from Dungiven the trail climbs over **Benbradagh Mountain** (An Bhinn Bhradach, meaning 'the treacherous/dangerous peak) and takes you onto the **American Road.** The road was built in 1967 by the US Navy to enable them to access the US Naval Communication Centre on the top of the mountain. The base closed ten years later.

The Grey Gables, (self-catering, minimum 2-nights stay), approx. €180 for 2 nights, bookable on AirBnb, located at the foot of Benbradagh (map 66).

Dungiven Castle

64

Dungiven

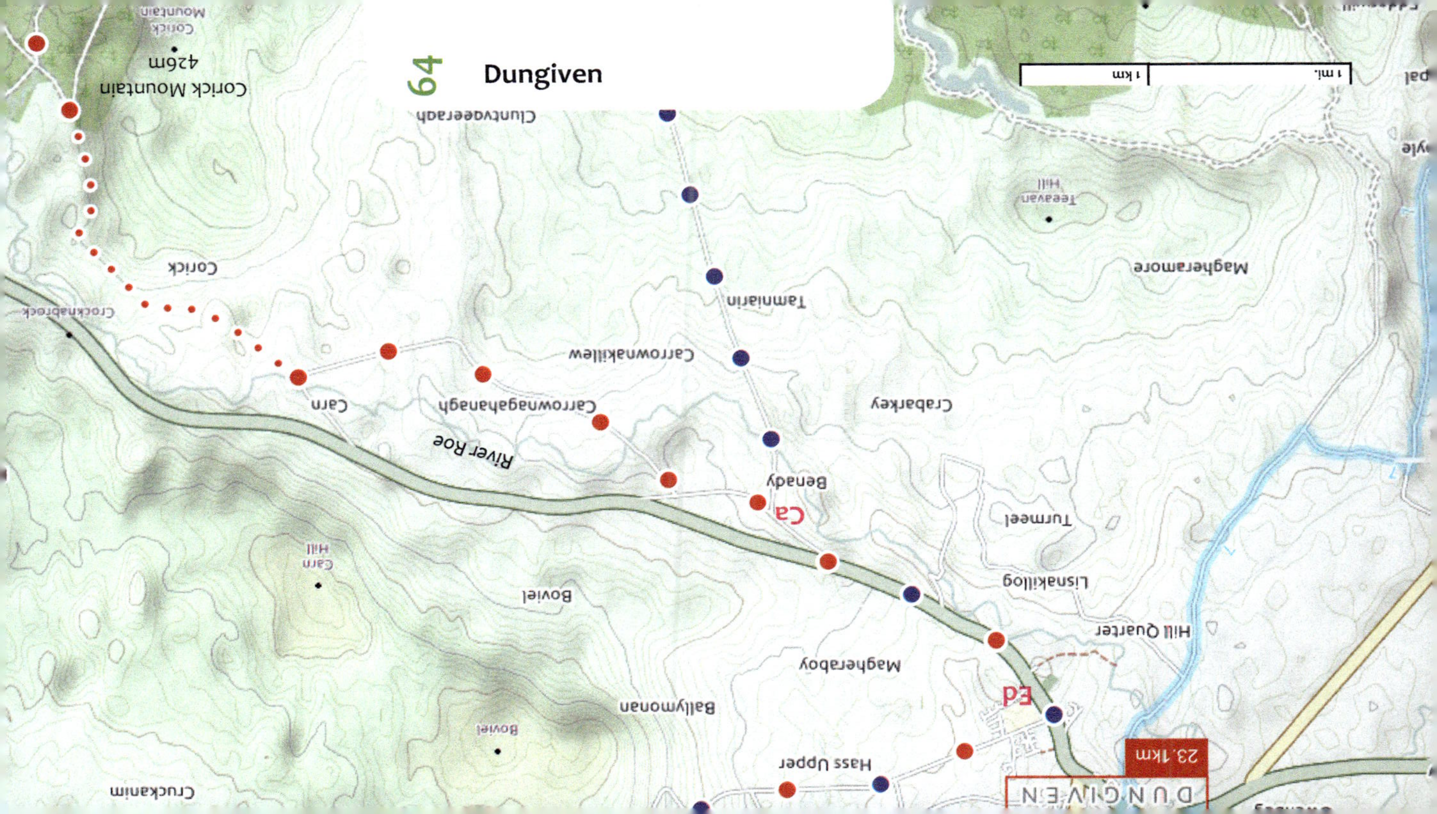

Corick Mountain
426m
Corick Mountain
Corick
Crocknabrock
Cluntvaeerah
Tamniarin
Carrownakillew
Carn
Carrownagahanagh
River Roe
Crabarkey
Benady
Ca
Turmeel
Carn Hill
Boviel
Lisnakillog
Hill Quarter
Magheraboy
Ballymonan
Ed
Boviel
Hass Upper
23.1km
DUNGIVEN
Cruckanim
Teeavan Hill
Magheramore
1 km
1 mi.

TIR NA NÓG - 'LAND OF YOUTH'

IRISH MYTHS & LEGENDS

One day, Oisín, a great warrior and son of Fionn MacCumhaill saw a beautiful white horse in the hills, and on its back a beautiful young woman. She told him that her name is Niamh and that her father was the King of Tír na Nóg. She had heard many wonderful stories of a warrior named Oisín and had come to take him back with her to Tír na Nóg.

Oisín fell in love with her and agreed to go with her, promising his father that he would return to Ireland to visit him soon. They rode the magical white horse across the sea to Tír na Nóg. It was a land where nobody aged, nobody knew of sadness and they lived forever.

After what seemed like three years, Oisín decided to visit Ireland as he was feeling homesick. Niamh reluctantly let him take the white horse back to Ireland, but warned him not to let his feet touch the ground or else he could never return to Tír na Nóg.

Oisín arrived only to find that 300 years had passed. The castle where he had lived was now in ruins. He was searching the hills for a familiar face when he came across some old men who were trying to move a large rock. He leant down from his horse to try to help them, but lost his balance and fell. As he touched the ground he aged 300 years.

Now a frail old man he asked the men he helped about his father, Finn MacCumhaill. They told him his father had died many years ago, old and broken-hearted. Oisín told the men magical tales about the land of eternal youth, Tír na Nóg, before he died. These stories are still told today.

65 Lenamore Forest

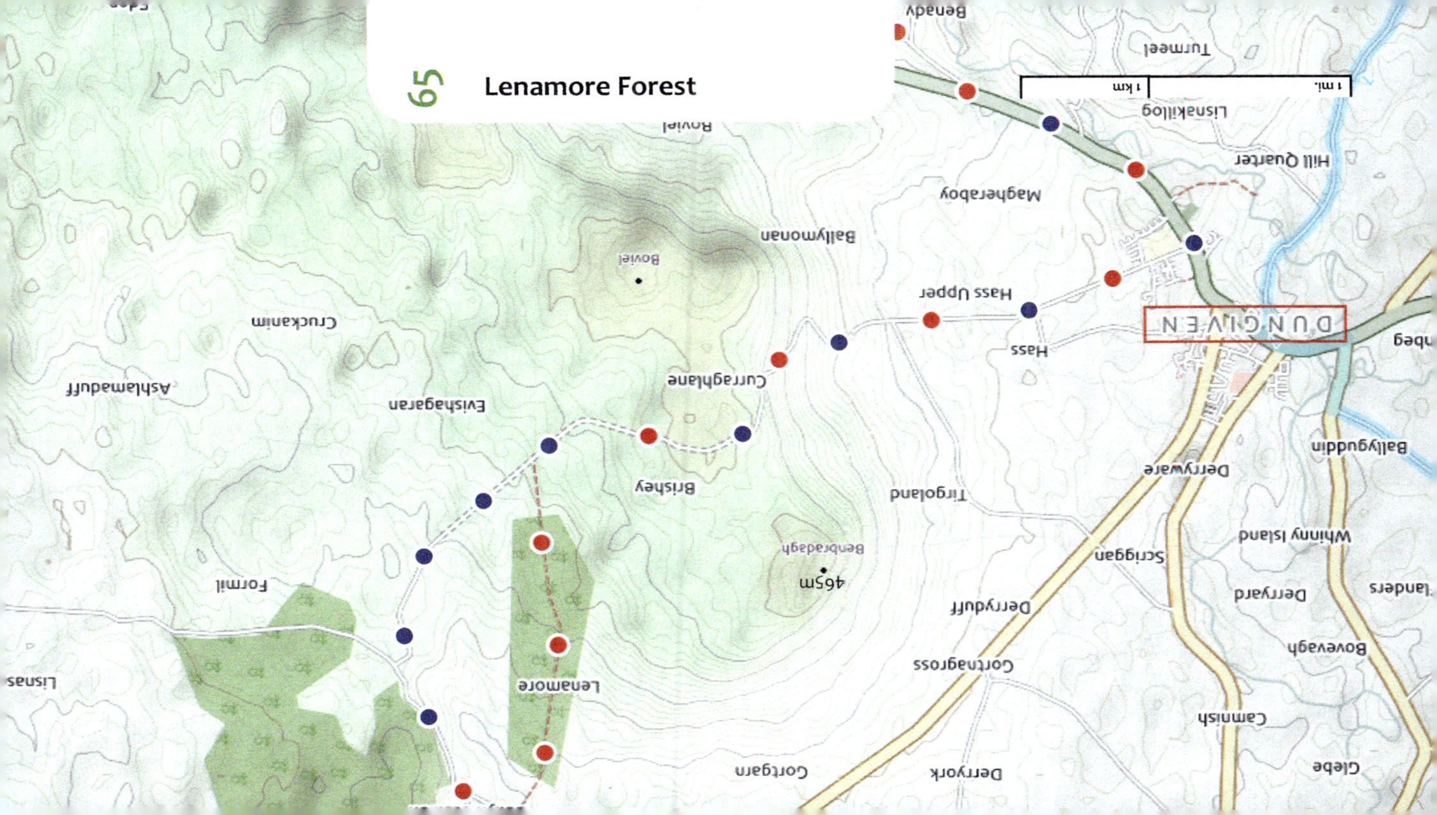

Forest at Lenamore. Photo by F. Richichi

Past Benbradagh you will come to **Legavannon Pot**, a plunge-pool formed as glacial ice melted. Further along the long laneway a grass track will take you to a road where you take a sharp left, and then right through farm gates towards Donald's Hill. This is one of the toughest parts of the trail with the steep ascent followed by a long stretch of bog over to **Rigged Hill Windfarm**. At the top of Donald's Hill you will be rewarded with breath-taking views of the Sperrin Mountains, Lough Foyle and County Donegal. Now for the bog-land trek across to Rigged Hill. There are no way-markers which makes this even more of a challenge. Using GPS with satellite view you may be able to locate the 'pathway' through the bog which greatly helps with some of this tough stretch. You will cross Temain Road followed by more rough and boggy terrain to the windfarm. A quiet road will lead you from the windfarm down-hill to Cam Forest. After Cam Forest you will reach the busy Ringsend Road.

(27.5km/17mi) Almost mid-way between Dungiven and Castlerock, from Ringsend Road, are some accommodation options off the trail. **The Weefield B&B** (3 km / 2 miles off trail), 113 Craigmore Road, Ringsend, BT51 4HS, +44 (0)28 7086 9255, www.hotelscombined.com or www.roomex.com. In Limavady (9 km / 6 miles off trail): **Alexander Arms Hotel**, £60, 34 Main Street, Limavady BT49 0EU, +44 (0)28 7776 3443 **Keady View Farm B&B**, Sea Coast Road, Limavady BT49 9DW, +44 (0)28 7776 4518, www.keadyviewfarm.com; **Whitehill Farm Guesthouse**, 70 Ballyquin Road, Limavady BT49 9EY, +44 (0)28 7772 2306; **Roe Park Resort**, £££, 10 Lisnakilly Road, Limavady BT49 9FB,

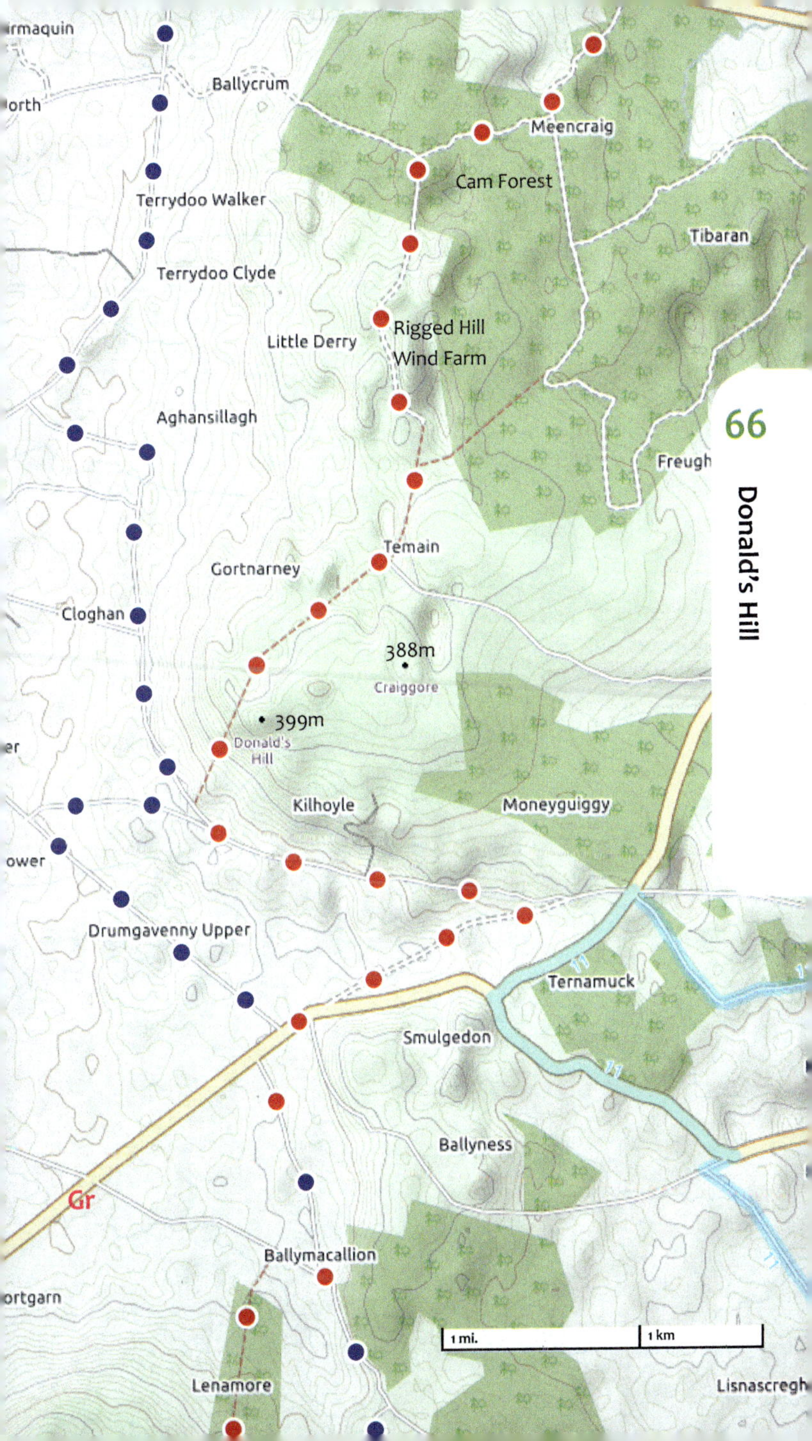
rmaquin
Ballycrum
orth
Meencraig
Cam Forest
Terrydoo Walker
Tibaran
Terrydoo Clyde
Little Derry
Rigged Hill
Wind Farm
Aghansillagh
Freugh
Temain
Gortnarney
Cloghan
388m
Craiggore
399m
Donald's
Hill
er
Kilhoyle
Moneyguiggy
ower
Drumgavenny Upper
Ternamuck
Smulgedon
Ballyness
Gr
Ballymacallion
ortgarn
1 mi.
1 km
Lenamore
Lisnascregh

+44 (0)28 7772 2222, www.roeparkresort.com or www.booking.com. Phone for a taxi to any of the above accommodations as the road is not suitable for walking. **Limavady Bells Taxi,** +44 (0)28 7776 8833; **Bells Taxis,** +44 (0)28 7776 3929; **Valley Taxis,** +44 (0)28 7772 2888.

From Ringsend Road, continue into **Springwell Forest** with a short walk on the busy N37 road in the middle of it. Leaving Springwell Forest follow Fermoyle Road around **Fermoyle Hill**. Take care on the busy Windyhill Road before turning right and then left into **Ballyhanna Forest**. Windyhill Road is also known as **Murder Hole Road,** so named after a highwayman named Cushy Glen from the 18th and early 19th centuries. He hid bodies of his victims in a bog hole until he was eventually shot in a failed robbery attempt.

"There is nothing so bad that it couldn't be worse."
- Irish Proverb

North Sperrins Way, towards Donald's Hill

Bratwell
Sconce
Altibrian
Grange Park
Ballyhanna Forest
Largantea
Formoyle
Dunmore
Gallows Knowe
Bolea
Dunbeg
Springwell Forest
Gortcorbies
Carrydoo
Limavady
27.5km
Weefield B&B
Leck
Ringsend Road
Drumramer
Craigmore Road
Kiltest
Tirmaquin
Ballycrum
Cam Forest
Meencraig
1 mi.
1 km
Terrydoo Walker
Tibaran
Terrydoo Clyde

Exit Ballyhanna Forest onto Bishops Road. This is a fairly long straight quiet road that will give you your first glimpse of the northern coastline and the Atlantic Ocean.

Along Bishop's Road enjoy views of **Binevenagh**, the last of the Sperrin Mountains, emerging to your left, **Lough Foyle** and the **Inishowen Peninsula** of Donegal, and the coastline and beach of **Benone.**

Take a rest at **Gortmore Viewpoint**. Standing on the hill here is the **statue of Manannán Mac Lir**, 'son of the sea', a Celtic Sea God from Irish mythology. The statue was created by John Sutton, who worked on the Game of Thrones TV show. The statue was stolen in early 2015, which sparked a campaign and Facebook page to bring the statue back. Police even launched a missing persons appeal!

Follow the road to the final forest on the Ireland Way, **Downhill Forest**. It is a pretty forest, unlike the large commercial forests you passed through today. The trail takes you by a fast-flowing river and around the large pond before exiting onto the A2 Mussenden Road. From the footpath you can get a glimpse of **Mussenden Temple**, built on the cliff edge by Frederick Hervey, 4th Earl of Bristol and Bishop of Derry. It is free to explore the grounds including the **Mausoleum** and ruin of **Downhill House**. At **Hezlett House**, a thatched cottage built in the 17th century, turn left onto Sea Road for your final approach to Castlerock and it's sandy beach.

Manannán Mac Lir (Celtic Sea God) at Gortmore Viewpoint

68 Binevenagh Mountain

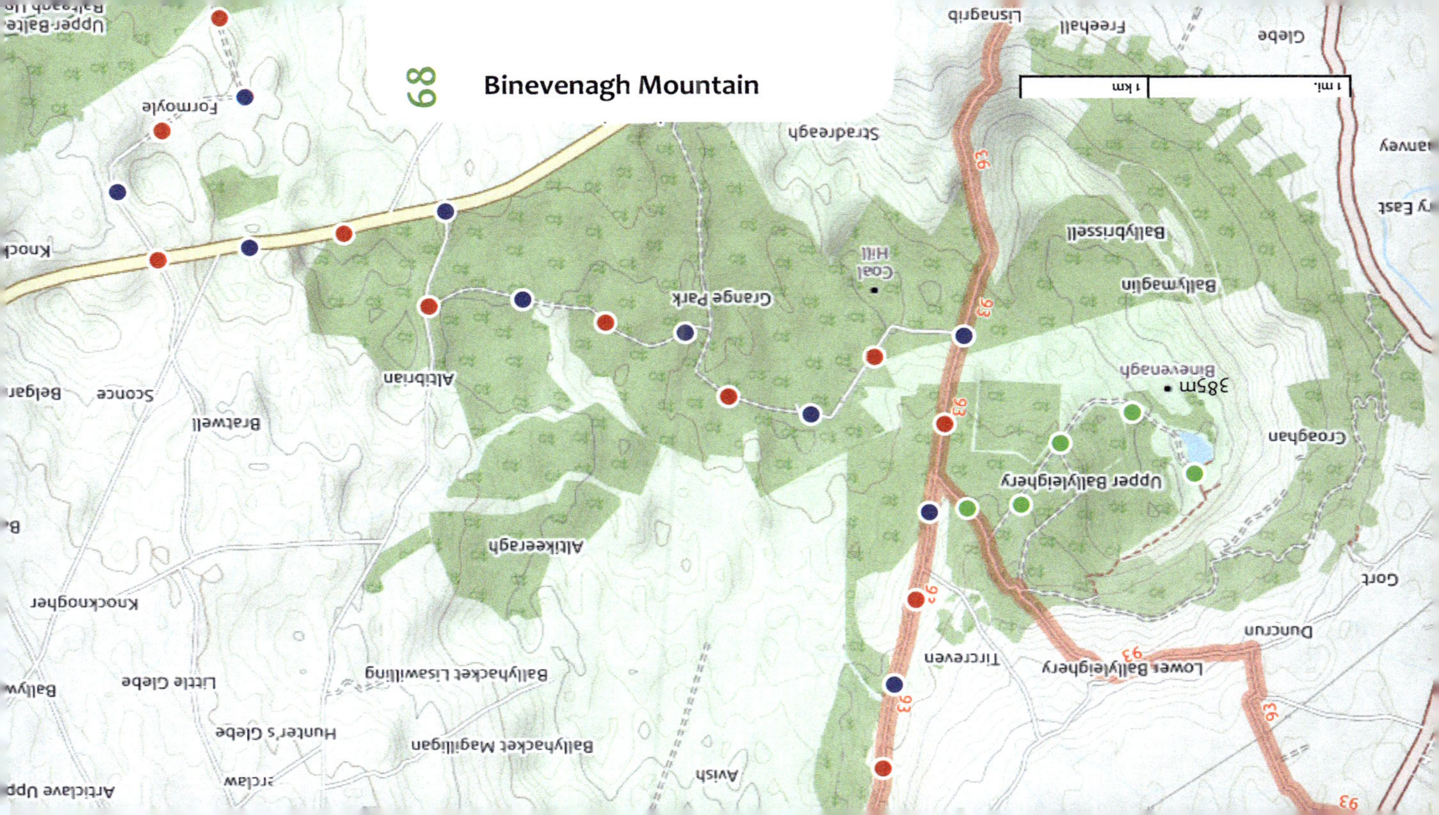

STAGE 19:

Castlerock - Portstewart

Castlerock - Coleraine - Portstewart

Distance:	16.2 km / 10.1 miles
Difficulty:	Link section, not for walking
County:	Derry
OSNI Maps:	Discoverer Series 4 & 5

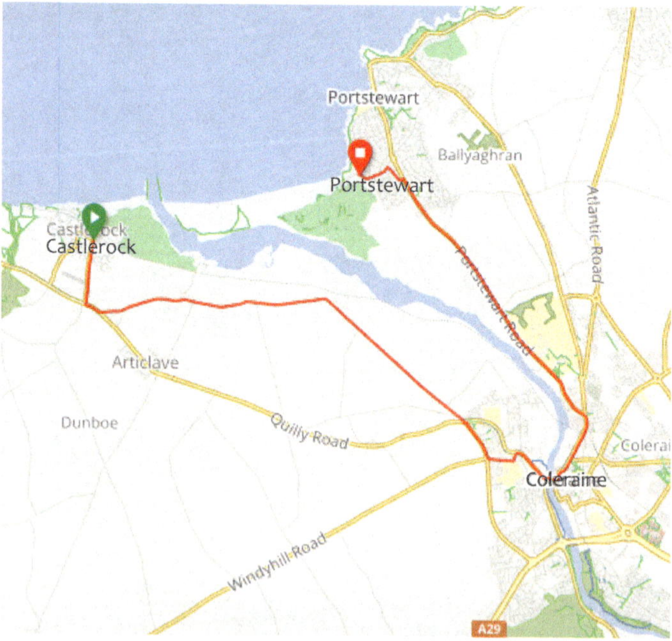

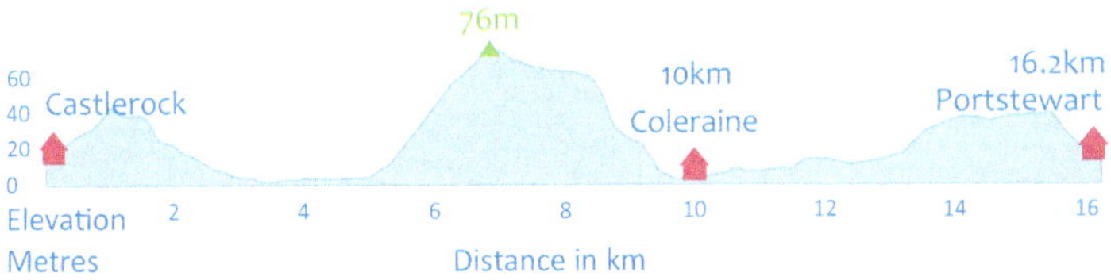

This 16.2km stretch around the river Bann does not have a suitable walking path and much of it is along roadsides. It is therefore recommended to use public transport for this section. A taxi takes about 20 minutes. Alternatively take the 134 bus or a train to Coleraine and the 140a bus from Coleraine to Portstewart. This will take around one hour depending on the day and transport times.

COUNTY DERRY / CONTAE DHOIRE

[28.6km/17.8mi] Castlerock A S R PO £ D P

Downhill Hostel, 12 Mussenden Road, Castlerock, Coleraine, BT51 4RP, +44 (0)28 7084 9077, email: info@downhillhostel.com, www.downhillhostel.com; **Carneety House B&B**, 120 Mussenden Road, Castlerock, Coleraine, BT51 4TX, +44 (0)28 7084 8640, www.carneetyhouse.co.uk; **Cranford House B&B**, 11 Circular Road, Castlerock, Coleraine, BT51 4XA, +44 (0)28 7084 8669; **Keeragh Lodge B&B**, 59 Altikeeragh Road, Castlerock, Coleraine, BT51 4SR,

River Bann, Coleraine

+44 (0)28 7084 8666, www.keeraghlodge.com; **Lonksview House B&B**, 10 Sea Road, Castlerock, Coleraine, BT51 4TL, +44 (0)28 7084 8755, www.linksview.co.uk.

Castlerock to Coleraine is all on quiet back roads and is an Ulster Way 'Link Section'. It is recommended on the Ulster Way websites to take a taxi directly to Portstewart although thru-hikers usually walk.

[10km/6.2mi] Coleraine

A S R PO £ D P

Breezemount House, 26 Castlerock Rd, Coleraine, Derry BT51 3HP, +44 (0)28 7034 4615, www.breezemount.co.uk; **Central B&B**, 14 Portstewart Rd, Coleraine BT52 1RN, +44 (0)28 7859 905512; **Carnadoon B&B**, Portstewart Rd, Coleraine, County Derry BT52 1RW, +44 (0)28 7035 7492; **Marina View B&B**, 22 Kenvarra Park, Coleraine BT52 1RT, +44 (0)7859 905512; **Premier Inn**, 3 Riverside Retail Park, Coleraine, Londonderry BT51 3AW, +44 (0)871 527 8262, www.premierinn.com; **The Lodge Hotel**, Lodge Rd Roundabout, Coleraine, Derry BT52 1NF, +44 (0)28 7034 4848, www.thelodgehotel.com.

Coleraine to Portstewart is all road but there is a footpath the entire way along the very busy A2 road.

Castlerock Beach

Mussenden Temple
Blue Link Section
Recommend Transport
46.1km
Castlerock
Benone
Umbra
Bennarees
Downhill
Freehall Watson
Ballwoolen
Liffock
Grange Beg
East Crossreagh
Crossreagh
Eagle Hill
Woodtown
Burren Beg
Ballywoodock
Artidillon
Exorna
Ardina
Pottagh
Gortgran
Craig
Burren More
Ballymoney
Articlave
Grange More Upper
Gortmore Viewpoint
& Manannán Mac Lir
Ballyhacket Glenahorry
Articlave Upper
Masteragwee
Ballyhacket Magilligan
Hunter's Glebe
Dartress
Blakes Lower
Ballyhacket Lisawilling
Little Glebe
Ballywildrick Lower
Upper Quilley
Dunalis Lower
1 mi.
1 km
93

THE CHILDREN OF LIR

IRISH MYTHS & LEGENDS

Lir was very disappointed when Bodb Derg was elected king of Tuatha Dé Danann, so Bodb gave him one of his daughters to marry. She was named Aoibh (pronounced 'Eve').

Aoibh and Lir had four children together: one girl named Fionnuala and three sons names Aodh, Fiachra and Conn. Aoibh died, so to keep Lir happy Bodb gave Lir another of his daughters to marry: Aoife (pronounced 'Eefa').

Aoife was jealous of Lir's love for his children and planned a way to get rid of them. When they were out one day, she ordered her servant to kill them, but he refused. She did not have the courage to kill them herself so instead she used her magic and turned the children into swans.

Under the spell, the children were to live as swans for 300 years on Lough Derravaragh, 300 years in the Sea of Moyle (between Ireland and Scotland), and 300 years in Irrus Domnann Erris near Inis Gluaire.

After the 900 years the children heard the sound of a church bell. They followed the sound and a priest found them. Some legends say that they were baptised and died, others say that they turned back into their human form and died as old and withered people.

Blue Link Section
Recommend Transport
6.2km PORTSTEWART
8.8km PORTR
10km Coleraine
Ballyreagh
Craigtown Beg
Carnalri
Maddybenn
Maddybenny
Nare
East Tullaghmurry
Garrylabin
Roseli
Bellemont Mo
East Crossreagh
Cappagh Beg
st Crossreagh
Cappagh More
Island Varc
Carnalbanagh
Ballygallin
Dooey Beg
Bannbrook Lower
Gortgran
Bannbrook Upper
Danes
Loug
Bellany
Ballycairn
Masteragwee
Millburn Road
Castletoodry
Waterside
Harpur
Upper Quilley
North Ballinteer
Lodge
1 mi.
1 km
93
96

STAGE 20:
Causeway Coast Way

Portstewart - Portrush - Portballintrae - Giant's Causeway - White Park Bay - Ballintoy - Ballycastle

Distance: 49.3 km / 30.7 miles
Difficulty: Easy
Counties: Derry, Antrim
OSNI Maps: Discoverer Series 4 & 5

Some people ask why the Ireland Way goes from south to north. The reason is mainly that the Beara-Breifne Way goes south to north, following the journey of Donal Cam O'Sullivan Bere. If I could chose the direction again I would still chose south to north. The south end of the trail is stunning but tough, the north end is stunning but with easy and fairly level terrain. After walking over 950 kilometres I am sure your legs or feet will appreciate that there are no more mountains to climb! They also may enjoy a relaxing dip in the sea and a stroll along the soft sandy beaches. This final stretch will take you through costal towns with several sites of interest along the way including **Dunluce Castle** and the famous natural geological site; the **Giant's Causeway**.

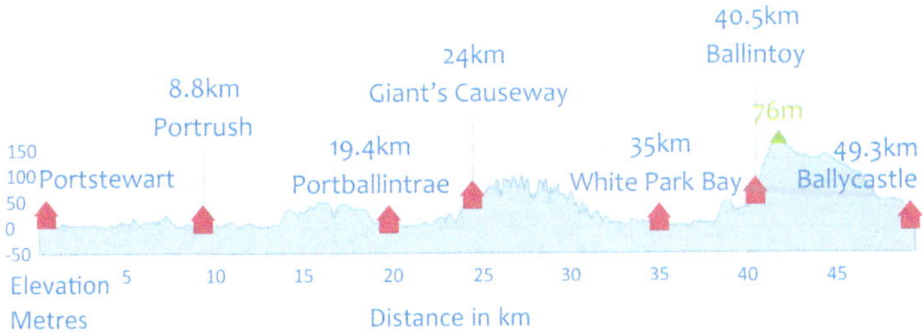

Ballintoy Harbour

[6.2km/3.8mi] Portstewart A S R PO £ D P

Carnalbanagh House, 192 Coleraine Rd, Portstewart, Derry BT55 7PL, +44 (0)28 70836294, www.carnban.com;
Kinvara Cottage Guesthouse, 6 Royal Ave, Portstewart, Derry BT55 7LE, +44 (0)28 7083 3567, www.kinvaracottage.co.uk; **Cromore Halt Hotel**, 158 Station Rd, Portstewart BT55 7PU, +44 (0)28 7083 6888, www.cromorehalt.co.uk; **The York Hotel**, 2 Station Rd, Portstewart, Derry BT55 7DA, +44 (0)28 7083 3594, www.theyorkportstewart.co.uk; **Strand House B&B**, 105 Strand Rd, Portstewart, Derry BT55 7LZ, +44 (0)28 7083 1000, www.strandguesthouse.com; **At The Beach**, 80A Strand Rd, Portstewart BT55 7LZ, +44 (0)28 7083 6510, www.at-beach.com; **Red Sails B&B**, 99 Strand Rd, Portstewart BT55 7LY, +44 (0)7551 843910; **Strandeen B&B**, 63 Strand Rd, Portstewart, Londonderry BT55 7LU, +44 (0)28 7083 3872, www.strandeen.com; **Ard Na Tra B&B**, 9 Seaview Drive-North, Portstewart, Derry BT55 7JY, +44 (0)28 7083 2768, www.ardnatra.com; **Craigmore House B&B**, The Promenade, Portstewart, Derry BT55 7AE, +44 (0)28 7083 2120; **Anchorage Inn Hotel**, 87-89 The Promenade, Portstewart, NIR BT55 7AG, +44 (0)28 7083 2003, www.theanchorbar.co.uk; **Wanderin Heights Hotel**, 12 High Road, Portstewart, +44 (0)28 7083 3250, www.wanderinheights.com; **Cul-Erg House B&B**, 9 Hillside, Atlantic Circle, Portstewart, Co Derry BT55 7AZ, +44 (0)28 7083 6610, www.culerg.co.uk; **Rick's Causeway Coast Hostel**, 4 Victoria Terrace, Portstewart, Derry BT55 7BA, +44 (0)28 7083 3789.

Fishing Boat Sculpture, Portstewart

Portstewart Town Map

On the Portstewart coastline is the impressive building of the Domician College. Follow along the rocky coastline to Rinadree Point for a nice viewpoint. Continue along the coast and you will arrive at West Strand beach, **Portrush** town and then East Strand beach.

COUNTY ANTRIM / CONTAE AONTROIM

[8.8km/5.5mi] Portrush A S R PO £ D P

Albany Lodge, 2 Eglinton St, Portrush, Antrim BT56 8DX+44 (0)287 082 3492, www.albanylodgeportrush.com; **Inn On The Coast**, 50 Ballyreagh Rd, Portrush, County Antrim BT56 8LT, +44 (0)287 082 3509, www.innonthecoastportrush.com; **Antrim House B&B**, 14 Eglinton St, Portrush, County Antrim BT56 8DX, +44 (0)287 082 3609, www.antrimhouseni.co.uk; **Clarmont Guesthouse**, 10 Lansdowne Cres, Portrush, Antrim, BT56 8AY,+44 (0)287 082 2397, www.clarmontguesthouse.com; **Mandalay B&B**, 50 Eglinton St, Portrush, County Antrim BT56 8DY, +44 (0)287 082 3572, www.mandalayportrush.co.uk; **Magherabuoy House Hotel**, 41 Magheraboy Rd, Portrush, Coleraine BT56 8NX, +44 (0)287 082 3507, www.magherabuoy.co.uk; **Links View B&B**, The Links, Portrush, County Antrim BT56 8SX, +44 (0)287 082 3769,www.linksviewportrush.co.uk; **Portrush Holiday Hostel**, 24 Princess St, Portrush, County Antrim BT56 8AX, +44 (0)28 7082 1288, www.portrushholidayhostel.com; **An Uladh**, 73 Eglinton St, Portrush, County Antrim BT56 8DZ, +44 (0)28 7082

The Arcadia, Portrush

Portrush Town Map

2221,www.anuladh.co.uk; **Pier 39**, 39 Kerr St, Portrush, Antrim BT56 8DQ, +44 (0)28 7082 3541, www.pier39portrush.com; **Ashlea House**, 52 Mark St, Portrush, County Antrim BT56 8BU, +44 (0)28 7082 3094; **Antique House**, 24 Portstewart Rd, Portrush, Coleraine, +44 (0)7526 898774, www.antiquehouseportrush.com; **Ramada Hotel**, 73 Main St, Portrush BT56 8BN, +44 (0)28 7082 6100, www.ramadaportrush.com; **Brae - Mar B&B**, 99 Coleraine Rd, Portrush BT56 8HN, +44 (0)28 7082 5224, www.brae-mar.co.uk; **Beulah Guesthouse**, 16 Causeway St, Portrush, County Antrim BT56 8AB, +44 (0)28 7082 2413, www.beulahguesthouse.com; **Portrush Townhouse**, 6 Bath St, Portrush, County Antrim BT56 8AW, +44 (0)28 7082 5699, www.portrushtownhouseaccommodation.com; **The Port Hotel**, 53-57 Main St, Portrush, Antrim BT56 8BN, +44 (0)28 7082 5353, www.theporthotel.net; **Atlantic View B&B**, 103 Eglinton St, Portrush, County Antrim BT56 8DZ, +44 (0)28 7082 3647,www.atlanticviewportrush.co.uk; **Harbour Heights B&B**, 17 Kerr St, Portrush, County Antrim BT56 8DG, +44 (0)28 7082 2765, www.harbourheightsportrush.com; **Royal Court Hotel**, 233 Ballybogey Road, Portrush, Antrim BT56 8NF, +44 (0)28 7082 2236,royalcourthotel.co.uk; **Anvershiel House**, Coleraine Rd, Portrush,

Dunluce Castle, County Antrim

County Antrim BT56 8EA, +44 (0)28 7082 3861, www.anvershiel.co.uk; **Aaranmore Lodge B&B**, Coleraine Rd, Portrush, Antrim BT56 8EA, +44 (0)28 7082 4640, www.accommodation-northernireland.com; **Eglinton Hotel**, 49 Eglinton St, Portrush, Coleraine BT56 8DZ, +44 28 7082 2371, www.eglintonhotel.com; **Prospect House B&B**, 20 Lansdowne Crescent, Portrush, Coleraine BT56 8AY, +44 (0)28 70 822299, www.bedandbreakfastportrush.co.uk; **Adelphi Hotel**, 67-71 Main St, Portrush, County Antrim BT56 8BN, +44 (0)28 7082 5544, www.adelphiportrush.com; **Causeway Cottage Mews**, 2 Causeway View Mews, Portrush, Antrim BT56 8PZ, +44 (0)7771 537987, www.causewaycottages.co.uk; **Oakdene Guesthouse**, 6 Lansdowne Crescent, Portrush, County Antrim BT56 8AY, +44 (0)28 7082 4629.

Back onto road, follow the A2 (Dunluce Road) and your next stop is **Dunluce Castle** (Dún Libhse), the ruin of a medieval castle which is accessible by a bridge. It was built by the MacQuillan family around 1500. You can download an app called Dunluce Castle to learn about its dramatic history and local tales. You can get some great photos from outside the castle, or alternatively there is a fee to enter and explore further. The A2 road takes you to the small village of Portballintrae and it's beach.

[10.6km/6.6mi] Portballintrae

A S R

Port Bhaile on Trá - "Port of the Beach Settlement"

Portballintrae is a very small quiet town with a beach.

Bayview Hotel, 2 Bayhead Road, Portballintrae, Bushmills, Antrim BT57 8RZ, +44 (0)28 2073 4100, www.bayviewhotelni.com.

Bushmills (cycle trail)

A S R PO

Bushmills is 3 km south of Portballintrae **Bushmills Whiskey Distillery** is the oldest distillery in Ireland. It is open daily to the public and provides tours. £7.50 entrance fee per adult. More information is available on their website www.bushmills.com/distillery.

Ballylinny Holiday Cottages, 7 Causeway Rd, Bushmills, Antrim BT57 8SU, +44 (0)28 2073 1683, www.giantscauseway.co.uk; **Cottesmore B&B**, 28 Castlecat Rd, Bushmills, Antrim BT57 8QY, +44 (0)28 2073 2122, www.cottesmorebandb.co.uk; **Rest a While**, 90 Castlenagree Rd, Bushmills, Antrim BT57 8XL, +44 (0)28 2073 2869, www.restawhile.net; **Carnside Guesthouse**, 23 Causeway Road, Giants Causeway, Bushmills, County Antrim BT57 8SU, +44 (0)28 2073 1337, www.carnsideguesthouse.co.uk; **Portcaman House**, 11 Priestland Rd, Bushmills, Coleraine BT57 8QP, +44 (0)28 2073 2286, www.giantscausewayhotel.co.uk; **Bushmills Inn Hotel & Restaurant**, 9 Dunluce Rd, Bushmills, County Antrim BT57 8⍰G, +44 (0)28 2073 3000, www.bushmillsinn.com; **The Smuggler's Inn**, 306 Whitepark Rd, Bushmills, Antrim BT57 8SL, +44 (0)28 2073 1577, www.smugglersinnireland.com; **Ulster Cottages**, 32 Ballywatt Rd, Coleraine BT52 2LT, +44 (0)28 2074 2276, www.ulstercottages.com; **Old Glebe**, 166 Castlecat Rd, Derrykeighan, Bushmills, Ballymoney BT53 8AP, +44 (0)28 2074 2148, www.oldglebebb.co.uk; **Meadow Cottage**, 31 Carragh Rd, Bushmills, Co Antrim BT57 8UE, +44 (0)28 2073 1837, www.meadowcottageni.com; **Causeway B&B**, 42 Priestland Rd, Bushmills, Coleraine BT57 8XB, +44 (0)28 2073 1909; **Bushmills Youth Hostel**, 49 Main St, Bushmills, Moyle BT57 8QA, +44 (0)28 2073 1222, www.hini.org.uk; **Seaview B&B**, Whitepark Rd, Bushmills, Co. Antrim BT57 8SN, +44 (0)28 2073 1621, www.stayatseaview.com; **Craig Cottage B&B**, 181 Whitepark Rd, Bushmills, County Antrim BT57 8SS, +44 (0)28 2073 1480, www.bushmills-accommodation.co.uk; **Causeway Lodge**, 52 Moycraig Road, Bushmills Co. Antrim, Bushmills BT57 8TB, +44 (0)28 2073 0333, www.causewaylodge.com; **Causeway Tavern B&B**, 241 Whitepark Rd, Bushmills, County Antrim BT57 8SP, +44 (0)28 2073 2224, www.causewaytavern.com.

Leaving Portballintrae, the next beach is **Runkerry Strand** and the impressive **Runkerry House** (privately owned). Not far past this is one of Ireland's most unique landscapes; the **Giant's Causeway**.

[4.6km/2.8mi] Giant's Causeway

A R

Clochán an Aifir/Clochán na bhFomhórach

The **Giant's Causeway** is a coastal area of about 40,000 interlocking basalt columns. They were caused by an ancient volcanic eruption, around fifty to sixty million years ago. In 1986 it was declared a World

71 Portrush, Portballintrae

Heritage Site by UNESCO. The **Giant's Causeway Visitor Centre** provides you with a headset for a guided tour. Adult admission to the Visitor Centre is £10.50 (cheaper if booked online at www.giantscausewaytickets.com).

Causeway Hotel, 40 Causeway Road, Bushmills, County Antrim BT57 8SU, +44 (0)28 2073 1210, www.thecausewayhotel.com; **Finn McCool's Hostel/B&B**, +44 (0)28 2073 2011, finnmccoolshostel.com: **Ardtrabane House B&B**, BT57 8SX +44 (0)28 20731007, www.ardtrabanehouse.co.uk; **Smuggler's Inn**, BT57 8SL, +44 (0) 28 2073 1577, www.smugglersinnireland.com.

The Giant's Causeway is followed by the ruin of **Dunseverick Castle** which has only a part of its walls remaining. Saint Patrick visited this castle in the 5th century AD. Pass by the small village of Dunseverick and the tiny Dunseverick Harbour. Not far after this is Portbradden and the beautiful beach of **White Park Bay**.

[11km/6.8mi] White Park Bay A

Whitepark Bay Youth Hostel, 157 Whitepark Rd, Ballycastle, County Antrim BT54 6NH, +44 (0)28 2073 1745, www.hini.org.uk; **Whitepark House**, 150 Whitepark Rd, Ballintoy, Ballycastle, County Antrim BT54 6NH, +44 (0)28 2073 1482, www.whiteparkhouse.com.

White Park Bay

FIONN MacCUMHAILL

IRISH MYTHS & LEGENDS

Gaelic mythology tells the tale of Fionn MacCool. He was a great warrior and leader of a group called the Fianna, protectors of Ireland's High King.

Fionn built the Causeway as stepping stones from Ireland to Scotland because the Scottish giant Benandonner had challenged him to a fight. When Fionn realised that Benandonner was a much larger giant than he, he asked for the help of his wife, Oonagh. She disguised Fionn as a baby and tucked him in a cradle. Then she baked a batch of griddle-cakes, hiding griddle-irons in some of them.

When Benandonner arrived, Oonagh told him that Fionn was out and would be home shortly. She offered the giant a griddle-cake and he chipped his tooth. She then gave one without an iron to the 'baby' who ate it easily. Having seen the size of the 'baby' and the strength of it's teeth, Benandonner reckons that its father must be a very large giant indeed and fled back to Scotland, destroying the causeway on his way so that Fionn could not follow him.

The Giant's Causeway

The trail takes you along **Ballintoy Harbour**. Ballintoy village is 1.8 km / 1 mile off-trail.

[5.5km/3.4mi] Ballintoy Harbour

Accommodation in Ballintoy Village + 1.8km off trail A S R

Bengore House B&B, Ballinlea Rd, Ballycastle, County Antrim, BT54 6NQ, +44 (0)28 2076 1005; **The Wee House**, 134 Whitepark Rd, Ballintoy, Ballycastle, County Antrim BT54 6ND, +44 (0)28 2076 2093, www.theweehouse.com; **The Fullerton Arms**, 22 Main St, Ballintoy, Ballycastle BT54 6LX, +44 (0)28 2076 9613, www.fullerton-arms.com; **Sheep Island View Independent Holiday Hostel**, Main St, Ballintoy, Ballycastle, County Antrim BT54 6LX, +44 (0)28 2076 9391, www.sheepislandview.com; **Glenmore Guest House & Campsite**, 94 Whitepark Rd, Ballintoy, Ballycastle, Co Antrim BT54 6LR, +44 (0)28 2076 3584, www.glenmore.biz.

Among the final sites of interest on the trail before Ballycastle are the filming site of *'Renly's Baretheon Camp'* in the TV series *Game of Thrones*, and just past it is the **Carrick-a-rede rope bridge.** You can cross the bridge to a tiny island called Carrickarede (Carraig a'Ráid - Rock of the Casting). It is believed that salmon fishermen built bridges to the island for over 350 years. You can buy your ticket there for £5.90.

Carrick-a-Rede Rope Bridge

White Park Bay

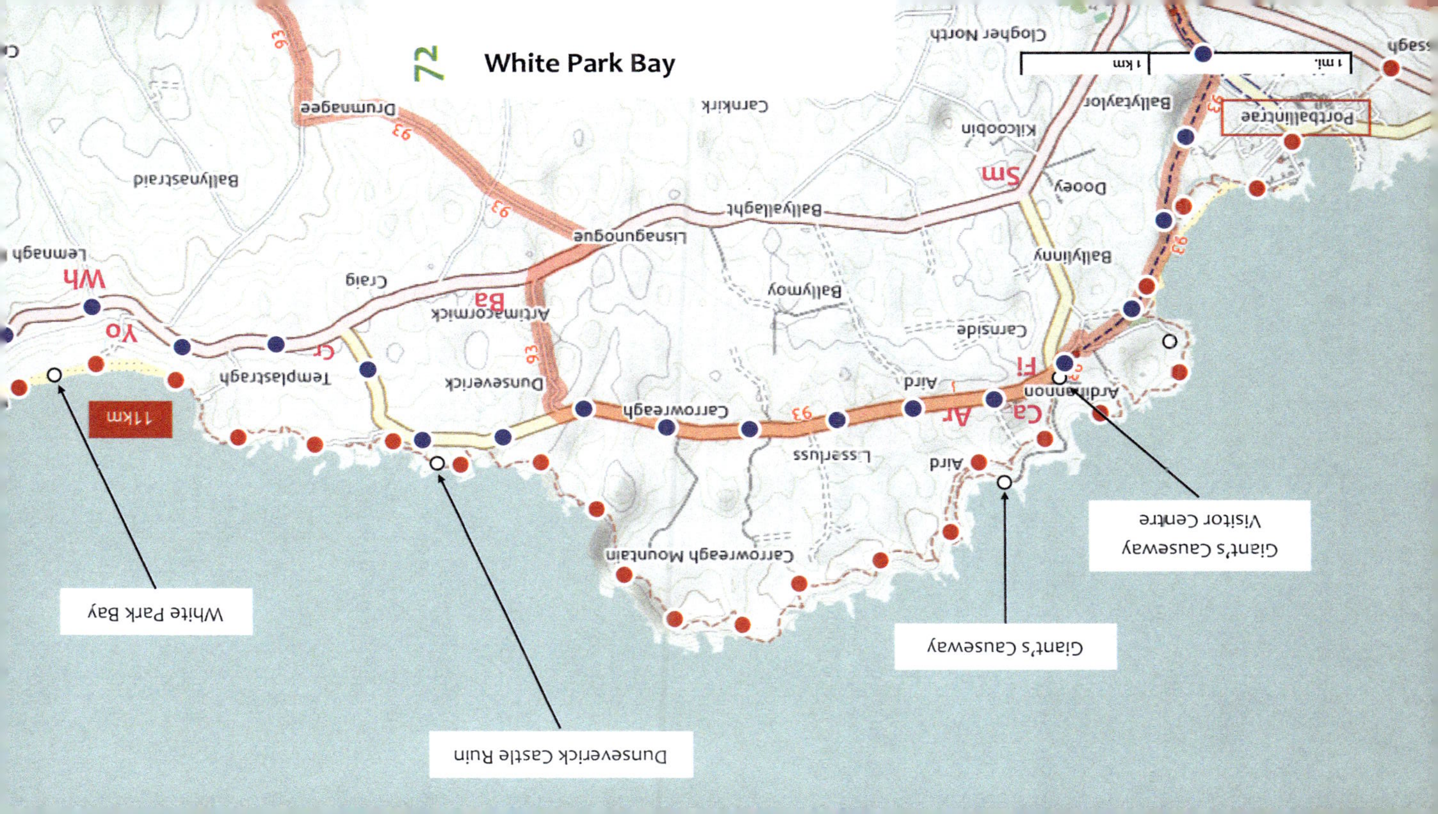

Further along the coast is the ruin of **Kinbane Castle** (Caislen Ceinn Bán - White Head Castle), named after the white limestone on which the castle was built. It was constructed in 1547 by the MacDonnells, and besieged by the English forces in 1551 and again in 1555. You can access the castle via steep steps but only some walls remain.

[8.8km/5.5mi] Ballycastle

A S R PO £ D P

Ballycastle is the final destination on the Ireland Way trail, with the end point at the **Children of Lir Swan Sculpture**. Out in the ocean you can see **Rathlin Island** and on a clear day you can see all the way to Scotland behind it in the distance. Take a day or two to rest here at this pretty seaside village. Congratulations on your completion of this epic journey!

Present your Ireland Way Passport at the Ballycastle Visitor Information Office to obtain your free Ireland Way Certificate.

End point of the Ireland Way, Children of Lir Sculpture

73 Ballintoy, Ballycastle

Ballycastle Backpackers Hostel, 4 North St, Ballycastle, County Antrim BT54 6BN, +44 (0)7773 237890, www.ballycastlebackpackers.net; **Kinbane Farmhouse B+B**, 85 Whitepark Rd, Ballycastle, +44 (0)28 2076 9947, www.kinbane.com; **Crockatinney Guest House**, 80 Whitepark Road, Ballycastle, County Antrim BT54 6LP, +44 (0)28 2076 8801, www.crockatinneyguesthouse.com; **Clare House**, 33 Whitepark Rd, Ballycastle BT54 6LL, +44 (0)28 2076 3889, www.clarehouseballycastle.com; **Clarewood House B&B**, Moyle Rd, Ballycastle, Antrim BT54 6LG, +44 (0)28 2076 2157; **J and J B&B**, 58 Clare Rd, Ballycastle, Co. Antrim BT54 6LQ, +44 (0)28 2076 9383, www.jandjguesthouse.com; **Causeway Coast Holiday Park**, 21 Clare Rd, Ballycastle, Antrim BT54 6DB, +44 28 2076 2550, www.hagansleisure.co.uk; **Hillsea Guest House**, 6 Rathlin View, Ballycastle, County Antrim BT54 6EN, +44 (0)28 2076 2385, www.ballycastle-accommodation.com; **Kenmara House**, 45 North St, Ballycastle BT54 6BP, +44 (0)28 2076 2600; **Ardaghmore B&B**, 35 North St, Ballycastle, County Antrim BT54 6BP, +44 28 2076 3329, www.ardaghmore.com; **Marine Hotel Ballycastle**, 1-3 North St, Ballycastle, County Antrim BT54 6BN, +44 (0)28 2076 2222; **An Caislean**, 42 Quay Road, Ballycastle, County Antrim BT54 6BH, +44 (0) 28 2076 2845; **Castle Hostel**, 38 Quay Rd, Ballycastle BT54 6BH, +44 (0)28 2076 2845; **Fragrens B&B**, Quay Rd, Ballycastle, County Antrim BT54 6BH, www.fragrens.co.uk; **The Old Manse**, 28 Quay Rd, Ballycastle, County Antrim BT54 6BH, +44 (0)28 2076 9503; **Ard-Na-Mara B&B**, 14 Atlantic Ave, Ballycastle BT54 6AL, +44 (0)7732 551692.

Author at the Children of Lir sculpture. Photo by F. Richichi

Ballycastle Town Map

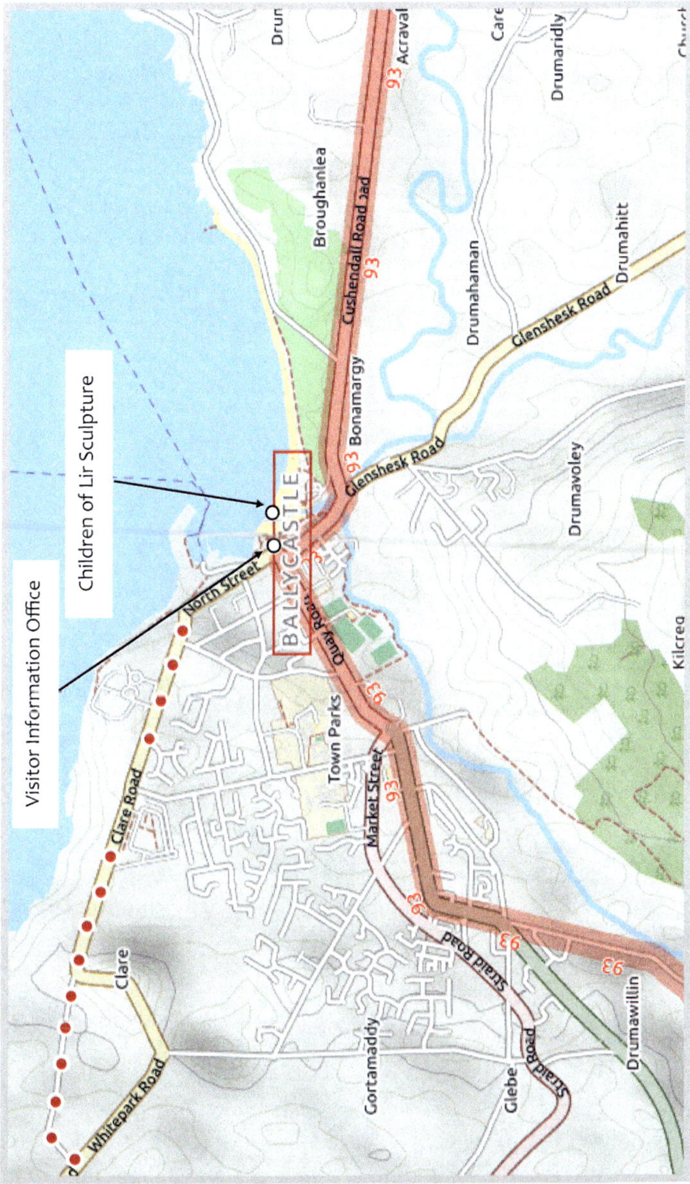

Stay in Touch

Your feedback will help keep this guidebook fresh and relevant for future walkers. Your comments and suggestions will be used to provide up-to-date information on www.theirelandway.ie/news. Please email me at caroline@theirelandway.ie.

If you would like to share your journey or stay in touch with fellow walkers, there is a Facebook group called The Ireland Way where you can comment and share photos of your adventures: www.facebook.com/groups/theirelandway, or tag us on Instagram or Twitter @theirelandway.

Slán abhaile agus tar ar ais arís go luath!

(Safe home and come back again soon!)

Further Reading

Annals of the Four Masters, translated by John O'Donovan. Hodges and Smith, Dublin 1851.

O'Sullivan, Philip, *Historical Catholicae Iberniae Compendium*, translated as *Ireland Under Elizabeth* by M. J. Byrne, Sealy, Bryers and Walker, Dublin 1903.

Somerville-Large, Peter, *From Bantry Bay to Leitrim - A Journey in Search of O'Sullivan Beare*, Victor Gollancz Ltd., London, 5324.

Carroll, Michael John, *March into Oblivion*, Bantry Design Studios Ltd., Cork, 2011.

O'Sullivan, Philip, *The Natural History of Ireland*, Cork University Press, Cork, 2009.

Berresford Ellis, Peter, *Eyewitness to Irish History*, John Wiley & Sons, Inc., New Jersey, 2004.

Image: Coomarkane, Glengarriff

Notes:

Notes:

Part 2: The Ulster Way
Portballintrae
White Park Bay
Portrush
Ballintoy
Portstewart
Ballycastle
Castlerock
Coleraine
Dungiven
Moneyneany
Gortin
Lough Bradan
Belleek
Pettigo
Keadue
Belcoo
Ballyfarnon
Blacklion
Highwood
Dowra
Castlebaldwin
Ballinagleragh
Ballinafad
Drumshanbo
Monasteraden
Leitrim Village
Ballaghaderreen
Loughglinn
Ballinlough
Ballymoe
Creggs
Ballygar
Ahascragh
Ballinasloe
Aughrim
Laurencetown
Meelick
Portumna
Lorrha
Ballingarry
Cloughjordan
Toomevara
Templederry
Upperchurch
Milestone
Cappawhite
Hollyford
Donohill
Tipperary
Lismire
Kilfinane
Galbally
John's Bridge
Ballylanders
Ballyorgan
Newmarket
Liscarroll
Churchtown
Millstreet
Ballyvourney
Gougane Barra
Ballingeary
Glengarriff
Kealkill
Adrigole
Castletownbere
Part 1: Beara-Breifne Way

Printed in Great Britain
by Amazon

28853418R00145